Successful Change Strategies

Chief Executives in Action

Edited by

Bernard Taylor

DIRECTOR BOOKS

Published in association with the Institute of Directors

First published 1994 by
Director Books
an imprint of Fitzwilliam Publishing Limited
Campus 400, Maylands Avenue
Hemel Hempstead
Hertfordshire, HP2 7EZ
A division of
Simon & Schuster International Group

The views of the authors do not necessarily represent those of the Council of the
Institute of Directors

Typeset in 11/12 pt
by Vision Typesetting, Manchester

Printed and bound in Great Britain by TJ Press (Padstow) Ltd, Cornwall.

British Library Cataloguing in Publication Data

A catalogue record for this book is available from the British Library

ISBN 1-870555-70-8

---

1   2   3   4   5   98   97   96   95   94

Contents

Notes on contributors

Charles Allen, Chief Executive of Granada Television and London Weekend Television, trained as an accountant before moving into personnel and general management roles and has built a strong reputation for managing change and developing people.

Before becoming Group Managing Director of Grand Metropolitan Innovations Ltd and the Compass Vending Group in 1986, he held financial positions in British Steel, TM Group and Grand Metropolitan plc.

Following the management buyout of Compass from Grand Metropolitan in 1988, he was appointed Managing Director of Compass. He managed the successful stock market flotation in 1989, and led the team which won the biggest services contract in Europe. He doubled the profit of the company in three years, before joining Granada Leisure as Chief Executive in 1991. Here he restructured the group of companies and improved the return on investment.

Charles Allen was appointed as Chief Executive of Granada Television in 1992, where he undertook a restructuring of the company, producing the highest profit figures and level of programme production in the company's history. He was appointed the first Chairman of Granada LWT International, the joint venture distribution company, formed in January 1993, which sells the programmes of Granada Television and London Weekend Television worldwide. In March 1994 he was appointed as Chief Executive of London Weekend Television, following Granada's acquisition of the company.

Kevin J. Bourke is Group General Manager, Corporate Relations, at Allied Irish Banks plc in Dublin. A career banker, he joined AIB in 1959 and spent his early years working in various positions within Retail Banking. From 1975 to 1982 he was Regional Manager for the Midland Region in Ireland. In 1986, after four years as Head of Public Affairs, he moved on to become Head of Group Marketing. He was appointed to his present position in 1990 and has responsibility for the development of corporate relations and communications with the 'Stakeholders' of the Group: shareholders, staff, customers and community.

Mark Brown is the founder and Managing Director of Innovation Centre Europe Ltd, an organisation researching and promoting innovation in organisations. He is also an Associate Faculty member at Henley Management College, and co-founder of the European Innovation Project.

His work involves management consultancy and training in the UK and overseas, writing management books and articles, and continuing research at King's College, London University and Henley on why some individuals and organisations are more creative and innovative than others.

His last major publication is *The Dinosaur Strain*, Element, 1988, and forthcoming titles include *Your Creative Edge*, Kogan Page, 1994, *Super Creative Teams*, Kogan Page, 1994 and the video *Ideas into Action*, Melrose, 1993.

Bob Chase, a chartered accountant, is the Group Managing Director of The Automobile Association, the UK's leading motoring organisation. He has responsibility for the performance of all commercial aspects of the AA, and reports to the Director General.

Before joining The Automobile Association in 1990, he was based in Hong Kong for eight years, latterly as Chief Financial Officer of Orient Overseas (Holdings) Ltd.

Before moving to Hong Kong he was employed as the Finance Director of Inchcape plc in Kenya, where the company undertook a wide range of trading and manufacturing activities. He was with Coopers & Lybrand in Norwich and London from 1964 to 1976, before going to Kenya.

Henry Curteis is an entrepreneur who during the 1980s built a new and successful business manufacturing and supplying jewellery chains to retailers.

He grew up on a small dairy farm in Shropshire in the village where Curteis Chains is situated. Academic promise suggested a career in law or diplomacy, but an interest in business came to the fore. After initial failure as a commission agent he spent 18 months in Procter & Gamble retail sales, coming top salesman in London North in his first year. He has contributed articles on an occasional basis to local magazines, newspapers, trade press and other publications – sometimes in a light-hearted vein. Recently he has taken an advisory role in the Department of Employment functional analysis project on the role of the company director.

Peter Ellwood is Chief Executive of TSB Group plc and TSB Bank plc. He was appointed Chief Executive – Retail Banking in May 1989 and in March 1991 took over responsibility for Retail Banking and Insurance which now comprises TSB's 1,400-branch network, the Insurance, Unit Trust and credit card businesses, and the finance house United Dominions Trust. His appointment to Chief Executive of TSB Group in August 1992 brought additional responsibility for Hill Samuel Bank – which provides merchant and corporate banking and investment management services – and TSB's Commercial Operations.

Peter Ellwood joined Barclays in 1961 where he gained experience in the Bank's Bristol District and the City of London, both as a corporate banker and as a General

Manager's Assistant working for the Senior General Manager and the Bank's UK Chairman. From January 1983 he was responsible for Barclaycard operations and in 1985 was appointed Chief Executive. In 1986 when Barclaycard became a central component of the newly formed Central Retail Services Division of Barclays Bank, Mr Ellwood was made Chief Executive.

Sir Malcolm Field is Chief Executive of W. H. Smith Group plc. He joined the company in 1963 and became director of its wholesale division in 1970. He joined the Group main board in 1974 and became Managing Director in 1982. He has been a non-executive Director of MEPC plc since 1989 and of Scottish and Newcastle Breweries plc since May, 1993. He was Chairman of NAAFI from 1986 until 1993. He is currently a Council Member of the Royal College of Art and was knighted in 1991.

Chris Gamblin is Managing Partner in Gamblin Associates, a firm of management and human resource consultants. At the time of writing, he was the Director of Human Resources for Bell Northern Research Europe, an organisation which provides the Research and Development for Northern Telecom. Both companies are wholly subsidiaries of Bell Canada Enterprises. BNR employs approximately 1,500 people in Europe. He was previously employed as a Human Resource Director for Northern Telecom in Europe.

He has had extensive experience in the IT industry, including eight years with Hewlett-Packard where his last role was Personnel Director for UK Sales and Marketing. He has also worked in a line manufacturing role for the Bemrose Corporation and previously worked in the public sector in Human Resources and Organisation and Development roles.

Dr Kevin Hawkins is Corporate Affairs Director of the W H Smith Group. He joined W H Smith in 1989 from Lucas Industries plc, where he was Director of Public Affairs from 1984. He was Director of the West Midlands Region of the CBI from 1982 to 1984. He is a member of the London Regional Council of the CBI and of the Council of the British Retail Consortium.

Martyn Laycock began his banking career in 1963 in South Yorkshire. He worked for National Westminster Bank in a variety of locations before joining Lloyds and Scottish Finance Group in 1970 where he managed branches in Durham and Newcastle upon Tyne.

In 1977 he opened Allied Irish Bank Group's operations in the North East of England. He took on sales and regional management roles in the South West and South East of Britain before moving to AIB's UK headquarters in Uxbridge in 1989.

As a member of AIB's senior management he worked in a number of divisional marketing roles, including market development and project management roles covering a number of key product development and management of change initiatives in the period 1989–92.

He left AIB in 1992 in order to achieve his ambition of working more closely with small/medium-sized businesses. In his new consultancy role he focuses on financial, marketing and strategic management.

George Medley joined the World Wildlife Fund in 1978 and was Director of WWF United Kingdom until he retired in July 1993.

In his early career he held management roles in the chemicals industry in Sri Lanka and India before returning to the UK in 1968 to Fisons International Division where he was appointed Sales Manager, Western Hemisphere, then Overseas Manager with responsibility for the agrochemical activities of all Fisons overseas subsidiaries.

He went back to India in 1971 as Deputy Managing Director of Glaxo Laboratories India Ltd, taking over as Managing Director in April 1973.

He was made a Trustee of the International Institute for Environment and Development in 1989 and was Founder Vice-Chairman of the Institute of Charity Fundraising Managers in 1983 and Chairman from 1984 to 1985.

Patrick Moylan has spent his career in consumer goods marketing and retailing. Following ten years with Woolworths, now part of Kingfisher plc, one of the UK's leading retail groups, he is now with Kurt Salmon Associates, an international management consultancy. He is responsible for the management of their Retail Group, which is a leader in the field. Their clients have included: BhS, Harrods, Marks & Spencer, Sears, Body Shop, Laura Ashley, Woolworths, Bally, the Burton Group, Coats Viyella and Courtaulds.

During the last three years, Kurt Salmon Associates' primary focus has been on improving customer service through superior management of the supply chain from the factory to the sales floor. Particularly important has been the development of Efficient Consumer Responsiveness, a programme of innovation in product planning, sourcing, operations and distribution.

Patrick Moylan has a degree in Economics and professional qualifications in Management Services and Resource Management. He travels extensively and lectures on contemporary retail issues.

Graham Pearson is UK Quality Manager, Business Management Systems and Quality Division, Rank Xerox (UK) Ltd. He joined Rank Xerox in March 1987, and managed the UK Sales Support Organisation until 1991, providing technical and business advice to the sales force and to customers. Then he moved to Business Management Systems and Quality Division to head up the drive for 'Quality'. He is responsible for the implementation of the Business Excellence programme throughout the UK company, and was responsible for Rank Xerox (UK) support in achieving the European Quality Award.

Before coming to Rank Xerox he spent many years with an international computer supplier, primarily in the areas of sales and customer support, specialising in the financial services market.

Brian Pitman took up his present position as Chief Executive of Lloyds Bank in December 1983.

He has spent most of his career with Lloyds Bank, and has had a wide range of experience in domestic and international banking, including spells in Europe and the USA.

In 1976 he was appointed an Executive Director of Lloyds Bank International, responsible for the UK and Asia-Pacific Divisions; and in 1978 he became Deputy Chief Executive. At the beginning of 1982 he was appointed Deputy Chief Executive of the Lloyds Bank Group.

He is a Director of Lloyds Bank plc, The National Bank of New Zealand Limited, NBNZ Holdings Limited and Chairman of Lloyds First Western Corporation; and a Fellow of the Chartered Institute of Bankers.

Gerald Radford joined the Dunlop Overseas Division in 1957. Following various posts in London, Italy and Argentina he became President of Società Italiana Dunlop in 1969. In 1980 he was appointed General Manager, Europe Sales Division and in 1981 Director and General Manager, Replacement, for Dunlop UK Tyre Division before becoming Managing Director of National Tyre Service, Dunlop's distribution chain, in 1982.

Following the takeover of Dunlop tyre operations by Sumitomo Rubber Industries of Japan, he became Managing Director of the new company, SP Tyres UK Limited in 1985 and Chairman and Managing Director in 1987. He is also non-executive Chairman of Motorway Tyres and Accessories Ltd, in which SP Tyres took a majority share in 1989.

Jim Rigby is a management accountant and has worked for Hewlett-Packard Ltd for nearly 30 years in a variety of roles. He is currently a Division Controller and he has undertaken overseas assignments in the USA and Europe.

He is well known internationally, speaking regularly at conferences on Activity Based Management, Total Quality Management and Performance Measurement. He is a Guest Lecturer at INSEAD on Strategic Cost Management and Executive Development Programmes.

Peter Siddall qualified as a chartered accountant and has been a professional management consultant for over 20 years. He has carried out assignments for major organisations in a wide variety of manufacturing and service industries in Europe, North America, Africa, Asia and Australia.

He founded Siddall & Company in 1978 which specialises in the management of change, in particular, organisation effectiveness and business processes in international companies and public sector organisations. Industry specialisations include oil and gas, telecommunications, electricity, chemicals, information technology and manufacturing.

Bernard Taylor is Professor of Business Policy at Henley Management College, Oxfordshire. He is Director of the European Council on Corporate Strategy, Editor of *Long Range Planning* and author of 15 books on Corporate Strategy. He is also a consultant to business and government internationally.

Before joining Henley Management College he held responsible positions with Procter & Gamble, Rank Xerox, the Chartered Institute of Marketing and the University of Bradford.

Patrick Tonks joined INS in 1987 at its formation. The company is now Europe's leading provider of EDI products and services. He has held a number of positions within INS including Marketing Manager, with responsibility for INS's Industry Sector Strategies. More recently he has been appointed to a position with responsibility for developing the INS software business in the UK.

He was educated at Manchester University where he gained a BSc honours degree. He joined ICL in 1982 and spent two years in the marketing and support of office systems hardware, software and services to a cross-section of UK businesses.

In September 1984 he undertook a six-month project within ICL to investigate the current and future trends in communications technologies and their role in the provision of Value Added Network Services.

Keith Willey is a director of Siddall & Company. He trained as a chemical engineer and then worked for an international paper company in technical, marketing and strategic development roles. He has an MBA from the London Business School.

His recent assignments include developing a global organisation in telecommunications, creating cost-effective structures for a new 15-country European oil business and assistance with post-merger organisation implementation of two companies in Spain.

Introduction

Bernard Taylor

'The ultimate, and largely ignored task of management is one of creating and breaking paradigms... When the competitive environment pushes an organisation to its limits, the old mind-set no longer holds... A discontinuous improvement in capability is needed, and it entails transformation. The trouble is that 99% of managerial attention today is devoted to the techniques that squeeze more out of the existing paradigm and it's killing us.'
Richard Pascale, *Managing on the Edge*, Penguin, 1991, p. 14

This is a book about the transformation of British business, and it has been written by the Chief Executives and the teams who are leading the change. The process has been called 'reinventing the corporation', 're-engineering the business' or 'breaking the paradigm'. These Chief Executives are all concerned with re-focusing, re-structuring and revitalising their organisations.

The new strategic leadership

This book is about revolution, not evolution, structural change rather than incremental change. It is not about squeezing out an extra 3 or 5 per cent productivity, a further 10 per cent reduction in costs, or selling more by 'trying harder'. Rather, it is about delivering a step-increase in performance — doubling productivity, halving costs, achieving market leadership.

Many of the companies described in the book are well known for their achievements.

- In 1992 Rank Xerox became the first winner of the European Quality Award.
- In the past ten years Lloyds Bank has increased share market value eightfold.
- Since Sumitomo Rubber acquired Dunlop UK Tyre Division in 1985, the productivity per employee has doubled and the amount of waste and returned products has been reduced by half.
- Through building stronger relationships with its customers, Allied Irish Bank has become the number one bank in Ireland.
- In the past three years the Automobile Association's profits have grown tenfold — from £2.7 million in 1989 to over £30 million in 1992.

1

- In 1991/92 BP Oil reduced its head office costs by 40 per cent.
- In George Medley's 15 years as Chief Executive at the World Wildlife Fund for Nature (UK), the charity's income has quadrupled.
- In the past ten years Tallent Engineering – a supplier of chasses to the car industry – has increased its turnover from £1.5 million with negligible profits in 1980 to £63 million and £3 million profits in 1992.
- Curteis Chains, a small jewellery manufacturer, is one of 3i's 'Superleague' high-growth companies. It has expanded rapidly despite the shakeout which is occurring in the British jewellery business.

Common themes

Each of these businesses has its own specific problems, and each of the Chief Executives has his personal leadership style, but there are common themes (see Figure I.1):

Stretch goals

Each Chief Executive has a clear set of corporate objectives. Brian Pitman's single-minded focus on shareholder value is enough to make any director pause

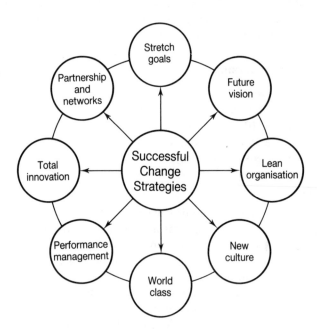

Figure I.1 The new strategic leadership

and take notice. It is difficult to find another bank which like Lloyds has increased its stock market value in the last ten years eightfold – from £770 million in 1982 to £6,760 million in 1992.

Future vision

Another common feature of high-performance companies is top management's ability to focus the efforts of their staff and to increase their employees' commitment, by communicating a credible vision of the company's future, and a sense of direction. The TSB Group aspires to be 'the UK's leading financial retailer'. Tallent Engineering wants to be 'the world's best manufacturer of chassis structures for medium size non-specialist cars'. The AA's mission is 'to be the UK's leading and most successful motoring and personal assistance organisation'. And they mean it! Their corporate strategies, change programmes and operational goals, and their employees' personal and team objectives all flow from these statements of intent.

Lean organisation

The introduction of a new leadership style and a new corporate culture usually involves the creation of a new organisation structure – with a smaller head office and fewer levels of management, also line managers who can be given total responsibility and can be held fully accountable for their business units.

In the last three years the TSB Group has had major surgery which included the following measures:

- The retail banking head office was moved from London to Birmingham.
- The branch network was redesigned, taking out 5,500 people.
- The Group head office was combined with the retail banking head office.
- Seven regional mortgage processing centres were combined into one.

In this book other executives report on the 'war against bureaucracy' at BP Oil, the Automobile Association, Hewlett-Packard and Granada Television, using modern techniques like Activity Based Costing and Business Process Re-engineering to slim down their head offices and to push 'dynorods' through their departmental structures.

New culture

In most of these companies the executive team has made a deliberate attempt to change the management style and the employees' attitudes. For the W.H. Smith Group of 29,000 employees, Sir Malcolm Field and his colleagues have defined explicitly the leadership style and the cultural norms which they want to instil.

They argue that 'empowerment' will 'increase the authority and responsibility of those closest to our products and our customers. By actively pushing responsibility, trust and recognition throughout the organisation, we can release and benefit from the full capabilities of our people.'

Similarly, the senior management of banks such as AIB, TSB and Lloyds have worked to reduce the bureaucracy and the remoteness of traditional bank cultures and to re-focus their employees' attention and their systems on delivering better service to customers at a reasonable price. This may seem incredible to bank customers who are used to standing in queues and talking to high-handed bank managers while groups of clerks shuffle papers in the background. But it is beginning to have an effect.

World class

Many of the companies represented in the book have already achieved 'World Class' and most of them are 'benchmarking' their performance against global best practice.

Manufacturing firms such as Xerox, Hewlett-Packard and Tallent Engineering use their affiliations with Fuji Xerox, Canon and Nissan to monitor their performance against the benchmarks set by leading Japanese producers.

Some companies – like Rank Xerox – set their senior managers performance standards, not just in terms of return on investment and market share, but also on customer satisfaction and employee satisfaction. Senior managers must reach their targets in these areas before they can receive their executive bonus.

Performance management

An essential requirement for achieving a dramatic improvement in performance is to obtain the commitment of each individual worker and each work team. This involves:

- Convincing each person and each team that they must take responsibility for their own performance.
- Teaching each worker how to produce a high-quality product and how to give an excellent service to customers.
- Providing them with regular feedback on their own performance.
- Recognising and rewarding excellent performance when it occurs.

Performance Management can be an expensive process to orchestrate. Xerox Corporation trained 125,000 staff in a Quality Through Leadership programme at a cost of around $200 million. The TSB Group trained 23,000 employees in Total Quality Management. However, partly as a result of these programmes, Rank

Xerox has steadily regained its market share and maintained its profits in spite of intense competition from Canon, Minolta and other Japanese companies. TSB has attracted £6 billion in deposits, and re-established its profitability in the highly competitive UK banking market.

Other companies which were once in intensive care like Colston dishwashers and Dunlop tyres have been resuscitated and brought back to life with Japanese production approaches such as Just in Time, Total Quality Management, and Kaizen (continuous improvement).

On performance-related pay, the benefits are also clear. But, as Chris Gamblin of Northern Telecom emphasises, pay is only one of a number of rewards which need to be considered. Pay and incentives must be designed as one element in a total system of 'managing for achievement'.

Total innovation

Also, there is the suggestion that Total Quality will not be enough. To maintain a competitive edge in the markets of the 1990s, companies must not just 'do things better' but 'do things differently'.

Mark Brown suggests that the challenge of the 1990s will be to 'tap every individual's creativity and intelligence. Involve everyone in the search for doing things better and differently in pursuit of delighting customers'. Henry Curteis, an owner-manager, explains how he has built an environment which is conducive to continual innovation. This involves moving people from a vicious circle of decline to a virtuous circle of growth.

Kevin Bourke writes about 'drawing on the creativity of staff' at Allied Irish Bank through a programme called Superthought which was 'conceived and delivered on a massive scale'. Ninety-eight per cent of staff and management were involved. They produced 1200 valuable ideas and harnessed staff enthusiasm for revitalising the bank and delivering an excellent service to the customers.

George Medley of World Wildlife Fund for Nature describes how 'flattening the pyramid' had the effect of 'releasing energy, talent, enthusiasm and skills that can take an organisation into a new realm of achievement'.

Partnerships and networks

To sustain a position of market leadership often requires investments and expertise which are beyond the reach of a single firm. So many businesses are forced to compete in world markets not as individual companies but as members of an alliance or partnership.

Strategic alliances are especially important in capital-intensive industries such as aircraft manufacture, airlines, trucks and automobiles, computers and telecommunications.

Xerox Corporation has two joint ventures: Rank Xerox in Europe and Fuji Xerox in Japan. TSB Group is the result of the merger and rationalisation of all the British Trustee Savings Banks. Tallent Engineering has built its world-class position through supplier-customer partnerships with Ford and Nissan, and collaborations with their other chassis suppliers in the USA and Japan.

Logistics is one area where Britain leads the world. This is largely through the efforts of our retail multiples. Patrick Moylan describes the efforts of Marks & Spencer, Allied Maples and Boots to compete on service delivery. Patrick Tonks explains how Tesco, Superdrug, Sony and ICL have used computer networks to speed up the communication and reduce stocks held in the supply chain.

Successful change strategies

How can we transform our organisations to compete successfully in the 1990s? According to the Chief Executives who report their experiences in this book, the answers will be found in one or more of these eight approaches:

- *Stretch goals:* Management must define their goals in terms of specific, measurable objectives.
- *Future vision:* Employees need to be shown a 'promised land' where the company will build a prosperous future.
- *Lean organisation:* Line managers need to be given a structure where they can take charge and can be held accountable.
- *New culture:* This requires a more open style of leadership, communicating values and working through teams.
- *World class:* To succeed, companies must 'reach for the stars' and measure themselves against the world's best.
- *Performance management:* This means involving every worker in delivering high quality products and services. It also means forming teams and giving them the training, the measures and the rewards they need.
- *Total innovation:* To compete successfully in the 1990s, it will not be enough to do the same things better. The challenge is to harness the creativity of the work force to do new things and to do things differently. This means tolerating a certain amount of chaos and disorder, relaxing controls and letting the employees 'take charge'.
- *Partnerships and networks:* To achieve market leadership, management has to learn to trust and to cooperate. They must form partnerships with their suppliers, distributors and competitors.

These eight approaches are given a different emphasis in each of the companies described in this book. Taken together they represent a new and more effective style of Strategic Leadership.

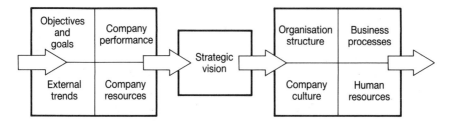

Figure I.2 Strategic management in practice

Implementing corporate strategy

Put in the context of Strategic Leadership or Strategic Management, the book deals with the crucially important area of communicating and implementing corporate strategy.

Figure I.2 displays the major processes involved in Strategic Management, in so far as they can be formalised. In practice of course the processes frequently occur not sequentially but iteratively and in parallel.

However, in trying to manage the processes systematically, it is important that they should include the following elements:

A. In *Strategy Formulation*
1. defining or reviewing *corporate objectives and goals* in the light of the requirements of shareholders and other stakeholders;
2. appraising the *company's performance* against these goals, and against the achievements of leading competitors;
3. assessing *trends in the business environment* (economic, technological, socio-political and competitive), and
4. appraising the *company's resources* (people, finance, technology, facilities, marketing and political influence) to determine whether the company has adequate resources to achieve its objectives.
5. From this situation analysis the management team can move on to define or review its *vision* for the future of the business. The vision should define in a short pithy statement how the organisation will focus its efforts to achieve a leadership position over competitors in specific product/market areas.

B. In *Strategy Implementation* the management team needs to consider four main areas:
1. What kind of *organisation structure* will be needed to sustain the company in the future? This means looking at the different kinds of structures (functional, regional, business unit, etc.), the number of levels, and the location of authority for key decisions.

2. What are the key *business processes* which need to be managed (e.g. order-to-delivery, or new product development)? It is important that these processes should be consciously managed in order to reduce waste and to cut down the 'cycle time'.
3. What is the *company culture* and how will it need to change? Traditional businesses are often focused around the production or operating system. To compete effectively these organisations need to become more customer-oriented. Also, mature businesses are often bureaucratic and they need to be more entrepreneurial and innovative. The process of changing staff attitudes at all levels can be time-consuming and expensive.
4. The final set of questions to be addressed concerns the *management of human resources*. To implement a new strategy in a highly competitive and rapidly changing industry often requires major changes in personnel policies — pay and conditions, selection and recruitment, training and development, rewards and incentives may all need to be changed.

This book is built around the theme of Implementing Corporate Strategy, and it is divided into the following four parts which cover the key areas where Chief Executives focus their efforts:

Part I   Building leaner, more flexible organisation structures
Part II   Re-engineering key business processes
Part III   Developing a continuous improvement culture
Part IV   The strategic management of human resources

The seventeen chapters have been allocated to the Part which seems most appropriate. In practice, however, the process of managing strategic change usually involves more than one area, e.g. a change of structure may be accompanied by a change of process, or a change of culture may require a change in human resources management.

Acknowledgement

This book would never have been completed without the solid support which I received at the office from my secretary Susanne Walton, at home from my wife Dorothy Taylor, and in business from the new generation of talented leaders and advisers who have written so frankly about their experiences. I would like to express my grateful thanks to them all.

Bernard Taylor,
Henley Management College, 1993

Building leaner, more flexible organisation structures

1 Restructuring and revitalising the TSB

Peter Ellwood

Executive summary

In 1989 the TSB was in urgent need of radical change. Activities were duplicated across the Group, there was a legacy of under-investment and costs were rising faster than income.

A four-stage strategic approach to tackling the problems was taken to create a vision, define the mission, develop the strategy and implement it.

This chapter describes the TSB Group's strategy of focusing on the core business of retail banking and insurance and the key techniques for successful change management: rigorous project management, good communications and resolute leadership.

In May 1989 I was privileged to become Chief Executive of a newly formed division of the TSB Group looking after retail banking. In the spring of 1991 I was asked to look after, additionally, its retail insurance businesses and in the summer of 1992 I accepted the post of Group Chief Executive at TSB.

Since I joined TSB, my team has restructured the retail bank, integrated the banking and insurance business to create the most advanced 'bancassurance' operation in the United Kingdom and, more recently, restructured the group and focused its strategy.

TSB's history

In April 1993, the TSB Group was capitalised at £2.4 billion, making it the 50th largest plc in the United Kingdom. It has 1.2 million shareholders, balance sheet footings of £31 billion, 33,500 staff, 7 million customers and 1,370 branches.

The largest part of TSB is its retail banking business. In 1989 it was a business in urgent need of radical change. Operating costs were rising rapidly and rising faster than income. Between 1986 and 1989 the important cost/income ratio had risen from 65.5% to over 72%. The bank's products were insufficiently competitive and we were losing market share. Our branches could not be described as attractive and they were smaller than the branches of our high street competitors, making economies of scale difficult to achieve.

On the plus side there were firm foundations on which to build. The staff were, in the main, keen, enthusiastic and had a strong empathy with the customers and there was a great deal of genuine customer care. There was a large, loyal customer base and sophisticated technology both in the branches and at the centre.

To some extent the problems were a result of TSB's history. TSB retained many elements of the federal organisation that had served it well since it was founded in 1810, and as recently as 1976 there were 73 separate Trustee Savings Banks. These were amalgamated, but when the TSB Group was floated on the London Stock Exchange in 1986 there were still four separate companies. Our federal roots had left us with a legacy of under-investment in the branch network, a many-layered management and skill shortages. Activities were duplicated in functions such as information technology, marketing and finance, and there was an unwieldy regional infrastructure managing the branch network.

The challenge in 1989 was compounded by an increasingly competitive market and the growing demands of customers throughout the financial service sector. They, quite rightly, wanted better value-for-money products and improved levels of service.

With a cost base – grown during years of combining dozens of small savings banks – masked by an unsustainable income stream flowing from uncompetitive products, the need for change could not have been more clear. But TSB was not alone. The whole financial services sector in the second half of the 1980s seemed to be waking, as if from a dream, to face the grim realisation that customers' needs were not being met. Everywhere one looked across the industry, there were signs of frenetic activity to redress the apathy of many decades.

Tackling the problems

It is easy to describe the problems, or 'challenges' as we like to call them! It is a little more challenging to deal with them effectively.

We took the following four-stage strategic approach to understanding how we would develop our business:

1. We created a vision of where we wanted to be.
2. We turned that into a mission to marshal hearts and minds within the company.
3. From our mission we evolved a strategy for achieving it.
4. We transformed that strategy into a series of specific actions.

To create a vision we weighed up the strengths and weaknesses of our company, and the opportunities and threats that lay ahead. Our strengths were clear: a large customer base; a branch banking computer system that was, and is, the envy of many of our competitors; a young and enthusiastic staff; a well-developed service culture; and strong empathy between the staff and their customers. The company's weaknesses, too, were clear: rising costs; duplication of jobs and functions; no long-term strategy; uncompetitive products; and more elderly customers than our competitors had. By looking at ourselves this way, we saw how to make the most of our opportunities and we knew where we wanted to put TSB in the market-place by building on our strengths. We had our vision of what TSB was and what it was going to be.

A mission statement conveys the vision to every member of staff, getting them to focus their sights and energies on achieving it. If people are to believe and accept it, the statement must be simple, it must be clear and they must feel part of it. It must set a common goal that everyone can recognise. Our mission statement met all those needs. It was and still is:

To be the UK's leading financial retailer through understanding and meeting customer needs and by being more professional and innovative than our competitors.

TSB staff recognise that statement and are committed to achieving the mission. They are aware that by 'leading financial retailer' we do not mean the biggest but we do mean the best. They know that 'understanding and meeting customer needs' means the customer always comes first. They realise that 'being more professional and innovative' means we are investing in people, in branch expenditure, in processes and in systems to create an organisation that is managed and staffed by people who all have a role that adds value to the organisation and who are all, therefore, important to its success. Implicit in the mission statement is the understanding that we cannot succeed unless we offer customers value-for-money products and excellence of service. Further refining that statement means meeting the basic financial needs of the man in the street. It is about emulating the best traits of the most successful retailers.

Three years ago, if you had asked a member of TSB staff 'Where is the business going?' they may have made some comment about becoming the fifth UK clearer. I can assure you that no one at TSB is now interested in being the fifth anything. Our mission is to become the UK's leading financial retailer.

But creating a mission statement does not make success happen. You must have a simple strategy for fulfilling that mission. Our strategy is to drive down costs and increase quality, sustainable income. It is simple, but it is powerful and it has driven TSB's transformation. We are rigorously driving down day-to-day costs so that we can afford to give a satisfactory return to shareholders and still invest in the business to give the customers a value-for-money deal and thus sustain long-term profitable growth. We are increasing income, not by widening margins and so creating uncompetitive products, but by adopting a marketing strategy that combines competitive, value-for-money products and excellent sales and service to our customers. This approach, in turn, gives us a greater share of total financial relationships for our customers and potential customers.

Managing change

Putting plans into practice is the hardest part of change. Our plans for TSB were to affect every corner of the bank organisationally, and many staff personally. It was crucial that those plans were carefully managed and vigorously communicated to the organisation, and that managers provided strong leadership.

I believe that the only way effectively to bring about large-scale radical change is to divorce the action of change from the day-to-day process of management. Responsibility for delivering the change should be given to dedicated, focused project teams using rigorous project management methodology.

Objectives must be specific and the milestones must be crystal clear. Senior managers at the highest level must ensure that appropriate resources are available and that projects cohere, fulfilling the corporate goal. Equally important, senior users should steer, bless and accept the work and as soon as possible it should be handed back to line managers, so that they 'own' it.

In 1989, at TSB, we launched *five major projects* with the aim of fundamentally reorganising the whole bank, reducing costs and focusing on the customer.

The Network Redesign Project rationalised branch and regional organisation; Head Office Review managed the relocation to Birmingham and a headcount review of all central functions; the Commercial Project rethought our strategy for commercial customers; we undertook a detailed analysis of customer and product profitability; and we carried out a programme of promoting the best-demonstrated practice within branches across the United Kingdom.

We set exacting project management standards, fixed the objectives firmly, tracked progress through senior steering groups and reviewed the deliverables regularly with the line managers who would have to use them. This degree of organisation meant that we knew where we were with the implementation at any given time. It may be true that revolutions never go backwards, but these thorough methods are the only way there is to keep them going forward, under control.

Change on this scale can be deeply unsettling. It is vital that even when the message will be a bitter blow to those who receive it, they must know as soon as possible. It should be communicated clearly and honestly. We use videos, conferences, team meetings and cascade briefings to make sure that every member of staff knows what is happening in their company. And when they have questions, if their manager cannot resolve them on the spot, they are fed quickly back to the top and answered.

As an example, our last year-end results were announced to the top 200 managers in the group at a conference and supported by a video, staff notices, in-house magazine feature and questions and answers designed to explain every aspect. *Within 24 hours all 22,000 divisional staff had received the information at face-to-face meetings.* There is no substitute for good communication, particularly at a time of corporate upheaval.

Radical change also demands resolute leadership – not just from the Chief

Executive. There must be a closely knit team of professional business people running the organisation. Such a team must be enthused by the corporate vision, they must support one another and they must be prepared to put the organisation first. The team should not be too large, because this inhibits the quick decisions needed to resolve issues. The directors of the senior management team at Retail Banking and Insurance are top quality professionals. It has taken some time to put this ideal team together – with some 'fall out'. But you cannot compromise when you transform a business.

Putting it into practice

TSB has earned the rewards of its endeavours over the last three years using these simple techniques and by sticking to the vision.

In the last three years we have reduced the headcount of the Retail Banking and Insurance division by over 5,500. We have cut the number of regional offices from seven to three and then from three to one, avoiding duplication and creating one bank, with a single focus. We closed our seven regional mortgage processing centres and amalgamated them to form a single centre in Glasgow.

In 1990 we went from 54 district offices to 21 area offices. Historically the district office manager had been responsible for some 27 branches and spent much of his time travelling from one branch to another. The area directors had a more manageable span of control, being responsible for some 8 branch clusters, with each cluster headed by a senior manager responsible for 8 smaller branches. During 1991 we rationalised even further, down to 16 areas. And in 1992 when we integrated our insurance and banking retail operations, the number of areas grew to 22. With each change, we have made sure that the organisational structure was made up of manageable units with clear responsibilities.

We reorganised information technology, finance, human resources and marketing, starting with a blank sheet of paper and building the optimum structure for each function, which was flatter and more effective. We relocated our entire Head Office from London to Birmingham and moved our clearing centre from a city location to a cheaper site in London.

To gain economies of scale in administering customer accounts, we moved 15% of back office work from our branches to 79 Customer Service Centres (CSCs). We used the flexibility of our technology systems to achieve this move quickly and to a greater degree than our clearing bank competitors. This change created a two-fold focus: staff in the CSCs could concentrate on process tasks, while the branch was freed from routine activities to spend time with customers.

Focusing on the customers and their needs

The traditional branch manager in TSB ran his or her branch as a micro business unit, with responsibility for administration and paperwork, lending within defined discretionary limits, staff training and development, handling customer queries, service levels, branch profit and loss and sales. His or her status and pay reflected the scope of the job, but distributing these responsibilities throughout our network increased TSB's cost base and diluted the time a manager could spend with the customers.

Taking work out of branches allowed the managers and their team to focus on customers and their needs. It also created more space that we used either to build more interview rooms or, in many cases, to refurbish the branch completely. The *new design branches* are open plan and more welcoming to customers, with enquiry counters, free-standing teller positions and more interview positions. Staff have more chance to be face-to-face with the customer, without a glass screen between them, and there is a greater sense of intimacy and personalisation of contact.

Our technology also gave us an edge in the interview rooms. Before, when our staff talked to customers about their financial needs, our traditional system of interviewing made sure that they covered all the relevant facts and offered the appropriate products. How effective this was depended on the experience and training of the interviewer. We have now introduced an expert system called *SuperService*, which guides the interviewer and shows the customer our information on their financial affairs. It also recommends relevant products to the customer and can even complete an application form for them to sign. SuperService is very popular with customers, it coaches inexperienced staff and it acts as an *aide-mémoire* for practised interviewers.

Integration of retail banking and retail insurance

Within the branches we had two separate sales forces – the banking staff who sold banking products and general insurance, and the insurance staff who sold life insurance and pensions products.

The Insurance arm of the TSB had been operating for 20 years, using the branch network for distribution and serving the needs of TSB customers only. Both the Life and Pensions business based at Andover, and the General Insurance business based at Newport, operated very much as stand-alone strategic business units, the former with its sales people working in branches and the latter paying commission to the bank on the products it sold.

In the spring of 1991, I was asked to take responsibility for TSB Retail Insurance as well as its Retail Banking arm. I saw this as a wonderful opportunity to offer the customer truly integrated products, whether they were short-term bank savings products or longer-term insurance savings products. Not only is this right for the customer but there would also be immediate cost benefits by removing duplication in sales management. The emphasis would be on giving the customer the product that he or she needs at the time they need it.

The plan was to move from separate businesses to the one powerful business of *Retail Banking and Insurance* (RBI). It is a process we started in 1991, first by putting all the information technology of the insurance business under the control of the RBI Information Technology Director and subsequently doing the same thing with Finance, Personnel and Marketing. Over time this removed a 'them and us' attitude between the bank and the insurance companies. We moved towards an integrated, dedicated sales and service staff operating from the customer side of the counter, to getting closer to the customer, understanding and meeting their needs, and building stronger, wider, more enduring financial relationships. We have now taken the first steps towards amalgamating the separate sales forces into a single sales force. This will be a first in the UK personal financial services market.

Better products

Being an integrated financial retailer calls for strong, value-for-money products and our product range is now more competitive than it has ever been. We have introduced a number of new 'champion' products that *since 1990 have attracted over £6.2 billion in balances.* As a result of this growth in deposit volumes, TSB RBI is able to develop these new customer accounts into fully fledged financial relationships while at the same time reducing the Group's reliance on the wholesale money market. But we will only continue to grow these balances by knowing more about our organisation and our customers. We have made large investments in improving our financial, marketing and customer information systems. These investments will go on. They must, because information is the life blood of any financial services organisation.

The benefits of all this activity have flowed to the bottom line. In 1990 we increased income by 18%, costs rose by just over 5% and profit before tax rose by 40%. In 1991 income went up almost 19%, costs by 3.8% and profit before tax by 17%. In 1992 income went up by 2.7%, costs actually fell by 1.4% and profit before tax was up 7.5% to £426 million. Good results but not as good as they will need to be in the white-hot competitive environment of the 1990s.

High quality service

Until recently, banking has been one of the classic examples of a supply-driven industry. We now face the challenge of being demand-led. Competition in product development and better cost management has dominated the last decade, but banking products are now commodities and cannot alone create or sustain competitive advantage. *The only thing that can create truly competitive advantage is service.*

Bankers have lived with a spurious sense of comfort by confusing customer loyalty with apathy. We have recently seen unprecedented fury vented on the banks by their customers. Although this is clearly fanned by hostile press coverage, it is a token of the present deep dissatisfaction with the quality of service.

Our own research shows that customers want specific improvements; more tills open at busy times; cash machines which do not run out of cash; clear information on bank charges; and fast and effective transactions. They also want better general treatment by courteous staff who respect their privacy and who sell them what they need, not just this month's special offer.

These issues will never be addressed by a quick-fix smile campaign. They require long-term training and management of quality. In two years almost all 23,000 staff in TSB RBI have been trained in total quality management – knowing what is required and meeting that requirement first time, every time.

And that is only the beginning of the quality process; it is a long journey, but one worth making. *Quality will be the major strategic differentiation in our industry –* those who achieve it will survive and prosper.

Focusing on our core business

Until now I have only discussed the Retail Banking and Insurance arm of the TSB Group – the TSB branded businesses. After its flotation in 1986, TSB made two widely criticised acquisitions – Hill Samuel Bank and Target Insurance. The strategy had been to build a diversified financial services group. This subsequently evolved into a two-brand strategy – TSB and Hill Samuel.

In the summer of 1992 I was appointed Chief Executive of TSB Group. We had a powerful group head office of some 100 staff who concentrated on defining high-level strategy, stewardship of the business, managing investor and regulatory relationships, planning, budgetary control and business monitoring. At the same time we had, in Birmingham, some 1,000 head office staff running the TSB Retail Banking and Insurance business.

It was clear that the TSB Group had to move to the next stage in its evolution, *fusing the group head office with the head office of its main operating unit.* This meant just one top team working together, with direct operational responsibility for all businesses within the Group.

The Group's strategy has also developed: our focus is now on the central business – Retail Banking and Insurance. Other parts of the Group are less central to our business but we continue to manage all parts of the Group for the benefit of shareholders.

Also, for the first time, we have announced that *we expect to deliver a 15% return to shareholders.* This is not an easy target and it will take three or four years to achieve. But when we have achieved it, I believe we will have done a good job for shareholders.

Conclusion

The financial services industry faces many years of great change. We are operating in an over-supplied market where margins are for ever under pressure from too many competitors chasing too few customers and striving to maintain or improve market share. Customers will continue to require better value-for-money products and better service, which they deserve. If they do not get it, they will quite rightly vote with their feet.

I am sure that in the next few years we will see a number of mergers between banks, between building societies and between banks and building societies. And I am confident that the shape of the industry we see today will be very different in five years' time.

The organisations which will still be around then will be those that have a clear vision of the future for their business and a clear strategy and action plan for getting there. They will be those who tenaciously seek to meet customer needs and expectations. They will need to be entrepreneurial, fleet of foot and totally committed to winning the race.

So what do I conclude from this? To be successful in restructuring and revitalising a company one needs analysis, vision, strategy, action, dedication, tenacity, discipline and a paranoia about success.

We at the TSB have those characteristics and go forward into the future with confidence.

2 Redesigning the head office at BP Oil – from hierarchies to networks

Keith Willey and Peter Siddall

'My co-authors and I downplayed the importance of structure in *In Search of Excellence* and again in *A Passion for Excellence*. We were terribly mistaken. Good intentions and brilliant proposals will be dead-ended, delayed, sabotaged, massaged to death, or revised beyond recognition or usefulness by the overlayered structures at most large and all too many small firms.'

Tom Peters, *Thriving on Chaos*, Macmillan, 1987

Executive summary

Successful companies adopt structures and processes to match their strategies – organisational 'fit'. But rapid changes in the external environment require equally rapid changes internally. The inability of many well-known large companies to do this has led them into difficulty and managers are now searching for ways of building the required flexibility into the fabric of the organisation.

This chapter is about changing the way large companies work. Underpinning the ideas are two basic assumptions – long-term profit and survival depend on satisfying the customer and the processes and structures which are built up to support this purpose over time will tend to become inefficient and misdirected.

Most large companies have a well-thought-out product market strategy and responsive, customer-focused operations. The problem they face is how to realign the processes and structures that link these two so that they will be low cost, effective and flexible. The processes described in this chapter show how managers can redesign their roles in a large company, drawing on the latest developments in organisation theory and recent practical experience.

Many of our best-known companies are experiencing extraordinary competitive pressures and exhibiting dissatisfaction with both their organisations and the pace at which they evolve. This has led to the current fashion for the introduction of major change programmes in the largest Western multinationals. These programmes are usually a series of initiatives under a single banner which calls for the whole company to change its ways. Perhaps the most famous is the US giant General Electric and its change programmes including 'Workouts', Global Best Practice and Process Mapping.

BP	Project 1990
Ciba Geigy	Vision 2000
ICI	Continuous improvement
Philips	Centurion
Siemens	Qualität Aktion
SmithKline Beecham	Simply Better

Figure 2.1 Some recent organisation change programmes

The programmes shown in Figure 2.1 are all about preparing the way for a fundamental realignment of management style and practice. The common starting point is that the company is believed to be too hierarchical and bureaucratic with high operating costs.

The origins of the problems are often historical. As new structures and processes slowly evolve, they add layers to those from previous eras. But this evolution can be uncoordinated, slow and counter-productive – so senior managers initiate change programmes which call for the levels below them to adopt dramatically different ways of working. Invariably it is middle management who are blamed for being intransigent and old-fashioned, getting in the way of progress.

At this time the internal links are provided by middle managers. As a group they are solid, loyal and often cynical. They are also now under threat. A common pitfall in creating change is to launch a 'big bang' attack on the bureaucracy and the hierarchy without really working out what will replace it. Such programmes run the risk of losing their way in the implementation stage. Resistance to change among middle managers is understandable because they are particularly sensitive to changes in process and structure. They have seen endless reorganisations for no apparent purpose. Attempts at 'scientific' management process changes often ignore the reality of managerial practice and attack their perception of personal autonomy.[1]

So to approach a change programme with a blank sheet for both process and structure is a daunting prospect. The high degree of commitment such programmes require means that the direction and the methodology must be adopted at the very top of the company first. The process is a long-term exercise which should feed from the strategy to the planning and subsequently to performance and consequent reward. Experience suggests that it requires an iterative process, with a degree of trial and error. By establishing an accepted methodology for carrying out these iterations, the company can build expertise in directing its own evolution.

Head office means bureaucracy

It is common for a head office to regard itself as an autonomous unit, responsible for its own size and shape, regardless of the duties of those who actually inhabit the building. Any sales office co-located there sees itself as the senior sales office, any

IT department as the corporate IT department. Increasingly it is realised that the design of the *head office influences the long-term success of the whole company.* There are common organisational factors that link the ability of the company to take a long-term view with management's inability to address short-term failure. Such situations can be understood better by examining what goes on in the head offices of large companies.

Experience of behaviour in big companies suggests that, among corporate staff groups, the managers' natural instincts to expand their roles, to promote organic growth and to be creative can often run riot in a head office. Also, senior managers are often more comfortable identifying with the head office itself rather than with the operating units. Many industries have experienced these happy times and managers hold fond memories of the corporate tower block. The pressures that bring them down to earth come from the following two sources:

1. The centre becomes a remote, bureaucratic place. A symptom of this is declining performance in the operating units, the cause of which is not to be found in the many reports and analyses which the centre commissions. The problem is really a lack of accountability, little operating autonomy, slow reactions and a lack of realism in financial projections.
2. The other shock is the cost of the centre itself. This cost consists of both the direct costs of head office *and* the costs generated in the operating units which have to respond to the bureaucratic routines. If we could ask where should we put our next new recruit – in the centre or in an operating unit, it is doubtful that an objective observer would perceive any extra value to be added in the head office. Yet somehow those central staff departments continue to create a demand for high-powered, well-paid individuals.

For many companies a recession and the consequent pressure to cut costs eventually embarrass head office. They are an overhead that simply gets in everybody's way. Suddenly the Chief Executive wants to commune again with all his old friends in the operating units. He has decided that the head office is not adding value to the front-line business. However, he would do well to be more selective in his assessment and examine just what goes on in the head office. An analysis of the objectives and processes which operate at the top of the business is an essential precursor to changing the whole organisation.

Changing the organisation

The key levers in an organisation are its structure, the management processes used, the information flows within it and its culture. These all serve to link a range of components together – business units, departments, individuals. A change programme acts on the links in order to increase the performance of the whole. The steps involved are as follows:

1. Define and separate the organisational building blocks.
2. Clarify the links between the blocks through process, structure, culture and information.
3. Add value to the whole company through networks.

The process is shown in Figure 2.2.

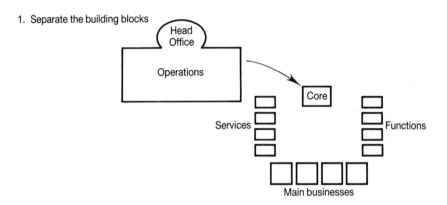

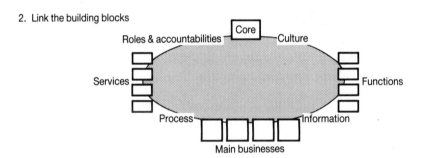

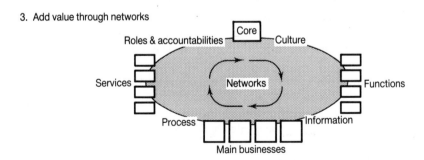

Figure 2.2 The three stages involved in redesigning a company

1 Define and separate the organisational building blocks

The operating businesses

The first step is to identify the most basic components of the organisation – the operating units – and isolate the links between them. Any company structure represents the latest preference for connecting a series of operating units. Divisions, subdivisions or other groupings of the operating units are designed to make the whole greater than the sum of the parts. The operating units however are fundamentally indivisible because they are adding value to a product or service for identifiable customers. Profit is made outside the company and they capture it. For them the rest of the company structure adds no value. Typically they will protest that they are the front-line troops and they do not need a head office. This is the most powerful argument for ensuring that any hierarchical layers are subjected to stringent tests to ensure that they add value to the operating units and that the units are of 'human' scale.

Clarity at this stage will help to overcome the confusion caused by differences in business unit size, blurring of boundaries between them and many intercompany transactions. However, *the principle of separation* is more important than getting the plea of 'what is a business' right first time.

The core replaces head office

The creation of the new 'core' corporate centre is the first task in designing a new organisation to link the operating units. *The Chief Executive selects his own small group to help him to carry out his own duties.* It is distinct from any centralised, shared activity or expertise and presents an opportunity to kill the concept of head office by taking away its head. It is also funded directly rather than sharing its cost among other departments. *This unit must also be seen not to manage any businesses.*

The Chief Executive's role is to lead by providing strategic direction, making the senior appointments, counselling the operating units in their planning, agreeing how to measure their performance and adjusting the strategy as a result of their performance. The key senior operational and functional managers work closely with him on these issues, providing high-level overlaps between the centre and the businesses.

Fundamental questions concerning the head office are: What does head office do and why? Who should be there? and, consequently, How big should it be? The order of these questions is very important. Imagine if they were reversed. If a head office of 1,000 people were to be created and filled with the top 1,000 managers they would still find plenty of important things to do. These embedded costs would be hard to shift. In other words, redesigning the head office should start with a vision of its role and what style to adopt. The literature on the style of head office is extensive. The options can be summed up in a simple and useful way. There are three alternatives as follows:

Strategic Planning This is about long-term investments, central coordination, highly influential staff jobs filled with business school-trained eggheads who anticipate everything for their subsidiaries in advance. Most multinationals adopted this style in the 1960s.

Financial Control This is the opposite. Hard-nosed, aggressive bottom-liners. Apparently deeply cynical of any manager who might stray from this month's working capital target or who dares to talk about 'long-term strategic advantage'. He might talk the share price down!

In the middle is *Strategic Control* which is a blend of the two.

Most of us can recognise these parodies of the two extreme styles. We would put, say, the big oil companies into the Strategic Planning pigeonhole and Hanson in the Financial Control category.[2] A full survey would probably reveal that the two extreme styles are really quite rare. Most companies are on the fence in the centre. They are trying to balance the long-run view with short-term results. At the same time they neither grant full autonomy to the business units nor take up the reins themselves.

Given the difficulties and contradictions that follow from this tension it is clear that this situation is the most demanding when designing the organisation. It is tempting to suggest that size is the outcome of careful analysis and consultations on style. In practice this is not always the case. Often the decision is an arbitrary statement about size, and the style follows.

Those companies who can still remember why the head office gained so much power will weigh up the costs against the undoubted benefits of the corporate role (see Figure 2.3). They will also remember that happy time when they made a series of strategic moves which caused a less sophisticated competitor to retrench or divest. Long-term plans can work – the problem is how to retain these without the bureaucracy, and the high costs of a large head office.

This is as far as the Chief Executive should go in prescribing a new organisation.

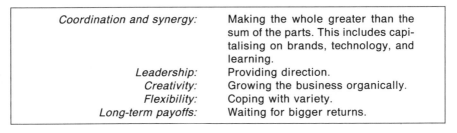

Coordination and synergy:	Making the whole greater than the sum of the parts. This includes capitalising on brands, technology, and learning.
Leadership:	Providing direction.
Creativity:	Growing the business organically.
Flexibility:	Coping with variety.
Long-term payoffs:	Waiting for bigger returns.

Figure 2.3 The benefits of a good head office

The rest of the ex-head office staff should then be encouraged to develop, jointly with the operational staff, the blueprints and models for their own futures.

The signal for managers to participate in the change programme is the change in Chief Executive's style, the effect of his or her new management processes and the clear statement of which posts he or she regards as part of the centre. The team approach creates powerful peer pressure not to ignore the various initiatives. Subsequent changes will then be evolutionary, resulting from the exchange of best practice and learning within these teams.

2 Clarify the links between the blocks

The centre should then be integrated into the rest of the company with new management processes and specific information needs to make the links to the businesses and the key functions. The Chief Executive must work hard to delegate within a clearly understood framework and build high quality into these processes to ensure that communication is fast, relevant and action-orientated.

The organisational structure and the key management processes must first be simplified. For each important activity (for example, business planning or human resource management), the key players must be brought to a consensus on how it should be done, based on clear accountability and de-layering. Business process diagrams help to pin down the exact detail of how each player will interact, for example to deliver the business plan or to ensure key jobs are filled. Such a process is described later in the section entitled 'Making it happen'.

Legitimate central roles — leadership

With the core of the old head office staff reduced, the next step is for the top layers of the business and functional hierarchy to realign. Any Chief Executive is understandably nervous about simply abolishing the central functional and business groups when they are so closely associated with the company's core competences. What then are the characteristics of the style he would like to see adopted by the other ex-head office components, and against which the Chief Executive can test the designs (see Figure 2.4)?

By this stage the Chief Executive has arrived at a firm idea about the size and role of the new, light corporate centre. The senior managers who are left — a mixture of functional and business staff whose roles in the organisation are confused and support staff who are not needed for the smaller corporate centre — must now undertake their own redesign, following the Chief Executive's lead.

The change is a delicate process to manage. The result often exposes many deputies and assistants — adders-up, checkers and second guessers who were often hired to sort out the mess that went before. The final result will be a corporate centre which can honestly say that it has minimised the waste created in its own

1. *They are small.* If there is a large department with its own hierarchy then either they're running a business or the bureaucracy has gone mad.
2. *They are never there.* These people are in the field preaching the gospel of sharing, openness and learning. They are building the special skills and knowledge into the operating management at large, not hoarding it in head office.
3. *There are no more cushy head office jobs to retire to.* Staff are only temporarily side-tracked, with a personal development plan which will take them back into the businesses.

Figure 2.4 Characteristics of effective central staff groups

structure and the waste created in its interactions with the rest of the company. However, this is only one side of the bargain – the rest of the company must also join in.

The initial task is now to extract any added value from the ex-head office group with the minimum of decentralisation of jobs. Merely pushing the jobs down into the operating level is not good enough (although some will inevitably find a place for themselves at that level). In fact the operating units probably have their own staff jobs with a similar mixture of added-value and waste-generating activity. The whole company must be involved in resolving this problem.

3 Add value to the whole company through networks

The changes so far have been largely focused on the centre. To make the whole organisation work, changes must be made to challenge both the established way of doing things and to encourage managers to agree new non-bureaucratic methods of operating – to achieve breakthroughs and commit themselves to continuous improvement.

Those head office activities outside the Chief Executive group are the functions and the support services. These two areas need different treatments, and must be clearly separated. For example, a function such as Human Resources often combines administrative support to the businesses for pensions and payroll as well as adding value through cross-business activities such as career development. Functions may be of the professional type – Human Resources, Accounting, Public Affairs; business stream-focused – Marketing, Manufacturing and Distribution; or they may deal with aspects of Technology or IT. The main sources of synergy across the businesses are found in these activities. If the processes in these areas cannot be clearly identified and managed then the suspicion must be that the synergies do not exist. Similarly, if the benefit of the activities reaches the customer through a tortuous route then the impact of that activity must be questioned.

For the functions, the balance shifts from the familiar large central staff to company-wide networks, with a building block in the corporate centre. The network members will agree together how much resource is needed at each other building block – the locally funded contribution to the cross-boundary effort.

A careful definition is needed before networks become a concept that managers can use. Networks are *groups of people with an agreed common purpose,* achieved through the individual authority to act of each member. Membership is determined by people's capability to contribute and each member will have reporting allegiances elsewhere. Thus the success of a network depends on trust, sharing and teamwork. The underlying benefit of a network is the focus on customer needs that it brings. It applies power and resource where it is needed and in a flexible way. It does not function on a 'hub and spoke' basis controlled by central staff.

The role of functions at the centre is to energise the network for the whole company, so that it provides leadership in setting common professional standards, excellence and learning at the point of delivery, the operating level. Suitable mechanisms for achieving this are benchmarking, the development of standards and the use of process re-engineering. For some, networks come naturally – people with information to share on technology or professions, such as engineers or lawyers, find it easier to talk to their counterparts in other parts of the organisation than to nearby colleagues in other disciplines. Technology can also aid networks – E-Mail, video-conferencing, faxes and other communication devices can be used by networks to great effect.

But many more critical activities should also be networked. Networking should be applied to those activities which aim to realise benefits from synergy, coordination, flexibility and creativity. To many people this sounds like a recipe for disaster – 'letting it all hang out' with no control of the business. But, in reality, controls are among the first things that have to improve to make it work. For example, the Chief Executive and the business heads form the most senior network. This network should allow the heads of the main businesses and functions to combine and cooperate with the Chief Executive in the development and management of the group.

How to build networks

Networks require careful attention to the areas of culture, structure, process and information. Organigrams mean nothing until they are brought to life with the details of how people will behave and how they will deal with the critical tasks. This is even more true when dealing with networks which are very unfamiliar to most managers and which, when presented pictorially, can take on puzzling forms.

It is said that a bureaucratic approach can kill networks. However, they can be implemented in a systematic way. The chief obstacles are listed in Figure 2.5. Many of these obstacles can be overcome by getting the 'mechanics' right – call it discipline in execution. A methodology is needed which is open and allows

Parochial attitudes – no concept of the pan-company team.
Introspective approach to problem solving – unaware of best practices.
Dependency on the local hierarchy – constant permission seeking, guarded
information sharing.
Arguments over funding and/or wrong incentives.
Poorly demonstrated short-term local benefits.

Figure 2.5 Networks overcoming the obstacles

managers to put forward their views on equal terms. The key players will be mainly the operational staff who might for the first time be challenged to identify how they can extract more customer satisfaction by interacting with the rest of the company. Even more challenging will be the need to tell distant colleagues about the best things so that other people can benefit from their experience.

However, to overcome all the obstacles, for most managers, involves a process of negotiation and a shift in behaviour which is difficult to achieve. Specialist and sensitive help is needed for this. Often, people have risen to the top of a company because they are the greatest exponents of the skills needed to succeed in the old hierarchy – but not in the new. Like middle management they may feel threatened by the new ways of working.

Services – align with customers

For the service groupings the debate is about whether there should be central suppliers serving the rest of the company. For example, frequently there are apparently strong economic cases made for having central IT departments. This is a legacy of the days when mainframe computing was a large fixed cost to be shared among the business units in order to realise economies of scale. The argument is given new life as expertise is built up and dependency develops.

At various points in time professional services such as lawyers will also be built up internally on the basis of a straightforward 'make-or-buy' calculation. Such departments can severely restrict the choice of buyers in the organisation. They also become orientated towards achieving an internal breakeven, losing any chance of being objective experts, and not motivated to achieve the greater benefit of the company.

The high costs and slow responses of support services in head offices are notoriously difficult to control. Where such non-core activities are carried out in-house there will always be a value-for-money debate. These services should therefore be ring-fenced and market mechanisms set up to focus them on their customers – the business lines. Such mechanisms may include market testing, outsourcing and a direct challenge from internal customers. The key priority is to ensure that their continued existence rests solely on these mechanisms. Today there are no strategic reasons why services should be located in head office, rather than be distributed or even outsourced; there is no blanket policy. Recent organ-isational research has identified a form of organisation where staff are not on the permanent payroll but part of the 'family', or a section of a clover leaf, which links expertise together in a 'virtual organisation'.[3]

Making it happen

Any change management project begins with a reason for change. Practitioners know that if there is no visible crisis or threat then they have to create a very attractive alternative. The techniques described in this chapter provide a potent mixture of the two. The Chief Executive takes away his patronage of the large head office staff and establishes his own system of control. But the others are not simply abandoned. They are offered an approach for creating new structures, processes, information and cultures for themselves. This section shows how such a methodology – the International Management Programme (IMP) as applied in BP Oil[4] – compels them to become intimately involved with, and responsive to, the operational units.

The value of the IMP programme is obtained through senior management participation and learning. A small team of senior managers works to define the key activities which together represent the major central management processes. The basis for the selection of activities is not restricted and it may be that some are chosen because they are undergoing significant change, they carry a high risk, are contentious or inefficient. In BP Oil, for example, these included the following:

- Investment Planning.
- Business Plans.
- Performance Measurement.
- Technology & Product Development.
- Health, Safety and the Environment.

These activities are then individually subjected to examination, to identify the component steps, the decisions, the management inputs and the timing. In particular, the perceptions at the interfaces between interested parties are explored so that mismatches can be clarified. This work is carried out using a combination of workshops and interviews with the managers affected. The activities are mapped so that there is a clear separation between individual managers or groups who are *accountable, responsible* and *contributing* (see Figure 2.6):

These distinctions are particularly useful in challenging some of the conventional assumptions about who does what and highlighting duplications, omissions and mis-matches. For example, one outcome of the programme for audit activities in BP Oil was to highlight that the accountable staff for the outcome of an audit were line managers and not, as previously understood, the audit staff. A typical diagram for the activity of Business Planning is shown in Figure 2.7. An essential

Accountable The key elements of accountability are responsibility for achieving a result, together with sufficient authority and power to take necessary actions and a degree of measurability of the result. Accountability may be delegated but may not be shared. It is not limited to short-term goals. In general 'line' management positions tend to have accountabilities.

Responsible A manager may hold a responsibility without having direct authority to issue instructions. It is exercised through influence, advice and if necessary the authority of the accountable person. All managers may have responsibilities outside their line accountabilities. For example, planning staff are essential in advising and helping in the planning process and are therefore responsible but line managers are accountable for the plan. In general, staff roles tend to carry responsibilities rather than accountabilities.

Contributing A contribution to achieving a result may be required from any manager. It concerns the provision of information, assistance and advice to those with the accountability and responsibility. Contributing is not optional. It is a required part of the manager's job.

Figure 2.6 Some definitions

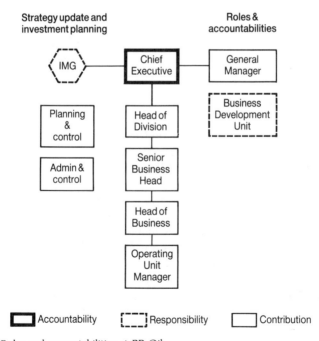

Figure 2.7 Roles and accountabilities at BP Oil

STRATEGY UPDATE & INVESTMENT PLANNING

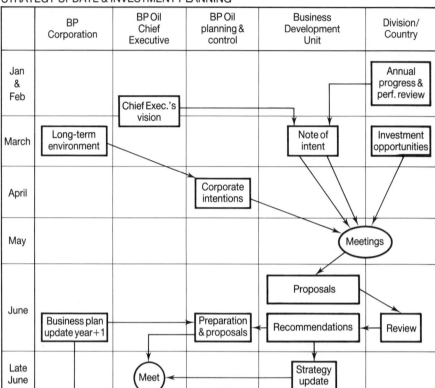

Figure 2.8 Process flows at BP Oil

element of the process is the creation of prototypes of definitions of activities and procedures which are then debated in order to develop consensus. The iterations are also important in allowing managers the opportunity to resolve issues outside workshops before the next draft.

Colour is used widely in the diagrams to communicate the different roles and accountabilities. Further distinctions are also used to indicate where a committee, an individual or a network is appropriate in any particular role. In addition to the assignment of roles and accountabilities *a map of the process* is made to indicate timings and key decisions (see Figure 2.8).

The changes to structure and process must also be accompanied by changes in information flows. Successful moves towards a less hierarchical structure and reduced bureaucracy are greatly assisted by greater delegation of authority and emphasis on openness and trust. Information sharing supports these objectives and is based upon the following six principles:

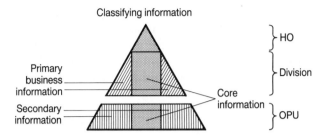

Figure 2.9 The information pyramid

- Openness and trust should be fostered through quality of information.
- Core information is commonly defined and freely available. It will always have the same definition when used at any level in BP Oil.
- Primary business information is the responsibility of and specific to the relevant network.
- Secondary information is decoupled from primary information and tailored to specific needs.
- Accountability is devolved as far as possible.
- Information should be used not abused; users provide quality not quantity, requesters reduce their demands to just the essentials.

The distinction between core, primary and secondary information within the existing management reports is illustrated in Figure 2.9.

Facing the consequences

The 'new style' head office, and the collective behaviours that it promotes, will change the culture of the whole company. With reduced layers of hierarchy and smaller permanent staff departments, it is inevitable that managers will move to project-based jobs. *Career paths must be found in the operating units, not at the centre and horizontal moves become career-enhancing not limiting.* Functional specialists will have few opportunities to manage departments but must persuade and influence their internal customers. Above all, managers must be more open and trusting and find new motivation in the challenges of continuous improvement and teamworking.

Within the company, staff and support roles must be reinforced with motivators other than that of building large departments and one-company careers. Business functional managers, such as Marketing or Manufacturing, must aim to become part of the operational team, to achieve credibility and acceptance with the line and to make agreements on how they serve the customer. Professional function heads, such as Finance or Human Resources, can add value by providing leadership and expertise to their equivalents throughout the company, constantly adjusting to address changes in the needs of line managers.

Shared and support services are different from the other groups. Their task is to identify their customers within the organisation, participating in a rigorous evaluation within the internal market for the services provided. Top–down changes rarely work here, instead, line managers must be involved in a process which allows them to make informed decisions about costs, increasing their control over them rather than just receiving allocations.

The 'bottom line' of these developments is that not everyone will be able to join in the changes. *A key result is the truncating of careers within a company.* For the individual, the prizes lie in taking skills and experience to a company that needs them at that point in time. He or she can add real value if they can demonstrate how to put the information they have been exposed to into action – useful knowledge.

These changes represent unprecedented opportunities for individuals to exploit their creative capabilities – hitherto largely untapped by organisations. Empowerment and accountability mean more than redefining jobs. It involves taking personal responsibility for delegated tasks and collective responsibility for the framework within which these tasks are executed. Put more simply, the challenge is to write the club rules and observe the disciplines implied – then enjoy the benefits, both personal and corporate.

The new organisation in context

The bandwagon of change which the big Western corporations have joined appears to be headed firmly in the direction described in this chapter and this trend is even more marked for international businesses. The prerequisites for building an efficient multinational structure have been explored extensively in management literature. In this context it can be seen that the power of the International Management Process lies in the practical application of some of these theories (see Figure 2.10).

For complex international organisations such forms have recently become known as 'Transnational' organisations. The process is described by Bartlett and Ghoshal: 'The centre must establish a new, highly complex, managing role to coordinate relationships in a highly flexible way ... create a context for the coordination and resolution of conflicts.'[5]

Companies such as the oil giant BP have been managing complexity and resolving conflict throughout their history but it is now realised that it is ineffective and too expensive to do this from the centre. The IMP provides a way of designing management systems for a complex organisation whilst achieving flexibility and low cost – especially critical features in new industries such as telecommunications where two years is the long term. It addresses many of the paradoxes which prevent organisations from transforming themselves for the business environment of the future such as the following:[6]

Requirements for 'Building the Ideal Organisation'[7]	IMP principles
Multiple advocacy	Senior management buy-in via use of iterative process prototyping, resolution of conflict via workshops and formal clarification of roles.
Fluid power structure	Extensive use of networking to short-circuit hierarchy. Delayering.
Legitimacy of dissent	Build openness and trust through sharing of information. Comprehensive consultation.
Discipline in implementation	Removal of ambiguity through Roles and Accountabilities. Detailed process driven by dedicated team of internal staff and consultants. Use of performance contracts.

Figure 2.10 The practical application of modern theory

- The need to foster internal stability to achieve change.
- Better control resulting from more delegation.
- Better measurement through fewer measures.

The key to change in organisations is to redesign people's roles and accountabilities and alter the way they must handle relationships with other people around them.[8] Sustainable changes result from creating an environment that promotes different behaviour through the resolution of the really crucial areas of conflict about the management process, rather than simply demanding changes in individual behaviour. The structure, process, information and culture can be changed in a systematic and proactive way designed to overcome the inertia inherent in large companies.

Notes

1. Mintzberg, 'The Manager's job – Folklore and Fact', *Harvard Business Review*, Jul–Aug, 1975.
2. Goold and Campbell, *Strategies and Styles*, Blackwell, 1987.
3. Handy, *The Age of Unreason*, Business Books, 1989.
4. Siddall, Tavares and Willey, 'Building a Transnational Organisation for BP Oil', *Long Range Planning*, vol. 25, no. 1, Pergamon Press, 1992.
5. Bartlett and Ghoshal, *Managing Across Borders – The Transnational Solution*, Hutchinson, 1989.
6. Peters and Waterman, *In Search Of Excellence: Lessons from America's Best-Run Companies*, Harper & Row, 1982.
7. Prahalad and Doz, *The Multinational Mission*, Free Press, 1987.
8. Beer, Eisenstat and Spector, 'Why Change Programs Don't Produce Change', *Harvard Business Review*, Nov–Dec, 1990.

3 Building an entrepreneurial organisation at WWF UK

George J. Medley

'Any institution has to be organised so as to bring out the talent and capabilities within the organisation; to encourage men to take initiative, give them a chance to show what they can do, and a scope within which to grow.'
Peter Drucker, quoted in James A. Belasco, *Teaching the Elephant to Dance*, Random House, 1990

Executive summary

The usual organisation for business is a pyramidical, hierarchical structure. This structure tends to stifle initiative from levels below senior management. This chapter describes a different structure designed to stimulate and encourage initiative and flair from middle managers. The structure is described in detail and the lessons learnt from its introduction into a medium-size charity business are discussed. Inevitably there are pitfalls to such a new approach and these are explored. In George Medley's view the pitfalls are outweighed by the benefits.

The majority of organisations base their structure on the traditional concept of a pyramidical hierarchy (see Figure 3.1). The Chief Executive (CEO) is at the top of

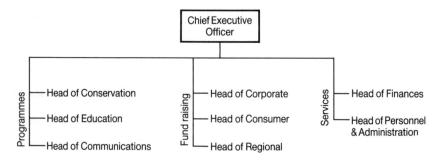

Figure 3.1 The old structure

the pyramid. Reporting to the CEO are the departmental chiefs and under them the managers, executives, and the remainder of the staff in a neat, clearly defined line. This structure has the advantage of clarity. Everyone knows exactly where they stand in relation to their superiors and juniors and to their peers. It has served industry well over the years, is quickly understood by anyone coming into the organisation and is transparent to anyone interested in finding out more about the particular company. Everyone feels comfortable with a simple pyramid. Everyone knows their place and the decision-making tree is quite clear. But the question has to be asked 'Does the pyramidical structure encourage entrepreneurialism?'

Where the pyramid fails

The most common answer to this question has to be 'No'. There is little chance of someone in tier three approaching the CEO unless he or she is positively encouraged to do so by those in tiers two and one. Such an occurrence is rare since this type of initiative would be seen as an attempt to subvert the normal channel of communication and an undermining of the 'power' exerted by those in the two tiers above the individual. Thus the pyramidical structure, for all its worth, tends to stifle those who may have more to contribute to their organisation than their position would suggest.

Where the fostering of individual initiative is not required the pyramidical hierarchy is probably acceptable but in the 1990s where competition is fierce, innovation is essential to the well-being of a corporation and flair and lateral thinking are most desirable attributes in key employees, the standard organisational structure fails the test.

What alternatives are there? One that has been tried by WWF UK (World Wide Fund For Nature) has certainly helped to build an entrepreneurial organisation but, it has to be said, with some difficulties in management control.

Frustration with departments

Up until 1990 WWF UK's structure was fairly standard for a not-for-profit organisation. The charity was divided into eight departments, each with a departmental head reporting to the CEO. There were three departments in programmes, Conservation, Education and Communications, three in fund-raising, Corporate, Consumer and Regional and two in services, Finance and Personnel. Beneath each head of department the structure was standard, with managers, executives and clerical and secretarial staff. Budgetary control was maintained by the department, each of which was made a cost centre or, in the case of the fund-raising departments, a cost and income centre. This structure was satisfactory while the charity was relatively small but the upsurge in public interest in the environment in the late 1980s, and the manner in which WWF had geared itself up

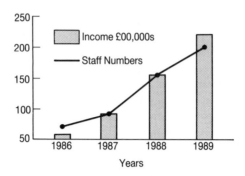

Figure 3.2 WWF UK income and staff numbers

to take advantage of this considerable public interest, led to explosive growth, both in terms of income generation and in staff numbers (see Figure 3.2). The complexities of service provision in the form of the programmes also escalated, with the charity turning its attention from the conservation of species to the much wider task of convincing decision-makers that fundamental change towards environmental matters was needed in the attitudes of government, industry and individuals.

The substantial increase in staff numbers in WWF UK included a large number of scientists who were hired for their ability to think laterally and to show a spirit of innovation and entrepreneurialism. This was needed to craft the reports that would have a chance of influencing those in positions of power in government and industry to take a more environmentally friendly and responsible attitude. It was inevitable that a degree of frustration would grow among such individuals if the structure did not allow them the freedom of expression that they had been led to believe was what was wanted from them. The departmental hierarchy was not serving them as they felt it should, and they believed that the heads of department were forming a barrier between them, their good ideas, and the CEO who alone could give them the freedom of operation that they desired.

These frustrations were expressed in the strategic planning sessions leading up to the Plan for 1990/1. The solution was to devise a new structure which would release some of the latent energy, entrepreneurial spirit and lateral thinking without losing the essential management control. A number of different ideas were considered, including divisionalisation by 'business mix' or conservation theme, giving each division its own programming, fund-raising and communications staff. This was rejected as an unnecessary complication for a small organisation of 150 people. Various permutations and combinations of the existing departmental structure were also considered, and rejected. The final proposal was radical, relatively untried and not a copy of any other structure known to be in existence at that time.

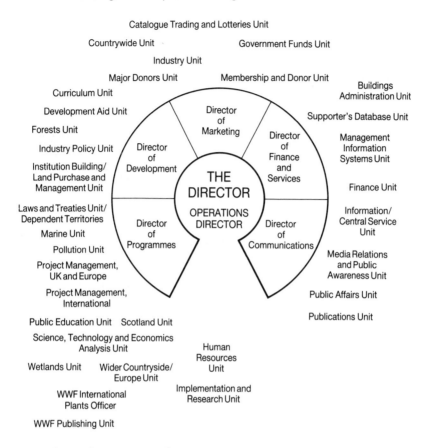

Catalogue Trading and Lotteries Unit

Countrywide Unit   Government Funds Unit

Industry Unit

Major Donors Unit   Membership and Donor Unit

Curriculum Unit

Development Aid Unit

Forests Unit

Industry Policy Unit

Institution Building/
Land Purchase and
Management Unit

Laws and Treaties Unit/
Dependent Territories

Marine Unit

Pollution Unit

Project Management,
UK and Europe

Project Management,
International

Public Education Unit   Scotland Unit

Science, Technology and Economics
Analysis Unit

Wetlands Unit   Wider Countryside/
Europe Unit

WWF International
Plants Officer

WWF Publishing Unit

Buildings
Administration Unit

Supporter's Database Unit

Management
Information
Systems Unit

Finance Unit

Information/
Central Service
Unit

Media Relations
and Public
Awareness Unit

Public Affairs Unit

Publications Unit

Human
Resources
Unit

Implementation and
Research Unit

Director of Marketing · Director of Finance and Services · Director of Development · THE DIRECTOR · OPERATIONS DIRECTOR · Director of Programmes · Director of Communications

Figure 3.3 The circular organisation chart

The flattened pyramid

The proposal was to flatten the pyramid, do away with departments and give a much wider range of managers responsibility for their own area of operation. Various methods were tried to depict this structure. The first attempt is shown in Figure 3.3. The central core of the structure is the Director (CEO) and the Operations Director (Chief Operating Officer or COO). This core is encircled by the five Functional Directors but with a gap at the bottom to show that the Human Resources Unit and the Implementation and Research Unit report direct to the core.

The outer circle contains the 36 units who all have a line responsibility to the COO but who are grouped according to their area to show that they have a functional responsibility to their respective Functional Director.

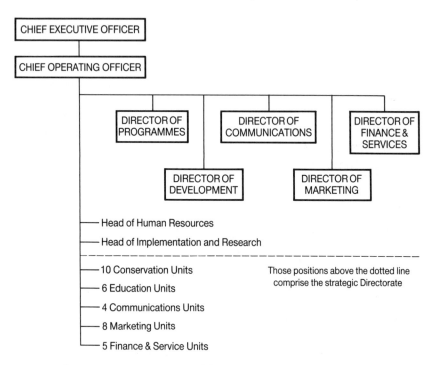

Figure 3.4 The new structure (conventional format)

This organisation chart was not easy to explain and a more conventional organogram was devised (see Figure 3.4).

The strategic directorate

The purpose of this structure was twofold. It enabled the CEO to be concerned with 'upward and outward management', leaving the COO to deal with the day-to-day management of the organisation and with responsibility for all the operations. The intention was for the 'Directorate', consisting of the CEO, the COO and the five Functional Directors, to be the strategic nucleus, concerned with planning, strategy and monitoring tactics but (other than the COO) to have no direct line responsibility. This would enable the Directorate to concentrate on the business as a whole without the day-to-day concerns and burdens of line management. The Functional Directors would be available for advice and guidance to the units in their area but line responsibility would be direct to the COO.

36 independent units

The 36 unit heads would each have complete responsibility for their unit, its operations, budgets and staff. They would agree their budgets and their objectives with the COO, together with their respective Functional Directors, acting in an advisory capacity. Once the objectives and budgets had been agreed the unit heads would have the freedom to operate within them. Their performance would be monitored using the management accounts which were to be produced monthly and which would be considered and debated carefully by the Directorate. Unit heads would be encouraged to use their new-found freedom to show initiative, flair and entrepreneurialism, but always within the agreed budgetary and objective limits. Once a year there would be a formal appraisal of their performance with a two-hour interview with the COO, attended also by their Functional Director, still acting in an advisory capacity. At this appraisal, performance against objectives would be assessed both by the unit head and by the COO. The two views would be debated, any disagreements reconciled and objectives for the next year discussed and agreed.

Advantages and disadvantages

This structure was put into effect on 1 July 1991. How effective has it been and what lessons can be learnt from its implementation and operation?

The first objective of freeing up the Directorate to concentrate on strategic and planning matters has been fully achieved. With the removal of responsibility for line management the Functional Directors spend much more time seeking more effective and efficient methods of operation, new concepts in fund-raising and service delivery, better use of management information systems, reappraisal of in-house operations compared to out-of-house and many other more strategic considerations. They have more time for making effective outside contacts, participating in and learning from discussions with other not-for-profit bodies both within and outside the areas of direct interest to WWF and keeping abreast of the latest developments in their particular areas of expertise.

For the unit heads the new structure has been largely a real success. Individuals who, under the old departmental structure, felt their initiatives and flair to be inhibited, have won new-found freedom. They are able to experiment, within their set objectives and budgets, in new methods of working. They have been released from the constraints imposed by the artificial boundaries of departmental structures, leading to much greater collaboration and cooperation, not just between units in the same area but, more importantly, across the whole business of WWF. Cross-cutting teamwork is the norm rather than the exception, with the benefit of real progress combining the best skills and thinking from all areas of the charity to reap success in achieving the Mission.

Two examples illustrate how the units have worked together to achieve success. The first was a campaign to persuade the government of an Asian country to become more concerned about the trade in endangered species being carried on in their territory. Many countries have signed the Convention on International Trade in Endangered Species (CITES) whereby the commercial movement of live animals, birds and plants in endangered categories, together with their skins, feathers and other parts, is strictly controlled. Unfortunately there are a few countries who, in spite of signing and ratifying the Convention, have not taken the necessary steps to put the Convention rules into practice. An initiative was proposed by WWF's Treaties Unit to bring pressure to bear on the Asian government to fully implement the CITES rules. The Treaties Unit organised a cross-cutting team with representation from communications, marketing and education which produced a plan, involving a major appeal to WWF's membership to write direct to the Asian government and to its representation in London. This appeal showed pictures of the plight of many endangered animals and birds in the bazaar markets and the skins openly available for sale.

The letter-writing campaign was coordinated by the cross-cutting team and resulted in a veritable flood of letters being sent to the Asian government's Prime Minister and to its representative in London. It was pointed out that the country had ratified CITES but that this treaty was being openly flouted in the bazaars. Within a month news was received that the Prime Minister himself had, unexpectedly, visited the bazaars, following which, laws were rapidly passed to outlaw such trade, a happy outcome from a well-coordinated campaign.

The second example is from a single unit, the Forests Unit. They had recognised that one of the best ways to stop the wholesale destruction of tropical rainforest was to target the end users of tropical hardwoods. They opened discussions with some of the UK's largest importers of hardwoods and, after many hours of talking over some months, succeeded in persuading one of these companies to agree that by the year 1995 all the hardwood they imported would come only from sources which were being managed sustainably. This was a major step forward, the first success in a new area and an example that has now been emulated by more than 15 companies who have all signed up to the 1995 target. Obviously the first company was seeking a commercial advantage whilst at the same time adhering to the best practices in environmental behaviour. This led to further discussions with the company's marketing department who were willing to provide financial support to WWF with the public relations benefits that such support would bring. This initiative might have arisen under WWF's old structure but the new structure clearly encouraged the unit to work out this proposal, to put it into practice and then to share the benefits with other colleagues in the fund-raising and communications areas.

The disadvantages of the new structure are that the role of the Functional Director is difficult for an ordinary member of staff to understand, a feeling that the Directors themselves have that they are not in complete control of their area because they do not have line responsibility for the units and the possibility of the unit heads using this confusion to play their Functional Director off against the COO to gain their own ends. *There have been a few unit heads who have used their freedom to initiate actions that have not been in the longer-term interests of the organisation.* These actions may have been correct when viewed from the narrow confines of the unit objectives but have not been justifiable in the overall interests of WWF UK. Because of the wide span of authority exercised by the COO, he has to depend to a large extent on the willingness of the unit heads to involve him in discussions on matters that could be outside the normal routine of the unit's objectives. A unit head who does not involve the COO in this way is clearly out-of-line but on a few occasions actions have been initiated that have not been cleared, leading to reprimand for the unit head. Whilst no irreparable damage has been done, the best interests of the organisation have clearly not been achieved in these cases. Very clear instructions have had to be laid down to ensure that repetitions of this behaviour do not occur.

The sudden elevation of executives to unit head, when the new structure was implemented, led to problems with some new unit heads that had had no formal management training. They were uncomfortable with their new responsibilities and, in certain cases, did not know how to achieve successful leadership for the staff that were responsible to them. They were all given training in the setting and use of budgets and objectives but this was insufficient to equip them all with the necessary skills to be a successful manager.

Whilst the Functional Directors fully understood their role, and by and large found the role to be stimulating and satisfying, they did miss the line responsibility which had, in the past, enabled them to keep a very close eye on the parts of the organisation that fell within their remit. Their styles of operation varied, naturally, and those that had a good rapport with the unit heads in their area found that they were able to fulfil a true functional role, giving help and advice to their unit heads whilst not stepping over the line of direct responsibility. Those that were less comfortable with their subordinates found the functional role more difficult, leading to a few cases of direct intervention in a line role with consequent conflicts with the COO.

The personality of the COO is crucial in this type of organisational structure. If the COO is decisive, clear and communicates well, both upwards and downwards, then the problems of the flattened pyramidical structure are small. If the COO lacks these qualities, however, then the organisation can get out of control, with separate unit heads doing their own thing without the central vision that will ensure the best for the organisation as a whole.

Essentials for success

If this structure is to work effectively, releasing the entrepreneurial spirit and lateral thinking that can take a business into a new dimension, the following key elements must be watched:

- The CEO must feel comfortable, delegating full line responsibility to the COO.
- The COO must likewise feel completely comfortable with the delegation of authority to unit heads, within agreed budgets and objectives.

- The COO must be decisive, have excellent communications skills and be sufficiently mature and numerate to be able to exercise control through budgets and through monitoring the achievement of agreed objectives.
- The COO must be respected and possess a character that will encourage the unit heads to bring their problems and their ideas that are likely to be outside the agreed parameters to him for discussion.
- The Functional Directors must be comfortable about relinquishing the role of line manager, concentrating their main effort on strategic thinking.
- The Functional Directors must be capable of building good relationships with their unit heads so that they operate as an adviser and guide, rather than as a line manager.
- Unit heads must have adequate management training.
- Budgets and budgetary control must be clearly understood by all unit heads and directors.
- Objective setting must be clearly understood by all unit heads and directors.
- The entire management team must be fully aware of and understand the new structure, its limitations and, most importantly, its advantages. Considerable effort needs to be expended to ensure such understanding.
- An effective and accepted appraisal system must be in operation, or be put into operation, to allow each unit head the opportunity to agree unit objectives and to be appraised on the achievement of those objectives.

Where these conditions apply, *this flattened pyramid structure can give significant advantages over the more formal pyramidical structure, releasing energy, talent, enthusiasm and skills that can take an organisation into a new realm of achievement.* There is a need to ensure that adequate monitoring is in place to avoid damaging initiatives from unit heads that are trying to 'play the system'. This monitoring should be capable of showing up the weaknesses in individual unit heads so that corrective action can be taken, either through more and better training for those who are less self-reliant or by some measure of restraint for those who are over-enthusiastic. WWF UK is beginning to see the benefits of these changes and has overcome most of the first obstacles that appeared after the new structure was implemented. There is a new spirit of entrepreneurialism, a new spirit of collaboration and a new spirit of achievement that could not have flourished under the old system. Teamwork has improved, inter-functional barriers have been broken down and, with careful monitoring systems in place, adequate management control is being exercised without inhibiting the essential freedom of expression that the new system was designed to foment.

4 Managing radical change in organisational structure and culture at The Automobile Association

Bob Chase

'Change has considerable psychological impact on the human mind. To the fearful it is threatening because it means that things may get worse. To the hopeful it is encouraging because things may get better. To the confident it is inspiring because the challenge exists to make things better. Obviously, then, a person's character and frame of mind determine how readily he brings about change and how he reacts to change that is imposed on him.'

King Whitney Jr, President, Personnel Laboratory Inc, to a sales meeting, quoted by *Wall Street Journal*, 7 June 1967

Executive summary

This chapter describes the cultural revolution which is taking place in The Automobile Association, involving:

1. Developing and implementing strategy and measuring progress.
2. Looking outwards instead of inwards.
3. Analysing the function of a head office.
4. Giving a head office a sense of purpose.

Steady growth in UK car ownership throughout the 1980s was matched by steady membership growth in The Automobile Association. But the abrupt economic slowdown at the end of the decade, leading into recession, *and* the effects of the technological revolution, brought the AA into the 1990s with problems that, in classic management-textbook style, we seized as opportunities.

Suddenly the AA faced *much* tougher competition in *all* its market-places. We recognised that, if we were to fight back quickly and successfully, we had to sharpen our focus, review our business and management structures and – equally important – fire up our staff, making them individually accountable for the delivery of quality service through innovative teamwork, and rewarding them for results. It was clear that we had quickly to implement and manage substantial change if we were to add value to the AA and ensure long-term survival.

Implementing change is never easy, and demands commitment from the top as well as the support of management and staff. The AA secured this, and in the last three years we have:

- Reviewed the competitive environment.
- Revised our marketing strategy.
- Re-focused our first business – Membership.
- Set a clear focus and mission for the AA Group.
- Refined our planning process.
- Transformed a collection of corporate activities into a strategic business unit.

This has enabled us to report record incomes and financial performance in each of the last three years, as well as providing us with the opportunity of implementing a significant investment programme.

The AA was formed in 1905, and is an unincorporated association whose affairs are managed by a Committee and put into effect by an Executive Sub-committee or board. AA Group turnover is in excess of £500 million annually. We are not a public limited company, and we do not have shareholders. *We are a club with 7.7 million members, and we have to give them a reason to renew their annual subscriptions by providing high quality and excellent value-for-money services wherever and whenever they need us.*

The AA is a service organisation: we deal with customers, not in vehicles or units sold. Some 14,500 staff have an important role in achieving our goals and satisfying our members' and customers' needs, and we recruit and retain high calibre people with the utmost care. We train and develop them to perform their duties to the best of their abilities, empower them to achieve their full potential, provide them with a secure and stimulating environment – and reward them for performance and competence.

Our uniformed patrol force of 3,600 is the biggest in the world and serves a third of all motorists in the UK. In 1993 we attended more than *4.5 million* breakdowns – an average of 514 breakdowns an hour, 24 hours a day, every day of the year.

Seven operations centres handle breakdown calls, and each achieved ISO9002 accreditation in 1992. We are able to fix 80% of the vehicle breakdowns attended at the roadside, and 93% of those attended at members' homes. And as the majority of AA members take the Relay option, they can rely on us to get them to their destinations whatever their difficulties.

Following business devolution in the 1980s, The Automobile Association is now organised in four business units: Membership, Insurance and Financial Services, Commercial Services and The Corporate Group (see Figure 4.1).

Membership provides roadside services to members and is responsible for marketing, new product development, and providing benefits and added-value services to personal members. It was created following a review of our competitive environment, and it represents a landmark in the implementation of strategy and successful management of organisational change in the AA.

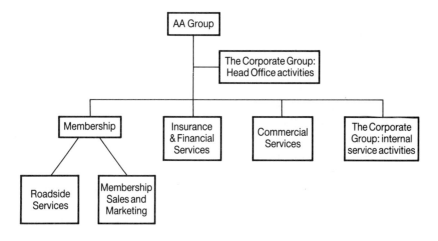

Figure 4.1 The AA Group Structure (June 1993)

Insurance and Financial Services provides a broking activity for motor, house and personal accident insurance. The business celebrated its 25th anniversary in 1992 and is one of Europe's largest independent personal-lines insurance intermediaries, with annual gross premium income of more than £500 million.

Commercial Services handles services and products that are not exclusive to AA members or packaged and delivered by our insurance business. The most well known are the market-leading AA Five Star Service, AA Roadwatch, AA Publishing, and the AA Driving School, which has grown impressively since its launch in 1991.

The Corporate Group provides services to each of the AA's main businesses through the Group Services Division. It also focuses on performance, strategy, policy and the overall governance of AA affairs through head office activities such as finance, internal audit, public policy, public relations, group marketing and international affairs.

The Group Services Division includes management services, which provides the businesses with the most efficient and latest computer systems and technology: we invest £1 million a week in running and improving our information technology infrastructure in an 'open systems' environment.

The welding together of all corporate activities into a strategic business unit has been achieved in a short time, and with remarkable success.

The competitive environment

Dramatic and highly competitive changes in the market place put pressure on the AA's businesses during the late 1980s – notably the breakdown recovery service, and Insurance Services. Research indicated that the following issues threatened our long-term survival:

- The market for AA personal membership had reached saturation – in 1969 the AA had 4 million personal members; 20 years later personal membership had only grown to 4.2 million.
- Most new cars in the UK were being sold with annual breakdown and recovery protection included in the price.
- Membership of the AA was linked to one product only – breakdown recovery – and this was the product under greatest threat.
- Aggressive price cutting by insurance competitors, and the offer of 'free' insurance with new-car sales by some motor manufacturers, had placed increasing pressure on our insurance business.
- Internally, we were probably not devoting sufficient resources to membership development and retention.

The marketing strategy

We decided to set up an action team to develop a medium- to long-term marketing strategy for the AA. It consisted of senior managers from each business, and their objectives were to:

- Review and refresh the marketing strategy.
- Identify sub-strategies that could be introduced immediately.
- Evaluate the risk of all recommendations based on environmental and competitive response scenarios.

The team identified, reviewed and quantified the issues facing the AA. It also commissioned independent market research to assess the image of the AA – and, encouragingly, it showed that we enjoy more public regard than many other large, high profile service and manufacturing organisations.

The Group mission

Within three months the team had completed its investigations and reported back to the Committee, recommending that the future mission of the AA should be to become 'the leading motoring and personal assistance organisation in the UK, providing information, advice and assistance to targeted customer groups for motoring, home and personal assistance needs'.

The AA's strengths are in the areas of *logistics, organisation, information technology, deployment, command and control, people skills* – and of course the *AA brand*, which represents 'Standards I can trust'. Future development was seen to rest on applying these strengths through a broader business base. As a result, we

---

AA GROUP MISSION

Our vision
To make AA membership truly irresistible

Our mission
To be the UK's leading and most successful motoring and personal assistance organisation

Our values
Courtesy and care for all our members and customers
Our people, and their skills
Our image of integrity and independence
Quality and value for money in all our services and products
Our business partners

Figure 4.2 The AA Group mission

reviewed our existing activities and refocused the Membership business in May 1991 with a mission to 'develop a highly valued range of member benefits and personal assistance services that will help to safeguard and build the position of the AA as the UK's leading membership-based organisation'.

The vision of a broader business base, reflecting the new focus and marketing strategy of The Automobile Association, had of course to be included in an AA Group mission statement (see Figure 4.2).

Each AA business was also asked to revise its mission statement, in line with the AA Group mission, and this delivered a change in strategic emphasis – from being product-focused to customer-orientated. In particular, the strategy for the Membership business was to enable the AA to achieve its ambition of offering superior services and products to selected customer groups in the motoring, home care and personal assistance markets.

As shown in Figure 4.2, the AA Group mission statement is divided into three sections: vision, mission and values.

Our values are the enablers of business strategy, the driving force. The quality of the service that we offer is essential to future success. And we aim to treat members and customers with courtesy and care at all times, seeking to make each contact an experience that justifies the claim that membership is 'truly irresistible'. Our values also give the AA brand its strong image in the market place, and represent 'Standards I can trust'.

We aim to protect and enhance this image, and to use it to promote the interests of our members and customers by acting as an opinion-former as well as an opinion-leader in all matters relating to motoring, safety on the road and the environment. And, of course, we also value our business partners, who contribute to our success.

Membership strategies

The Membership business set the following strategies to achieve its mission:

- The repositioning and reinforcement of the AA brand.
- The strengthening of the link between the AA and its personal members.
- The creation of new profit streams for the AA Group.

Another strategy is to foster common understanding throughout the AA Group, so that, working together, the four businesses can protect and enhance the AA brand.

Membership, as a concept, is fundamental to our future strategy, shaping consumers' perception of the AA brand and building long-term relationships with members as individuals.

A deliberate attempt to *manage* the brand, rather than letting it simply drift, was judged to be vital. Repositioning it to become more relevant to a member's or customer's home and family needs, as well as motoring needs, would create opportunities to develop new profit streams for reinvestment, and valuable additional member benefits and services.

New product development

The AA has also introduced *new* services and products, the most significant being the AA Magazine, AA Callsafe, and the AA Driving School.

The magazine was issued to all personal members in June 1992. Successor to *Drive*, it is an additional member benefit, and an essential tool in strengthening the long-term relationship between the AA and its members. The publication enables us to market our services and products, to provide information and advice, and to deliver a consistent message to members.

The second issue featured Callsafe, the AA phone that enables stranded motorists to summon help without leaving their cars, children or personal belongings, by connecting them directly with an AA operations centre or the emergency services. Already, some 17,000 members have purchased this new product.

From a zero base, the AA Driving School now has a team of more than 600 instructors providing high quality tuition to learner drivers, with a pass rate of over 50%. As with any new product development, it is currently losing money but, as the recession ends and the business expands, it has a very promising future.

We have only just begun to introduce new services and products to target markets – motoring, home care and personal assistance. They will help to differentiate us from our competitors, and reinforce the reasons why motorists should join and remain in membership of the AA.

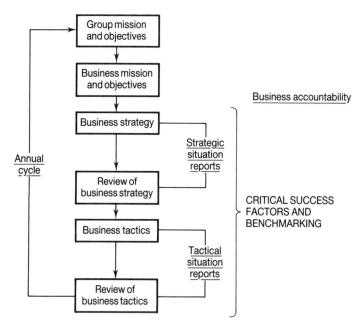

Figure 4.3 The AA planning approach

With major developments taking place within the AA, the need to change our annual planning process quickly became a priority...

The planning process

The process was, over many years, a forms-driven exercise — mechanistic, and lacking the real capacity to add value to the organisation. Intense effort was put into 'getting the numbers right'. The corporate plan was a 'bottom-up' routine, with a consolidation of business plans that focused on short-term financial performance.

Our new planning process has two stages: strategic and tactical (see Figure 4.3). Once the AA Group's objectives have been set, businesses are required to outline their own missions, objectives and strategies for the next five years.

Formulating strategy is difficult and time-consuming but absolutely essential for future success, and strategic business plans are reviewed by the Executive Sub-committee to agree the long-term direction of the AA Group, and by each of the businesses before they prepare tactical plans incorporating detailed financial projections.

Now that we have separated strategy from tactics, the focus has shifted to measuring strategic progress. For without measurement systems no one can be held accountable for progress, there is little scope for effective strategic discussion, and we cannot be sure how well we are managing change. We have, therefore, created a planning environment in which managers understand exactly what is required of them, and this is increasing their commitment to the process.

In each planning cycle we require the businesses to revisit their existing strategies and to provide a report on the progress that they have made. We call this a *strategic situation report*, and a similar report is required at the tactical stage of the planning process. We have also introduced *benchmarking*, having first identified critical success factors for each business.

Clear and effective planning, communication and leadership are the prerequisites for managing change. And it was in the development of Roadside Services and the formation of The Corporate Group that we applied them to manage both organisational and cultural change...

Roadside Services

The Automobile Association has always had a strong marketing base through direct mail, a sales force and a chain of retail shops. The emphasis on marketing also exists in our Membership business, which has two principal activities: Roadside Services, delivering roadside assistance; and Membership Sales and Marketing, providing a coordinated approach to membership sales and new product development.

The AA not only provides assistance to personal members in the breakdown assistance market, it goes to the rescue of fleet and company customers too. Membership Sales and Marketing manages the relationship and develops the communication strategy with personal, company and fleet members, as well as satisfying their changing needs through new products and services.

Over the years substantial investment in deployment technology and systems networks had been undertaken in Roadside Services. However, with *nine layers of management* between head office and the AA patrols serving our members' needs, progress towards achieving our strategic objectives was hindered, and Roadside Services lacked a clearly defined, quality and customer-service culture.

During the planning process we identified the following key weaknesses that had to be addressed if the AA's reputation and service delivery were to be enhanced:

- Managers and supervisors needed to anticipate rather than react to members' needs.
- The duplication of management and administration had to be eliminated.
- Support services were too big and far too remote from members.
- Two-way communication channels did not exist.

A flatter organisation

A first task was to flatten the organisation structure and make it more dynamic and responsive to members' needs. We removed four levels of management – 650 supervisory and management positions – in the space of 18 months, and were able to find alternative positions for many staff elsewhere within the AA Group.

We also rearranged our geographical boundaries, eliminating two regions and streamlining the support services required, and moved head office staff to fill strategic positions in the field, strengthening our customer-service delivery mechanisms.

Team-building

These changes gave us a clearer identity and a sharper focus on our members. But we still needed to build self-confidence among staff, and to improve communication, innovation and teamwork.

We achieved this through the creation of effective and highly motivated teams. For example, AA patrols, who had previously worked in isolation, were formed into small teams managed by an inspector who became wholly responsible for their performance and motivation. Team spirit was raised with outward-bound programmes in the Scottish countryside. And the introduction of team briefings made sure that all members of staff were aware of performance, administration, procedures and developments at national and regional levels.

Upward communication

Upward channels of communication were created through *Talkback*, the business magazine, and regular phone-ins that gave staff the opportunity to voice their concerns, to ask questions and to raise new ideas with senior management – with the guarantee of an answer; and Teams in Action, group discussions exchanging ideas and information on the best practical solutions to local problems, were introduced.

All these moves have helped to empower staff and to boost their confidence, and they played a critical part in the success of the AA during the recession.

The results of the changes speak for themselves. We reduced duplication and administration. 90% of our problems are now solved by innovative local teams. And there has been a significant improvement in the quality of member service.

The Corporate Group

'Corporate activities' in the AA formerly represented an unconnected collection of internal services for our businesses and a range of head office functions. More than 1,000 staff were employed, and the internal income was more than £60 million.

By far the largest area was Management Services, among whose responsibilities was the provision of cost-effective information technology – achieved through the corporate network, with 8,000 telephones and 7,000 kilometres of cable supporting 16,000 terminals 24 hours a day, and the operation of a substantial private radio network, enabling our operations centres to handle 7 million calls a year and our Insurance business to provide more than 3 million quotations.

The role of head office

In 1990 corporate services needed direction, structure and identity. It was not a business as we know it today. It did not have a clear strategy, and it did not fully understand its relationship with and the needs of the AA's businesses. But before we could implement change we needed to define what role a head office should have in the management of the AA's affairs.

Traditionally, the head office had adopted a 'running' style of management, with all major operating decisions made by the executive team and all corporate activities provided from the centre. We moved to a 'guiding' style of management, with head office critically evaluating the strategies of individual businesses, and some services provided on an 'as-needed' basis.

At a stroke, the AA Group management took a more 'hands-off' approach. They were primarily responsible for assessing the thinking behind the strategy and the major decisions of the individual businesses. We then worked hard to try to categorise all corporate activities under one of two headings: Stewardship or Service.

Stewardship activities are those involved with the formulation and implementation of strategy, performance and fiduciary control: for example, group finance and internal audit. *Service* activities are contracted as they are used, and are obliged to survive by delivering good quality products and services that are cheaper than those available in the external market. Examples of central services are management services, property and logistics and procurement.

Once the concepts of stewardship and service were established, we were able to determine the following:

- What corporate activities were required for the head office to carry out its 'guiding' role.
- What stewardship activities should be discontinued.
- What was an acceptable cost for stewardship activities.
- What services should be centralised or devolved.

A business

We also decided that the annual increase in the cost of stewardship activities should not exceed the rate of retail price inflation; that the prices charged for

---

THE CORPORATE GROUP

MISSION STATEMENT
* We are committed to the success of the AA.
* We provide services that are valued by our customers, and give direction to and set standards for the AA Group.
* Our people come first, and are rewarded for performance and customer care.

Figure 4.4 The Corporate Group mission

service activities should be less than market prices; and that service activities should be operated on a breakeven basis.

Immediately, the collection of stewardship and service activities that we decided to treat as *a business* under the title The Corporate Group began to have a clearer focus, and this was reinforced when we introduced a mission statement (see Figure 4.4).

The nine objectives for The Corporate Group were sub-divided into the following three areas:

Stewardship objectives concentrate on:

* the establishment of a framework of standards for the AA Group, and
* guiding the AA to achieve its mission of personal assistance, caring, integrity and independence.

Service objectives include:

* the provision of value-for-money services and products to the internal customers of The Corporate Group, and
* improvements in productivity and operational efficiency.

Internal objectives are directed towards staff in The Corporate Group by:

* the creation of a challenging and rewarding environment, visibly putting people *first*, and
* the development of a customer care programme to encourage and ensure service excellence.

We have subsequently grouped all service activities to form the Group Services Division, and this has given even clearer focus and understanding of our business.

Customer care

With this sound framework in place, we had then to engage the *commitment* of staff through a customer care programme.

This initiative had already been used successfully in The Automobile Association — Travel in 1985, Roadside Services in 1986, and our Insurance business in 1987 — but it had always been directed at our external customers, never focused on our internal customers.

In 1991 all the staff in The Corporate Group attended a customer-care course, aimed at improving performance by clarifying objectives and enhancing relationships with other businesses in the AA Group. Each delegate was asked to make suggestions for improving the AA, and doing our existing tasks better. The responses included:

- Raising the visibility of senior management.
- Improving the working environment.
- Enhancing knowledge of individual departments within the Corporate Group.
- Improving communication throughout the organisation.

In response, the following 'people initiatives' were quickly introduced: Corporate Care in Action, team briefing, personal performance reviews and team building exercises.

Corporate Care in Action took place in a centrally heated marquee in our Basingstoke backyard in December! Staff were shown how Management Services was using the latest information technology to provide better solutions to its business customers. They also visited a 'trade show', where people from their own business explained their departments' roles — there were demonstrations from property, logistics and procurement, personnel and training, and others.

The managing directors of the AA's three main businesses were given the opportunity to specify what *they* wanted from The Corporate Group — high quality at low prices, of course — and at the end of the conference we asked our people for their response to the day. 83% told us that the conference had been a good opportunity to meet people, and 72% thought that it had made them feel part of The Corporate Group.

Team briefing

Soon afterwards we introduced team briefing — to increase the cooperation and commitment of staff by making sure that our people know exactly what we are doing, how we are doing it ... and the reasons why.

Corporate Group team briefings take place monthly, and within 72 hours of the issue of a 'core brief' the latest information is given to all levels of staff. Although the emphasis is on downward communication of new information, there is also the opportunity for discussion of relevant issues, and staff questions are referred back to the source of the core brief — the Corporate Group management team.

Personal performance review

The AA is a service organisation, and service is delivered by *people*. We consider ourselves to be a fair employer, and we make a substantial investment in our people, for they are a key asset in our strategy. We have also given them a sense of purpose and direction through the introduction of the personal performance review.

PPR requires staff to make a self-appraisal of their performance, and this is used as a basis for discussion with line management. The PPR also enables the manager and the individual staff member to assess the individual's skills and abilities prior to a development plan being created, setting out training and development objectives for the short- and medium-term.

We have now completed three cycles of PPR, and the latest has placed increased emphasis on the individual's competencies. Rewards are now clearly linked to performance, and this is reflected in our bonus scheme. Staff have a greater sense of purpose and achievement.

A sense of achievement is also being increased via greater emphasis on team building, and during 1992 many of our people in The Corporate Group attended outward-bound programmes, working in groups to improve their teamwork and understanding. Everyone also attended a customer-care update course in 1993.

The results

These initiatives, and the framework that we established for The Corporate Group at the outset, have helped us to raise performance markedly. The results are reflected in the following:

- The improved quality of the service and products provided by The Corporate Group to other AA businesses.
- A clearer focus on what services are required by our business units.
- The disposal of 'inappropriate' businesses, such as Business Travel.
- The development and enthusiasm of the staff through 'people initiatives'.
- Enhanced efficiency because we always question the way that we do things.
- Improved teamwork, and, of course,
- Better financial results which are helped by continuous improvement programmes.

In 1989 the AA reported a group profit before tax of £4.9 million. In 1993 the profit of the group is expected to exceed £30 million.

The successful management of our organisational change has made a significant contribution to improving financial performance. So too has the disposal of a minority interest in our Insurance business to Eagle Star, which has enabled us to earn substantial interest income on the proceeds.

As you would expect, change remains a constant in The Automobile Association. Very recently we have introduced a new AA Group mission statement (see Figure 4.5); and we no longer require the separate businesses of the AA to work to their own mission statements.

The new group mission places emphasis on reliability, accessibility and the fullness of the AA offering, and builds-in the phrase 'Standards I can Trust', which has become an essential part of our new culture.

Our task now is to maintain the momentum, building on our successes, winning and retaining new AA members and customers, and persuading those customers who are not members to join us. AA membership *is* becoming irresistible.

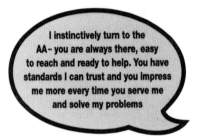

When every member and customer can say this, we will be irresistible

Figure 4.5 AA Group Mission

Recommended reading

Hugh Barty-King, *The AA – A History of The Automobile Association 1905–1980*, The Automobile Association, 1980.

Bob Garratt, *Creating a Learning Organisation*, Director Books, 1990.

Michael Goold and John J. Quinn, *Strategic Control Milestones for Long-term Performance*, Hutchinson Business Books, 1990.

David Kaye, *Game Change: the impact of information technology on corporate strategies and structures*, Heinemann Professional Publishing, 1989.

II Re-engineering key business processes

5 Activity-based costing and process re-engineering at Hewlett-Packard

Jim Rigby

'Create best practices across functions to translate new ideas into successful products. Make these efforts pay off in half the time it currently takes.'
John Young, CEO, Hewlett-Packard, quoted in Gregory H. Watson, *Strategic Benchmarking*, John Wiley, 1993

Executive summary

The demands on managers to control and reduce costs have intensified dramatically in the 1990s. Traditional cost planning and control procedures have been supplemented with swingeing cuts in employment levels, as the solution to profit shortfalls.

At Hewlett-Packard, management have pursued a more controlled analytical evaluation of its cost structure, focusing on the causal drivers of costs, identifying inefficiencies through activity analysis, eliminating waste using TQM methodologies and encouraging continuous process improvement through relevant performance measures. Organisationally, the historical vertical functional structure is being overlaid with multi-function process-focused teams.

The Hewlett-Packard Company achieved sales of over US $16 billion in 1992, employing over 92,000 people. There are three key types of organisational units that make up the corporation – manufacturing divisions, selling companies and support centres. The manufacturing divisions, about 60 of them, are semi-autonomous businesses with product line charters to meet the needs of worldwide market niches. For example, our Scottish Division specialises in meeting customers' test, measuring and monitoring needs in the world telecommunications Industry. Product Development, Manufacturing, Marketing and Administration are standard divisional functions. Product divisions are grouped into sectors for control and strategic coordination purposes. The selling organisations are geographic units operating in 116 countries and they sell the complete product range output from the 60 manufacturing divisions. The support centres co-exist with the sales companies but they are in divisional sector groupings, and they provide local customer support and services.

```
►Downsizing
►Reduce costs by 10%
►Stop all recruitment
►Halt capital projects
►Switch off lights
```

Figure 5.1 Traditional cost control methods are of limited value

Business climate

Worldwide trading and economic conditions changed dramatically in the latter half of the 1980s. The need for competitiveness in technology, value and service compounded the challenges for management. Cost control and cost reduction became a permanent feature of financial and business planning. The traditional reactions of management are shown in Figure 5.1.

These tactics may provide temporary relief and improvement, but the real opportunity and challenge are to recognise the level of waste and inefficiency in an organisation's business processes and find substantial improvement. This is especially true in the electronics and computing industry where we face constant shortening of product life cycles. *70% of Hewlett-Packard's revenues in 1993 will come from products launched within the last three years.* Technology advances of bewildering scope, pace and cost, deliver more processing capability for a lower product price every year. Significant changes in manufacturing skills and processes, changes in sales and distribution channels, technology partnerships and new niche competitors have all demanded a different approach and new kinds of financial support from accountants. 'The same old way' just does not work in our industry if you want to be successful.

ABC – activity based costing

In 1985, one of our computer product divisions learned a tough, expensive lesson at the hands of a competitor. Essentially, the new product cost and price, resulting from our existing overhead allocation approach was too high, so the product failed to meet its market share and contribution targets. Investigations revealed that, as the new product passed through the manufacturing process, it was absorbing costs that it simply did not incur. The logical extension of this discovery was that other products were being under-loaded with cost. 'Cost drivers' were then analysed to recognise and apply the overhead, based on the consumption of resources rather than the allocation of labour and material costs. By 1988/9 ABC had become HP's standard policy for costing, reporting, pricing and inventory valuation with greater accuracy than before. We discovered product cost distortions in excess of 20% when we converted to 'cost drivers', which was vital information especially in our large volume businesses.

DFM – design for manufacture

The ability to change significantly the manufacturing costs of products, particularly those with short product life cycles, is negligible after launch. Cost drivers were therefore a vital influence on design engineering decisions – 'design for manufacturability' being a fundamental basic technique in HP. We were able to tell engineers that it costs, say, 4 cents to 'auto insert' a component versus 70 cents to hand load and solder onto a printed circuit board, and that it cost 18 cents to procure components from a multinational partner with corporate price agreements, EDI, no inspection, etc., versus a local supplier with low volumes where the procurement cost can be as much as 50% of the purchase value of the material unit costs. Armed with this type of data, the engineer's decisions and selections can be valued in cost terms.

A word of caution at this point – the relative success of ABC in HP's manufacturing environment owed a lot to two key decisions. The first was to view the ABC introduction as a team concept and solution, with R&D and manufacturing representatives working with accounting to specify the processes to be monitored and the cost drivers to be used. *It was not presented as an accounting tool* – we got 'buy in' across the organisation for ABC as a significant improvement on the old method. Secondly, we started simply, with only seven or eight cost drivers, mastered the techniques and reports, then became smarter and more complex at later stages. We took only three to four months to convert to the new approach and we did not spend much in system changes, much being done off-line on spreadsheets.

It is important to understand that the 'cost pools' remain the same irrespective of overhead recovery system. But the visibility provided by ABC encourages management decisions that lead to lower cost structures. However, to present ABC as a cost and people reduction programme is inappropriate and potentially damaging to some organisations, and the communication of the change to employees has to be handled carefully.

CPI – continuous process improvement

The natural extension of ABC from manufacturing is to recognise it can be applied to other functions within the business. For HP we had the benefit of two major influences on the attitudes of our employees and their receptivity to change. Through our profit sharing programme with all employees and the share participation scheme with about 75% of employees choosing to be shareholders, their interest in improving the company's competitiveness and profitability is high. Secondly, HP has been heavily committed to Total Quality Management since the 1970s. I prefer to use the words Continuous Process Improvement as being more descriptive, i.e. the elimination of waste, refining processes, methods and movements so that 'cycle times' and 'time to market' are optimised.

Whilst there is a good overall record of improvements, HP, like most other companies, has approached CPI on an unprioritised, somewhat random fashion, based on individual initiatives rather than a valued, controlled and directed process. Our manufacturing function has been the most responsive and participative in CPI — but then the measurement of performance is an integral part of the manufacturing mentality. The tools are there — we just needed accounting data to support and prioritise the opportunities for waste reduction and elimination.

Researchers claim that most organisations have a minimum of 30% waste in their cost structure, yet typically accountants have not seen waste elimination as a major source of profit improvement. When you consider that HP in 1992 was a $16 billion company spending $8 billion in expenses, then if our wastage was 30% it represented a $2.4 billion opportunity for profit improvement. This dwarfs the impact of downsizing and the other techniques that finance directors and managements introduce (see Figure 5.1). In our case, whilst profit improvement would always be welcome, the opportunities to reinvest more efficiently in, say, R&D would stimulate higher growth and profit. We always have more ideas than resources.

Process management

TQM teaches that everything we do is part of a process. Yet accountants and management teams typically continue to plan, monitor and control their businesses on a functional, departmental basis. We analyse and measure *what* type of expense we have spent rather than *why and on what* business process. This ignores the cross-functional, interdepartmental activities and their contribution to key processes.

In our division, the functional managers debated and discussed what we thought were the key business processes and our conclusions were refined to six key processes (see Figure 5.2). The control process is internally focused, i.e. meeting fiscal, reporting and control requirements and includes activities such as financial accounting, human resources, etc. The other key processes tend to be

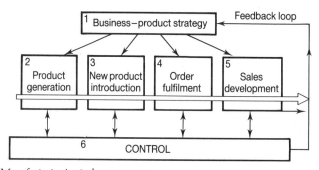

Figure 5.2 Manufacturing's six key processes

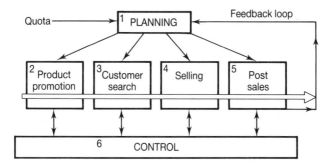

Figure 5.3 The selling company's six key processes

(ILLUSTRATION ONLY)					
KEY PROCESS	**MFG**	**R&D**	**MKTG**	**ADMIN**	**TOTAL**
Business-product strategy	20	500	320	100	940
Product generation	500	3800	400	50	4750
New product introduction	340	340	810	40	1530
Order fulfilment	2520	10	30	240	2800
Sales development	100	50	1100	70	1320
Control	800	200	300	690	1990
Total	**4280**	**4900**	**2960**	**1190**	**13330**

Figure 5.4 The costs of the six key processes by function (£1,000s)

customer-focused, market-driven. Our UK selling company also followed this approach and concluded they too had six key processes (see Figure 5.3).

The task now was to restate our functional cost structure into a process matrix (see Figure 5.4). This proved very illuminating to management. The major surprise was the extent to which our costs and people resources were consumed by the control process. A similar picture emerged in our selling company, as illustrated by the people matrix (see Figure 5.5).

Activity analysis

The process matrix was developed by means of a comprehensive interview with each department. The finance staff knew the departments' annual cost plan, asset base and human resource plan. In advance, we asked each manager to think through, sometimes with key staff, the tasks and activities undertaken and the key processes that initiated or benefited from the work. The actual interview took two to three hours and after a further two-hour cost evaluation exercise in finance, we produced for each department an analysis by activity of their cost plan. This

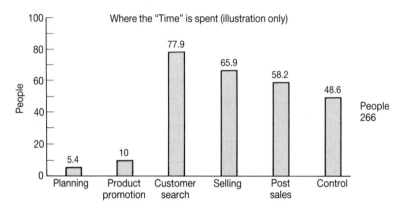

Figure 5.5 The key process analysis

allowed the key processes to be evaluated by activity. All along we accepted that 'near enough was good enough' – none of the typical accountant's fixation with fourth decimal place accuracy!

As the analysis developed, the 'gut feel' reaction to the costs of the activities certainly stimulated debate and in many cases, serious consideration of the value of some activities being done at all. 'If that's what it costs, I don't need it', was a typical management reaction. Another benefit was to recognise the linkages between departments. Who was the customer for the output and did it meet the needs? The exercise contributed significantly to the recognition that we had a top heavy organisation with too many departments.

'Non-value added'

The other key element to the activity analysis was an effort to identify the 'non-value added' element in each activity and process. Our definition of non-value added for this phase was *waste* or *duplication* or *cost of inefficiency*. For example, having to re-layout a printed circuit board design or rewrite test procedures or rerun a computer analysis or report. In other words, rework of any description. Each department gave a fairly honest appraisal of their activities, in many cases the evidence of the supplying and receiving departments supported or contradicted the evidence. Once again, the results were fascinating (see Figure 5.6).

It came as no shock to find the manufacturing element of the order fulfilment process to be most efficient. After all, production departments have a historic fixation for variance and standards deviation reporting. Also, they are usually the people who readily apply TQM to process improvements – unlike R&D, Marketing and Admin who are too busy to improve. If only they knew.

The analysis indicated our most precious resources of R&D and Marketing to be

PROCESS	OWNER	TOTAL	VA*	NVA*
		£1,000s	%	%
Business-product generation	GM*	940	70	30
Product generation	R&D	4700	50	50
New product introduction	MKTG	1510	60	40
Other fulfilment	MFG	2800	85	15
Sales development	MKTG	1320	50	50
Control	ADMIN	2060	60	40
		13330	**60**	**40**

* General manager
* Value added
* Non-value added

Figure 5.6 Process cost indicators (illustration only)

the most wasteful. For us, it was less important to cut their budgets and improve the bottom line. What we wanted was improved 'time-to-market', and more products available to get higher sales growth and let the profits flow from there.

Process engineering

The results of the analysis helped to stimulate thoughts about restructuring the organisation – away from a functional focus into an empowered process team, cross-functional so that process and performance improvements could be generated and implemented. The secret is to use Activity Analysis to indicate where the opportunities are and to allow management to direct and influence the priorities for improvement. TQM provides the tools to achieve the improvements and selecting the correct performance measures to check progress completes the improvement cycle (see Figure 5.7).

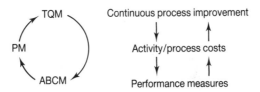

Figure 5.7 The improvement cycle

6 Using EDI to re-organise the supply chain

Patrick J. Tonks

'What defines humanity is not the capacity to create a second nature – economic, social or cultural – beyond a biological nature; it is rather the capacity of going beyond created structures in order to create others.'
Maurice Merleau-Ponty, *The Structure of Behaviour*, Beacon Press, 1963

Executive summary

The pressures to improve inter-company communications, across the business networks in which companies operate, is encouraging the development of the 'intelligent business network'. This is a group of cooperating companies or 'business partners', using EDI technology to create a closely coupled supply chain or a more complex 'business network'. The resulting capability for redesigning business relationships has been identified by MIT in their 'Management in the 1990s' research programme as a key strategic success factor for business in the 1990s.

This chapter examines the impact of Information Technology (IT) and in particular Electronic Data Interchange (EDI) on distribution in three sections as follows:

1. *Intelligent business networks* assesses the potential impact of IT on traditional supply chain relationships.
2. *EDI in practice* describes how companies are using EDI to achieve improved efficiency in their supply chain.
3. *Tesco: breaking down the barriers of trade* shows how EDI is being used in one of Britain's leading supermarkets, and the benefits the system has brought.

Intelligent business networks

'Management in the 1990s' is the largest, and most authoritative, research programme yet conducted into the impact of information technology upon organisations and their abilities to survive and prosper in the competitive environment of the 1990s and beyond. The five-year, $5 million programme was conducted as a partnership between a number of large corporations and the Sloan School of Management at MIT. Some of the key conclusions of the programme were recently published in *The Corporation of the 1990s*. International Network Services Ltd (INS) became involved in the research programme in 1989, as a result of our experience in the application of EDI to business – which had already been identified by MIT as a key enabling technology for 'business network redesign'.

In order to assess the likely future impact of information technology upon businesses, MIT first carried out a number of detailed studies of major technological innovations of the 1980s; the resulting business benefits; their impact upon competitive advantage; and the success, or failure, of the participants. From this work they were able to draw a number of important conclusions concerning the impact which IT will have upon businesses, and to construct models which better enable business leaders to visualise and influence the resulting changes.

The fundamental premise is that it is no longer a question of *whether* IT has a strategic role but of *how* to exploit IT in the strategic management of the business. How is it possible to identify the strategic IT applications, to reconfigure the business to exploit IT capabilities and to use IT to differentiate your company from your competitors?

MIT classifies these changes into five levels of business transformation (see Figure 6.1).

1. *Localised exploitation* This is IT implementation within a business function and within one organisation, typically to improve the efficiency of a particular task: the installation of a PC-based, purchase ledger or a customer database system, for example.

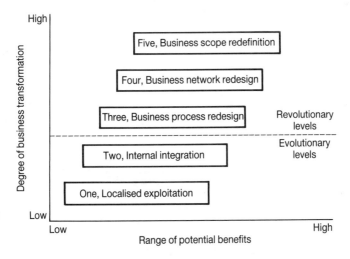

Figure 6.1 How IT can transform a business

The benefits at this lower level are localised, producing improved efficiency in a narrow area of a business.

2. *Internal integration* This level extends localised exploitation by integrating key internal applications to establish a common IT system for the business – by means of local area networks or corporate databases, for example. Typical applications are integrated sales forecasting and production scheduling, or integrated ordering and warehouse systems.

   The benefits of this approach are, typically, increased efficiency information sharing and responsiveness to customer demand.

These first two levels are 'evolutionary', requiring relatively small changes to the business processes. In contrast, the remaining three levels are 'revolutionary' – requiring radical changes in business practices. At levels 1 and 2 IT is an administrative resource, used to *support* existing business strategies. At the higher levels IT is a *strategic investment* which enables new business strategies to be implemented.

3. *Business process redesign* The central premise at this level is that IT is a platform for designing business processes and that it should not be simply overlaid on the existing organisation. Now it is possible to start restructuring business processes and aligning the IT infrastructure with them.

   The key IT applications at this level include the implementation of EFTPOS, barcoding, and EDI and which may allow JIT ordering and self-billing.

   The opportunities at this level are for the creation of a major improvement in capability, for example, improving inventory management and gaining competitive edge. This is the level at which most of the EDI activity to date has been concentrated. The major retailers' implementations of EDI for store-re-plenishment ordering provide examples of successful business process redesign.

4. *Business network redesign* Thus far we have seen IT-based change *within* a single organisation. The fourth level represents the use of IT for redesigning the nature of exchange among a number of participants in a business network, changing the boundaries between one organisation and another and thereby creating a more effective business network.

   The key IT applications are based on communication networks and include EPOS, EFT, E-Mail, Database Enquiry and exploitation of EDI.

   New strategies that result from these changes include QR (Quick Response), CALS (Computer Acquisition and Logistics Support) and other supply chain management approaches. These provide better operational efficiency, more effective market positioning and greater opportunities for business partnerships. Current case examples are: the Supply Chain Integration approach now being adopted by Tesco, and the AA's relationship with its panel of insurers. For such strategies to succeed it is essential that the potential benefits are fully understood by *all* members of the supply chain (or business network in MIT terminology).

5. *Business scope redefinition* The highest level represents the enlargement or shifting of the business scope by the substitution of traditional capabilities by IT-based capabilities, for example, EDI, Systems Integration and Information Databases.

   Effectively, level 5 offers the potential for redefining the business. A classic early example of this approach was American Airlines' reservation system, SABRE. By using information databases, EDI and telecommunication networks, SABRE was transformed from an internal seat reservation system, supporting the sales of American Airlines, to a service for American's industrial competitors – where it developed into the most profitable unit of American Airlines! British examples of business scope redefinition, enabled by EDI, are already emerging. The case study of EROS, the electronic record ordering company, describes one such initiative. Another example is INS itself!

   The benefits provide opportunities for growth, added value and new business development. It is very difficult to anticipate such developments, but the MIT results can help in the identification, and evaluation, of opportunities.

Redesigning the business network

There is no *sustainable* competitive advantage to be gained from information technology. The pace of technological development means that innovative IT solutions can be reproduced, or substituted, at lower cost by responsive competitors. This is, however, not the *whole* truth, as identified by the MIT programme. Technological innovation allows an organisation to create an enhanced competitive position, which may then be exploited to redesign processes and establish new types of business relationships which then prove *extremely* difficult for competitors to substitute or copy. Thus, by continual IT-based innovation, very strong market positions can be created.

A good example of this approach can be found in the ASAP system, implemented by Baxters in the US medical supplies market. In the same way, EDI and other business network services may be employed, and then exploited, to integrate, reposition, and even eliminate, business processes *between* organisations within the supply chain. So the type of business relationship to be established with key members of your business network must be considered alongside the role of IT integration.

Figure 6.2 illustrates the following strategic options for business network redesign, with regard to these two basic considerations:

1. *Electronic infrastructure* The position currently adopted by the majority of users of EDI services is characterised by the use of public data standards and a

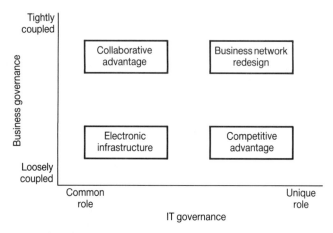

Figure 6.2 Options for a business network

common role for IT; with loosely coupled business relationships. Although there may be some barriers to entry for new participants, there is little room for new advantage among existing players.

2. *Competitive advantage* By employing a proprietary linkage, or proprietary data structures, it is possible for the 'first movers' to gain some (albeit very short-term) competitive advantage or they may lock in suppliers. This position is difficult to sustain and is increasingly unacceptable to business partners.

3. *Collaborative advantage* This is the position to which several of the British EDI 'Hubs' are moving, with certain of their key suppliers. Whilst still employing common electronic trading technology, they are forming commercial relationships which allow the technology to be exploited for mutual collaborative advantage. This may be accomplished by removing redundant, or overlapping, processes between the trading partners – e.g. through the use of self-billing, exchange of forecasting data, or account reconciliation.

4. *Business network redesign* In this position the IT infrastructure is exploited to strengthen and modify relationships between members of a 'business network'. Experience suggests that information technology should be used for added-value applications and/or functionality rather than to establish proprietary links or standards if this position is to be sustained. Proprietary IT solutions will be strongly resisted by business partners and will be overtaken by the development of open solutions.

With a closely coupled business relationship it may be possible to maintain this IT 'added value' through sustained innovation and it is possible to develop business relationships which may achieve a *sustainable competitive advantage*.

Table 6.1 The roles and benefits of electronic trading

Roles	Operational efficiency	Market positioning	Partnership conditions	Strategic capabilities
1. Transactions	Operating cost savings	First mover advantage; possibility of creating industry standard	Generally unrestricted	Low
2. Inventory	Benefits drift downstream	Opportunities for weak differentiation	Restricted through standard contracts	Low to medium
3. Process	Accelerates downstream drift	Opportunities for stronger differentiation	Restricted through specialised contracts (strategic alliances)	Medium
4. Expertise	Savings in time and costs are secondary	Opportunities for unique relationships	Specialised cooperative network arrangements	High

Towards the intelligent business network

The MIT programme contains a considerable volume of material which identifies and explains the key considerations in business network redesign; examines the roles of the business network and relates both of these to the potential business benefits. Whilst the implementation of EDI for 'electronic trading' suggests benefits arising from administration and inventory, it is important to recognise that process linkages and information/knowledge sharing up and down the supply chain can ultimately yield a more sustainable competitive advantage.

Table 6.1 summarises the various roles of electronic trading or, more generally, electronic integration in business network redesign. The MIT report concludes that these roles are hierarchical – offering increasing levels of strategic capability, or opportunity for sustainable competitive advantage.

The roles are categorised as follows:

1. *Transactions* The use of EDI to exchange the equivalent of paper transactions – order and invoices, for example. The benefits of this approach are largely in operational efficiency, accuracy and reduced administration costs. There is some market positioning advantage in being a first mover and hence, to create or influence the industry standard. There is little reason to be selective in terms of trading partners and the longer-term strategic impact is likely to be low.

2. *Inventory* The electronic trading relationship makes inventory available and visible to both parties. Information on stock levels is enhanced and the movement of goods is triggered – enabling JIT manufacturing, for example.

   Inventory tends to be forced back upstream and so the benefits may drift downstream. There may be significant benefits to the consumer through the progressive reduction of inventory and/or work in progress (thus cost) in the supply chain. The shifting of costs will generally need to be reflected in the contractual relationships – or in the trading discounts.

   This role of electronic integration is not generally relevant in financial services, for example, where there is no physical inventory, which might explain the slow adoption of EDI in this sector.

3. *Process* This role emerges where individual trading partners integrate their business processes through electronic links, so removing redundant or overlapping processes to create a new and more efficient supply chain. This type of relationship will require a partnership approach and will be adopted only with key members of a business network. The MIT case study on GE–Lighting is a classic example of this role of electronic integration in the retail industry.

4. *Expertise* In this role, skills and expertise are shared among the members of a business network. Very close, and specialised, commercial relationships will be required and the cooperating organisations may establish a sustainable competitive advantage. An example of this is the unique relationship between Courtaulds and Marks & Spencer for clothing design. By using CAD/CAM and EDI technology, retailing, design and manufacturing expertise are shared electronically.

EDI in practice

We are seeing a series of dramatic changes; changes that vary from industry to industry, yet have a common underlying theme. Companies are forming closely coupled communities of businesses using electronic technology for all inter-company communications, using electronic trading to reshape the boundaries between companies, to form business networks with cost taken out to the benefit of all the parties.

The following are some examples from retailing, which has been one of the strongest and most effective exponents of EDI since the late 1970s:

1. *Tesco* – probably Europe's leading exponent of EDI and Quick Response – has over 1000 trading partners exchanging an increasing variety of business documents electronically. An example of the erosion of boundaries in retailing can be found in the exchange of forecast information. This is being undertaken by Tesco for both short- and long-life products and results in suppliers having the ability to plan their production more efficiently, to reduce stock holdings, to

increase service levels, and to eliminate obsolescent stock. The net result is that members of the business network are working to accurate and timely information, and taking cost out of their joint operations.

Nearly all British multiple retailers are using EDI. Such is the pace of change now that companies can make rapid progress in the formation of *intelligent business networks*. A detailed case study of the use of EDI at Tesco is included in the next section.

2. *Superdrug* set themselves a target of 12 months to establish a community of 100 trading partners but they achieved it in 6 months. The network represents over 80% of Superdrug's orders by value.

Such is the penetration of EDI and Quick Response in UK retail multiples that any major retailer which is not involved is at a competitive disadvantage.

The principles of Quick Response are not limited to retailing. In *manufacturing* they call it 'Just In Time' (JIT). The electronics industry is another major user of electronic trading in companies such as ICL, NCR, GPT, MITEL and Sony.

1. *Sony's* Bridgend manufacturing plant produces one-and-a-quarter million televisions a year. Their implementation of EDI has been focused on supporting their JIT strategy. As a result Sony now order over 750 components via EDI, representing over 50% of the orders placed with local suppliers. As in Quick Response, the focus of JIT has been to reduce lead times. Using EDI Sony has reduced their order-to-delivery cycle by approximately two-thirds. This has been achieved by the fast and accurate exchange of information, the early identification of shortages or mismatches and the resultant timely delivery of *quality* components.

2. *ICL* has also adopted EDI as a strategic policy. The ICL objective is that: 'Everything except hardware and people will be capable of being distributed electronically by 1995.' At the end of 1990, ICL was already exchanging over 30% of purchase orders via EDI. They had reduced their order cycle by over 80% and were sending more than 80% of all air freight bookings electronically. As a key player in an increasingly global market ICL have also implemented international trading relationships via EDI in countries such as UK, USA, Taiwan, Japan and France. In international markets, the ability to break down the barriers between organisations can often bring greater gains.

The achievements of the retail and electronics industries are not isolated, they are mirrored in other industries such as publishing, pharmaceuticals, health care, insurance, home shopping, oil and stationery. Companies like W H Smith, John Menzies, 3M, ICI, Glaxo, the AA, Littlewoods, Freemans, BP, Esso, Conoco, Castrol, Spicers and DRG are using EDI to redefine the boundaries and scope of their business networks.

In the 1990s there are three major *growth opportunities* for EDI as follows:

1. *International Networks* We are witnessing the removal of barriers to trade across Europe – this, combined with the increasing adoption of global sourcing, means that companies are looking to standardise their business networks regardless of geography.
2. *Financial EDI* There is a great deal of interest in the potential to include the payments cycle and other financial services in the EDI loop – for example, Spar's paying over £100 million per annum to its suppliers and Littlewoods exchanging EFTPOS data with its card acquirer.
3. *Government* Whilst there are already a few users in local and central government, e.g. HMSO, government must be one of the biggest potential users of EDI. The organisational dynamics are different but the potential for change is equal to many areas of the private sector.

In summary, there is a wealth of EDI activity in industry and commerce, and the activity is focused on improving the communication between companies in their business networks. However, there is still a great potential for the use of EDI. To quote the MIT report: 'EDI is not a choice . . . [it is] the inevitable way business will be done.'

Tesco – breaking down the barriers of trade

Tesco is one of Britain's largest food retailers with 390 stores and 84,000 staff serving 8 million customers each week.

In the last decade the company has been completely transformed – the number of stores has declined but the development of superstores has greatly increased floor space; inside the stores the old emphasis on price has been traded in for a new emphasis on quality.

As Howard Bryant, Tesco's Trading Director, explains: 'Whereas in 1982 we stocked 5,000 food items, we now offer over 16,000 food lines plus a wide range of household, health and beauty products, wines and spirits. In the past eight years we have enjoyed dramatic growth, doubling margins and trebling profits.'

Tesco attributes its recent success in part to a crucially important ingredient – its commitment to Information Technology (IT) and to Electronic Trading in particular. Tesco's use of IT is well illustrated by the model developed by the Massachusetts Institute of Technology as part of its 'Management in the 1990s' research programme (see Figure 6.1). This model depicts the initial use of IT in only one business function of an organisation to solve local business problems, e.g. a local accounting system. There then comes a move to more integrated systems, as individual applications are linked over local networks, for example, in order to share information. It goes on to show how IT is used to change the business process and redefine the areas of organisational responsibility in order to gain competitive advantage.

Ultimately, IT can provide the opportunity to change the nature or scope of an organisation. A good example is the way IT has enabled retailers, like Tesco, to offer 'cashpoint' banking services through their Electronic Point-of-Sale (EPOS) tills. The model itself has to some degree shaped Tesco's progressive use of IT and Electronic Trading through Electronic Data Interchange (EDI). It has led the company up the model's route, from the first step of changng from paper to magnetic tapes to major advances in the management of the supply chain. Tesco has by no means reached the end of the road as yet – further exploitation of IT and EDI is planned.

Early days – receiving invoices

Tesco took its first steps into EDI in the days of direct supplier deliveries when each of its 2,000 + suppliers produced one invoice a day for 350 stores. This represented literally millions of invoices per week from suppliers for Tesco. The paper mountain problem was obvious! Checking invoices and matching them against deliveries was a mammoth task.

Tesco's first solution was to start receiving invoices from large suppliers on magnetic tape, taking advantage of an amendment to the Finance Act in 1980 which allowed VAT invoices to be exchanged electronically. The saving on data preparation and eliminating input errors from this move alone was massive. Although expanded to cover ten suppliers, this route was limited by the procedures required to handle all the tapes. 'EDI is a far more efficient and less cumbersome process and we are confident that most suppliers will accept that EDI is the way of the future,' states David MacInnis, Director of Inventory Management.

Now, a project is under development for the receipt and automatic matching of suppliers' price files. 'This will allow mismatches to be resolved before invoices are received, reducing Tesco's and suppliers' administrative costs and also benefiting suppliers by smoothing the payment process,' adds Stephen Hyde, Trading Accounts Director.

Transmitting

Of greater impact on existing trading practices was Tesco's move in 1984 to eliminate the need for sales reps to collect orders from stores by sending store orders electronically to a central order processing system. Orders were then transmitted to ten major suppliers linked to Tesco's central computer by leased lines, resulting in reduced levels of both inventory and out-of-stocks.

But as Systems Controller, Geoff Warburton recalls,

Electronic order transmission for direct delivery suppliers became the accepted way forward, but setting up and managing individual links into our computer was not easy. Managing and supporting such a system was horrendous – our network analysts were already an overstretched resource and there was a lead time of 2–4 months for installing a leased line!

Tesco found an attractive alternative solution in using an EDI service which enables a single communications link to provide access to an unlimited number of suppliers. The move to the new service in April 1987 caused minimal disruption and it took no more than four months to bring each trading partner on to EDI. Tesco has recently installed high speed communications links to allow large volumes of data (20 megabytes per hour) to be transmitted. The benefits to Tesco from this development were clear. According to David MacInnis, 'The move to Electronic Trading has meant that stores are able to place orders as close as possible to the time of sale.'

Centralised distribution

IT and EDI have also played an important part in a complete change in Tesco's distribution system and the underlying business process away from direct stores ordering. In 1982 80% of dry grocery was distributed direct to stores from suppliers and 20% from the central warehouse. Today Tesco distributes more than 90% of dry grocery goods from its own distribution centre.

The decision about what and how much to buy is now taken centrally by a new Stock Management function rather than by individual store managers. All deliveries are made to Tesco's distribution centres so products are delivered to stores as they are needed, cutting stocks held by stores. Receiving a single order over EDI for each warehouse rather than each store results in substantial savings in distribution costs for suppliers, providing an opportunity for Tesco to negotiate advantageous terms.

Holding stocks centrally means smaller store backrooms, a greater floor area for selling and a minimum number of deliveries each day, already quality checked, thus increasing revenues and reducing handling costs simultaneously. If a product sells out it can be replenished from the warehouse, rather than waiting a full week for new stocks under the old system.

Short-life products

The next logical step was to achieve central control of short life products, but this presented a new set of problems for Tesco – lead times are shorter, conditions of storage vary, distribution problems differ, quality control is vitally important and reaction times are shorter.

In terms of physical distribution, Tesco operate eight composite warehouses to store products in temperatures ranging from − 20 C to + 10 C, each serving 50 stores and handling a million cases per week in peak periods. Specialised vehicles designed to maintain different product temperatures in transit ensure all goods can be delivered to stores in a single vehicle. This enables Tesco to deliver goods to stores as they are required to meet customer demand – in other words, 'Just in Time'.

In terms of the ordering process, electronic ordering was introduced for bread, for example, only in 1989 and resulted in reduced ordering time, out-of-stocks, wastage *and*, most importantly, increased sales. As with other direct delivery goods, each store uses a portable data capture unit to enter and transmit its requirements to Head Office, where the order is processed and sent to any one of five bread suppliers via EDI links. Tesco now believes other fresh products delivered direct, such as wet fish and milk, could easily follow the same electronic route.

Eight years ago no short life products were distributed centrally; now they all are. Eight years ago 50 million cases of goods were distributed from central warehouses; this year the figure will rise to well over 400 million. As David MacInnis explains: 'We now have fewer deliveries, but a better range and quality of goods in each store. With good experience of using EDI with direct delivery suppliers, we were confident that using it with our warehouse suppliers was a good idea.'

Furthermore, Simon Marshall, Stock Control Planning Manager, believes that:

EDI has solved the short-term problem enabling Stock Management to respond to rapid development in other areas of the business. Eliminating the clerical tasks in Stock Management, such as telephone orders, means we can devote more time to analysis and planning for both ourselves and our suppliers.

Electronic trading grows

David MacInnis states:

Since 1988, through a series of supplier seminars, we have built up a community of approaching 400 suppliers all of whom receive orders with many sending back invoices using EDI. For warehouse orders this accounts for 70% of long life product orders and 50% of short life product orders. Through 1991 and beyond, our ultimate aim is to increase our Electronic Trading community to all our suppliers.

The introduction of Electronic Trading for ordering and invoicing at Tesco has now been extended beyond trading document exchange to improve other areas of business. For example, in October 1987 the first of a new EPOS system – 'Checkout Plus' – was installed resulting in speedier, more accurate transactions at the checkout, helping customers and enabling stores to run more efficiently. By September 1992 Tesco had 390 stores representing 96% of turnover using the system, making it the largest food scanning operation in the UK.

'Checkout Plus' incorporates an EFTPOS (Electronic Funds Transfer at Point-of-Sale) system which can receive instant electronic authorisations for credit or debit card payments. This means customers can pay for their shopping and, at the same time, receive up to £50 cash from their debit card in a single transaction. Its scanning facility also removes the need for individual pricing; stores produce shelf edge labels using up-to-date price information transmitted regularly from Head Office.

'The increased accuracy resulting from scanning means we have extended our ordering systems to use sales data as the basis for ordering products from the depots. Using constantly updated sales information means we are able to respond more accurately to fluctuation in demand,' claims Ian O'Reilly, Computer Systems Director. 'By combining EPOS, EDI and sales-based ordering we have vastly improved our ability to respond to customer demand.'

Information for suppliers

Tesco's replenishment systems incorporate sophisticated future demand predictions using sales history data, seasonal factors, local knowledge, planned promotions, stock building decisions, etc. Lead times, load sizes, delivery frequency and current stock are also taken into account before a final forecast is produced for the supplier.

Tesco is using EDI to communicate forecast information to suppliers to save time and as part of a move to a more open business strategy. As Barry Knichel, Head of Inventory Planning explains,

Traditionally companies have released only minimum information to the outside world. But where retailers and suppliers need to work closely together to achieve their common aim of providing an excellent service to the customer, the more open approach we are currently pursuing is paying dividends.

This is particularly important for short life products where time is of the essence and forecasts are used for production and delivery scheduling. For long life goods the next 13 weeks are normally forecast, while short life goods are forecast one week in advance to cover each day of the following week. If selected suppliers are unable to meet provisional orders, demand is spread among alternative suppliers. Since forecasts form the basis of the final order, suppliers can plan production more efficiently and lead times can be reduced by as much as half.

According to Barry Knichel:

This represents a further reduction in stockholding without any drop in service levels. Indeed, the service often improves because suppliers are no longer dependent purely on their own forecasting – there are fewer surprises and we are developing a better understanding of each other's business.

Understanding the supply chain

Having examined its internal business process, the next step for Tesco was to develop a better understanding of the whole supply chain and determine how EDI could be used to improve it.

As Geoff Warburton points out:

To gain the full benefit of Electronic Trading we need to develop trust and co-operation with our trading partners.

Already we have had discussions about how we can take cost out of the business to the benefit of us, our suppliers and our customers. This often means removing the proliferation of checking and replication of documentation between us and our suppliers.

For example, if a supplier sends a delivery note ahead of the vehicle Tesco can react to shortages more quickly when placing the next order, as well as streamlining the depot's goods-in process. Anomalies due to breakage or quality control can be reflected on the goods received note transmitted back to the supplier as confirmation of delivery. Payment can then follow automatically and electronically on the due date with the bank advising the supplier of the credit to his account. Electronic payments require less administration, are more secure and reduce the potential for fraud.

For all this to be effective there needs to be agreement on product information, including the coding of consumer units and traded units, pricing, case size, weight, volume, etc. Most of this data belongs to suppliers and Tesco recognises the need to provide suppliers with an exchange of product code data – ensuring that all products are recognised means deliveries can be accepted at goods-in. As Geoff Warburton puts it,

The consumer benefits because there will no longer be unknown product codes at the checkout. But more importantly, by redesigning the business process with our trading partners we will have taken cost out of the supply chain – a benefit that ultimately will be passed on to the customer.

Electronic trading in the 1990s

Tesco has come a long way since replacing the first paper invoices with magnetic tape. Technologies such as EDI, EPOS and scanning will continue to play a major role in the redefining of their business processes to gain competitive advantage – a fact summarised by Ian O'Reilly: 'If Tesco can be more effective in communicating with suppliers than our competitors, then our business partnerships are strengthened and we get a better service, the benefits of which we pass on to our customers.'

He goes on: 'We have made considerable progress in improving the efficiency and effectiveness of the supply chain and have plans for still more. Even beyond that is the scope for changing the nature of our business.' But that is for another day!

Recommended reading

Michael Scott Morton, *The Corporation of the 1990s*, Oxford University Press, 1993.
'Electronic Business Exchange', Conference Proceedings, 10, 11, International Network Services Ltd, June 1993.

7 Building a world-class manufacturing company through strategic partnerships

Martyn Laycock

Executive summary

In 1981 the turnover of Tallent Engineering Ltd was under £1.5 million, and its profitability negligible. It had no organisational strategy or direction. The order book was rapidly diminishing and workforce morale was low. With the UK economy in severe recession Tallent's future looked bleak. Opportunities were hard to come by and there were few funds available for investment. *Today, Tallent has a turnover approaching £60 million a year, profits exceed £3 million.* The Company has strong and successful business strategies and – despite another difficult recession – has continued to grow rapidly. A recent survey judged Tallent to be one of only 2% of companies in UK manufacturing currently achieving 'world-class' standards.

Martyn Laycock describes how, through a bold strategic initiative, skilful investment in state-of-the-art technologies, and using techniques which today might be called 'business process re-engineering', the company transformed its systems and processes, reshaped its 'organisational architecture', pared down its costs, improved productivity and product quality and – helped by a policy of close collaboration with its customers, employees and suppliers – carved for itself a profitable and growing niche within the fiercely competitive automotive components sector.

End of an era

When I first encountered Tallent Engineering in 1972 they were a small but well-established company making decent – if unspectacular – profits. As a wholly owned subsidiary of the privately owned Colston Group, they had developed core competencies in engineering and heavy metal pressings. They existed largely to meet the needs of their parent company – manufacturers of a range of domestic appliances. I was arranging finance for a new 200-ton press required to improve output and streamline production flows.

In 1979 Colston decided to sell their appliance business to the Italian manufacturer Ariston. As Britain's smallest domestic appliance manufacturer Colston had few economies of scale, no competitive edge. They had failed to make the volume breakthrough they had pursued for years with their patented domestic dishwasher and were simply too small to compete with major suppliers such as Hoover, Hotpoint and Zanussi. Under the terms of the sale Colston would in future simply receive royalties from Ariston for the use of their designs.

All of this was to have a significant impact on Tallent's business strategies for the future. They managed initially to replace much of the Colston output with work for Talbot's motor assembly plant in Linwood, Scotland but rumours were growing that the plant would close as part of a worldwide rationalisation. *This closure would bring serious problems for Tallent for, by 1980–1, over 50% of their £2 million annual output was going to the Linwood plant.*

In the midst of severe economic recession new work was extremely hard to come by and new opportunities were few and far between. Unless Tallent could find new applications for their skills and experience, their future, like that of many other manufacturing firms at the time, would begin to look decidedly bleak.

A window of opportunity

I visited Tallent again in 1981 – this time to discuss financing of a very different nature. Following a thorough review of their operations and markets the company had decided to pursue bold new strategies. *They were planning to invest around £3.5 million – one-and-a-half times their annual turnover.* Much of this was for state-of-the-art plant and machinery – including the very latest robotics. In the midst of a severe economic recession the scale of this proposed investment seemed remarkable – especially as neither Tallent, nor their parent company, had significant funds to put into the project themselves.

Tallent had appointed a new Managing Director in 1980. Bernard Robinson had joined the company as an apprentice tool-maker in 1956. Since then he had worked his way up the company ladder – become a production supervisor in 1965, Works Manager in 1972. On his appointment as a director in 1977 he had decided to take night-classes in order to obtain an accountancy qualification. As a production engineer he felt he needed to understand the figures – the financing and investment side of the business.

When assembling his new management team in 1980 Robinson had recognised an urgent need to find new, longer-term business. It was only a matter of time – no more than two years he reckoned – before the Linwood plant would close. But he had looked on this eventuality as a possible window of opportunity for his company – perhaps a 'one-off' chance to find a new direction, develop new long-term strategies, before the Talbot business came to an end.

Without the reliable Colston business, the company were – to use Michael Porter's phrase – 'stuck in the middle'. They had neither low-cost edge, nor specific contracting edge, nor any differentiation of product or quality from their competition. They lacked any clear business focus, any strategic direction. At this stage Bernard Robinson sensed something radical was needed:

We had a strong asset-base, good freehold buildings, room to expand, some useful plant and machinery. Morale at the time was quite low but we had a loyal and committed work-force – some valuable core skills in areas such as pressing and basic engineering. I felt we had an urgent need to 'do something different'. We needed to look not only at products – but also at *processes* – at how we were doing things – how we could do them better. The world was changing, old standards were no longer good enough. We needed to find a way to differentiate ourselves from other manufacturers serving our types of markets.

It was Robinson's vision, together with the commitment of his management team, which was to establish the company's successful business approach into the future.

A glimpse of the future

Robinson believed solutions would lie in the achievement of *quality* and *price* advantages over traditional engineering products offered by Tallent's competitors. That would mean making some fundamental changes.

Among many industry sectors he and his team considered was the automotive industry. In Britain in 1980 this was in turmoil. There was overproduction throughout Europe. Michael Edwardes was tackling appalling labour-relations and low-productivity problems at British Leyland. Chrysler were expected soon to close their remaining UK plant. Even major producers like Ford and Vauxhall were finding things tough as the recession put new pressures on productivity and cost reduction.

Robinson had been to Germany and to Japan to see what was happening there. In Germany he had seen prime engineering skills, better organised production. But in Japanese car plants he had seen robotics and new production processes. He had witnessed close attention to quality, noted the coming together of functions such as design and production, seen how *cooperation* was making things easier, more effective, for the manufacturers *and* for the customers. He had been impressed. Robinson's team sensed that eventually there would emerge a new industry structure; fundamental changes occurring at that time would bring new opportunities. *Globalisation* was starting to have a considerable impact.

Tallent's board looked at other industries – consumer electronics, IT, DIY. They even contemplated manufacturing presses for others. But most of this work required short production runs to match frequent specification and model changes. This would mean constant set-up changes and, almost inevitably, lower productivity for Tallent.

Their detailed research suggested that the troubled motor sector could well provide Tallent's best opportunity for the future. Robinson explains:

We didn't look just at Britain. We looked at Europe and beyond. We looked at the world-wide direction of motor manufacturing and considered the possible future structure of the industry. We saw that the Japanese influence was making its presence felt almost everywhere. It was even being rumoured that the Japanese may set up factories in Britain. We realised if we were to have any part in the future motor industry we would need, ourselves, to take a different approach – to respond positively to the changes taking place. The old traditional methods of engineering production were being overtaken. Old comfort zones were rapidly being eroded. To have any chance Tallent would need somehow to become part of the 'new tomorrow'.

So it was that the company boldly decided to set its major focus on the manufacture of motor components. Tallent's management sought the largest components they could competently handle. They wanted high-volume work suited to their core pressing and engineering skills and needed to combine this with low variety. There was a need for long and uninterrupted production runs if they were to succeed. As Robinson explained:

We decided that *chassis-structural components for mid-market, non-specialist cars* was what we needed. Such models tended to have 5–10-year lives, sell in volume and, typically, whilst there would be several body and interior changes, usually the chassis and sub-frames tend to remain unchanged.

We'd need to achieve consistently *high quality* if we were to succeed. We'd need to change our whole approach – introduce new technologies and processes – we'd have to reorientate ourselves, get the workforce to accept new work practices – adopt *greater involvement* in our business.

Selling the vision

Robinson knew that Rover, now part of the beleaguered British Leyland, were set to introduce new models, and that Ford were working on the design stages for the Cortina replacement: 'We went to Rover, told them of our skills and our plans for the future, and, quoting pretty competitive prices, managed to persuade them to give us a try. We clinched an order to make cross-members for the new SDI model.'

Tallent were soon able to increase their share of production of cross-members for Rover from 30% to 50% – eventually they became 100% suppliers. But the company needed more of this type of business. They decided to pitch for some of Ford's future business. Tallent had to have large, ongoing, *volume* orders if their bold investment plans were to be justified. Two members of Robinson's management team were ex-Ford and knew the company were taking the growing threats to their business from Japan seriously. Tallent's detailed presentation to Ford explained how by adopting the very latest manufacturing and production technologies – robotics from Japan, software from Scandinavia – and by introducing new work-practices and management control procedures they would be able to achieve both economies of scale and high-quality output.

Tallent's major goal was a contract to manufacture components for the new Sierra, due for launch in 1983.

Raising the finance

For their bold new plans to succeed Tallent would need a period of rapid, even spectacular, growth. Their 1981–2 business plan – a weighty and detailed document some 94 pages long – recognised the risks the company was taking:

The textbooks are full of case-histories highlighting the high risk of business failure associated with high gearing, particularly in periods of recession. The gearing of European, American and Japanese competitors is considerably higher than in the UK. There is little doubt that the risks of high capital investment in a recession are high but the rewards of stealing a march on competitors are equally high.

Critical to the plan would be the establishment of *credibility* with banks and investors, and with customers, especially potential new customers such as Ford.

It became Finance Director Alex Worrall's primary responsibility to explore all the avenues of funding – to seek as much 'leverage' as possible. Worrall takes up the story:

I started with the Department of Trade and Industry. They were introducing various initiatives designed to encourage new attitudes in British manufacturing industry at the time.

I made sure their office in Newcastle knew Tallent intended to be part of this new approach. We took our business plan to them, assured them we believed in it, gave them a realistic summary of our relatively few strengths and, at the time, our many weaknesses. We stressed our belief that, with the right backing, our plans could be achieved – that, as a management team we were committed to them. Most importantly, we sought their advice. This was a critical part of our strategy and it worked.

The DTI helped Tallent to negotiate a £1.2 million European Investment Bank loan at a heavily subsidised 4% p.a. This allowed the company to present their ambitious new plan to a number of lenders. Eventually four key lending sources – two American, one French, one Irish – agreed, through Worrall's strenuous efforts, to back the company. Despite the severe recession in the UK they liked the ambitious hi-tech plan and had confidence in the capability and dedication of Tallent's management.

A £20 million contract

When a Ford delegation visited Tallent's Aycliffe site in 1981 and saw the management commitment and the dedication of the workforce, they awarded Tallent the contract they so needed – the supply of 800,000 pairs of rear suspension arms for the new Sierra model. The contract was worth £20 million over a four-year period and, at a stroke, unlocked Tallent's ambitious investment plans.

Soon, based on the quality of their production for Rover, they also negotiated additional work for British Leyland to manufacture sub-frames for the LM10 and

LM11 (Maestro and Montego) models which were to replace the ageing Ital, Maxi and Allegro saloons.

As a precaution however Tallent decided to restrict their output for the automotive sector to *not more than 50% of their annual sales* in the early stages. They therefore also sought business from locally based manufacturing firms such as Thorn Lighting, Black and Decker and IBM in order to build up the non-automotive side of the business.

A Japanese approach

Bernard Robinson was convinced that quality of output would be critical for Tallent's success. In visits to Japan he had seen that if consistent *quality* was to be achieved then the approach needed to permeate right down to the shop-floor. Operatives had to be given the power to control the quality of their own output. He recognised the need to look at entire *processes* right through the factory – from the ordering and receipt of stock through to the eventual packaging and despatch to the customer.

Having risen from the shop-floor himself, Robinson realised the organisational problems he would need to overcome. There would have to be many changes and reorganisations. His experience told him there would be resistance to this at shop-floor level:

Many of the processes being used in Japan were quite alien to the traditional British engineering approach. Knowing my work-force well and, acknowledging their low morale, I realised that the introduction of these new processes would take time. Much patience and retraining would be necessary. I could see huge opportunities but I could also foresee some of the problems of bringing in new systems and getting them to work. I and my Board and production colleagues did a lot of 'management by walking about' in those days. We needed to think the entire production processes through and to decide what changes would be feasible and how best they could be implemented.

Robots and human beings

When Tallent introduced the first robotics line the workforce were rightly sceptical, as Robinson describes:

They thought the machines were going to take their jobs. But we were able to disprove that theory quite quickly – there's actually plenty of room for both men and machines in modern manufacturing – so long as you get the blend right and use the machines for the right reasons. *I had learned from my visits to Japan and elsewhere that human beings are best at tasks which call for variety – modern computer-controlled machines are far better at repetitive tasks.* Once they're set up, and properly maintained, they simply go on producing what they were designed to produce – *what* is wanted, *when* it is wanted – and with virtually no need for rework.

Once our robots were settled in (we did have a few problems at first) the inspection process became virtually built into the system. Then we could start to focus our workforce on the critical areas *between* the hi-tech production processes to improve the work-flows and overall efficiencies. We first introduced a simple enough technique that the machines were kept 'in true'.[1] It was a basic discipline but a good introduction to change. Once the lads had come to terms with this and seen the benefits then we began to introduce to them the concept of *continuing improvement* – something I personally felt very passionately about and still do!

Tallent's approach to employee relations was maintained well into the future. Strong, positive leadership and good communication have been features of their style. Robinson believes in encouraging worker participation and employee involvement. *Employee numbers have grown from around 150 in 1981 to over 700 in 1993 and the firm continues to have a completely strike-free record.* There are productivity and bonus schemes. The workers operate in customer-focused 'cells' which encourages them to focus on their end customers – and they are encouraged to suggest improvements at any time. Robotics are a common feature now across Tallent's 18-acre site – Bernard Robinson reckons that *for every new robot installed the company creates five new jobs.*

Introducing just-in-time

By 1983 Robinson's management team had become increasingly aware of the 'Just-In-Time' techniques which lay at the heart of the Japanese manufacturing approach.

The Just-In-Time (JIT) system pioneered in Japan, notably by Toyota, focused on the 'management of inventories' and the 'reduction of waste' – a concept founded upon the concept of 'visibility' – the ability to *see* what is going on. Simplicity and synchronisation are two of its key features. Based on lower batch sizes – the ability to achieve a smooth and efficient *continuous* production process – it was the opposite of traditional 'batch processing'. To be successful it requires high degrees of cooperation with both suppliers and customers.

Tallent's high gearing and continually stretched cash flow meant that the JIT system had considerable appeal and Robinson and his team prepared eagerly, if somewhat cautiously, for its introduction. Robinson had made a strategic management appointment a year earlier. He had brought in Simon Flunder from Ford and had given him responsibility not just for purchasing but for the entire flow of goods and inventory through Tallent's manufacturing processes.

With the UK economy still in recession, however, Ford's 1983 Sierra launch brought disappointing news. The new model did not sell in the numbers that Ford, or Tallent, had expected. With their funding and fixed operating costs geared to higher output levels Tallent's cash flow became increasingly stretched. Other new contracts had been won – from Rover and Jaguar – and the *diversified* strategy was working quite well. Non-motor business was being handled for Black and Decker,

Samsung, Goldstar and IBM. But with the Ford work critical to Tallent's cash flow, bankers and lenders had to be warned in 1984 that loan interest and repayments might prove difficult to meet. In the meantime, management earnestly examined all aspects of the business in a search for ways to improve matters.

Alex Worrall explains:

Our 'backs-against-the-wall' analysis showed that over a number of years we had simply become used to carrying ever-increasing levels of stock and to debtors paying late and management was spending much of its time chasing outstanding accounts. We always seemed to be trying to sort out foul-ups of one sort or another. Often we seemed to be doing things not once, but twice – sometimes more.

Pioneering EDI

Worrall's growing interest in Electronic Data Interchange (EDI) was to prove a key to solving these problems.

During 1983 he had become aware of the ODETTE initiative then getting underway in the motor industry. The concept of electronic data exchange was new and Worrall soon became convinced that JIT techniques alone would not fully solve Tallent's cash flow problems.

He began to see the wider and long-term benefits of EDI: improved ordering and stock control at one end of the process and streamlined billing, accounting and the electronic collection of money at the other. He felt these could eventually form a platform on which to establish closer, more effective relationships.

In the meantime the expected changes in the structure of the UK motor industry were beginning to materialise. The large manufacturers were actively reducing their numbers of component suppliers; they were offering increased volumes to those suppliers who were prepared to invest in new processes. In response to the threats from Japan there was also a new focus on quality within the industry. Manufacturers such as Ford, Rover and Jaguar were concentrating more and more on producing the major components, and on *assembly*. They began to offer their first-tier suppliers more of their business if they were prepared to invest in new cost-efficient production and management processes.

Tallent were by now convinced that they had adopted a winning strategy. Increasingly positive talk about Nissan's plans to open a factory in the North East simply reinforced this view. The *future* looked good – but first they needed to solve the critical problems of the present.

In 1985 Tallent became the first ever user to access Istel's EDICT system via PCs. They became EDI *pioneers* – using PCs because they had no funds to buy a mainframe. Their EDI links cost only £5,000, plus a lot of management time, and were, according to Alex Worrall, one of the best investments the Company ever made. Today he admits:

I don't personally believe we would be in business now if we had not allied the benefits of EDI to our efforts to introduce Just-In-Time.

It provided us with critical communication links with both our customers and our major suppliers, helped us build a platform for greater co-operation in the future. It also began to provide us with critical, hard, reliable information.

Some suppliers were less willing than others to cooperate with Tallent's new system. Some, like British Steel, were simply not prepared to make the necessary changes. So important though were these changes to Tallent that they decided to re-source their steel – through stockholders who *were* prepared to work the JIT system. Simon Flunder says:

We quickly realised that good communications are a prerequisite for improved supplier–customer relationships. Soon we were receiving up to six, sometimes eight, deliveries of steel a day.

We began to *manage* the production flows through the factory. Traditional mass-production techniques had meant splitting the process down into small, manageable sections but it is perfectly natural to take a hard look from time-to-time at the entire process – examine how things 'fit together'. Many firms seem to build complex structures – lots of 'specialist' departments – which then spend much time fighting each other, contesting ownership of information. We've always had a small and very cohesive team at Tallent – that's certainly been an advantage over the years.

Tallent's entry into EDI, coupled with their JIT initiative, brought improvements in stock turn from six times to fourteen times each year. It has since improved significantly further. Far less capital was tied up in stocks and work-in-progress. And, through EDI, money started to come in on due dates and much less management time was spent sorting out errors, chasing up outstanding accounts. Cash flows improved significantly.

Eric Forth, Parliamentary Under-Secretary of State for Industry and Commerce, presenting Alex Worrall with a *Data Communications Manager of The Year* Award at the EDI '89 Conference at London's Savoy Hotel in January 1990 said:

EDI is not primarily about technical issues; it is about applying the best management practice. The most tangible benefits are seen in cost reduction, the control of resources, accuracy of data transmission and the speed of response, all of which lead to better customer service and gaining that most valuable asset, the competitive edge.

Autonomous work groups

Through Simon Flunder's ongoing work on Tallent's *processes*, management began to set themselves targets in a number of key areas. The danger, Flunder recognised, was to try to do too many things too quickly:

You have to be very careful about the degree and pace of change. Too much too quickly and the organisation and its people can't, or in some cases, won't, accept it. So we looked at key areas one-by-one. We'd start off with ball-park targets in particular areas, for example, not more than 100 tons of steel in stock at any one time. Then we'd look at how this could be achieved and track the likely ramifications right through the production process. A primary objective was to synthesise purchasing and logistics into a new *skill* and to do this we obviously needed to work closely with our suppliers. We also needed to improve communications with, and between, our own people.

The development of a 'cell management' approach proved helpful. Management created separate 'cells', or process *teams*, to carry out interlinked processes. They encouraged each 'cell' to look at how stocks in their areas could be reduced, production flows, and quality, improved and how waste could be eliminated. *Each cell was encouraged to take full responsibility for its own output and eventually for its own costs and overall quality.* Key control information was given high visibility using charts at key 'cell' control points in the factories.

In this way the workforce began to adopt 'ownership' of the work which they carried out. They worked more harmoniously with management to help to raise the efficiency of the production process, to improve the quality of the output, to eliminate waste, and to drive down the inventories, and costs, as a result.

Continuous improvement

Robinson began to get obsessive about quality:

The introduction of JIT was our starting point but, in seeking the required continuous flow of production and the absence of inventories we also highlighted a lot more weaknesses.

Originally we hadn't quite grasped that JIT was inseparable from quality – it isn't just a technique or a process – it's an entire new way of doing things. We found that JIT simply won't work unless you *build in* quality. There is precious little room for error and no allowance for rework.

He stepped up training for the workforce, introduced new internal communication systems and developed a more 'open' style of management. He and his fellow directors did even more 'walking about', got involved with the cells and the teams and encouraged the whole Company to start *thinking* quality.

Simon Flunder discovered another benefit of JIT:

Over time we found we needed less space for stock and work-in-progress; we could start thinking more about factory layout – about linking the various processes in a more logical fashion. Our teams came up with some good ideas in these areas. As we phased in improvements we saved precious space and became more efficient in this area too. Our preferred suppliers took greater interest and cooperated in many of the changes which we implemented. As we continued to grow we translated the improved systems into our *new* factory layouts and into a true system of continuous improvement – one which we continue to this day.

Although today Tallent's focus on processes and on improving the overall business structure might well be labelled 'business process re-engineering', it is important to realise that, beyond the joint introduction of EDI and JIT, Tallent's has been a *continuous*, ongoing process of change. A sharp strategic focus was achieved through a flexible approach and the ability to respond positively to changing conditions and to new technologies.

Strategic partnerships

Another concept used successfully in Japan and adopted by Tallent has been 'partnering': the strategic setting up of joint ventures and alliances whereby firms in the same, or related, supply chains cooperate to add value to each other's operations. It is a concept gaining rapidly in popularity and use in the 1990s, not least where internationalisation, in many cases *globalisation*, is occurring as a natural extension of trade.

Nissan opened their UK assembly plant on Wearside in 1986. This helped to put Tallent's quality approach even more fully under the spotlight. By a stroke of good fortune one of Japan's leading exponents of JIT, quality and continuous improvement had arrived virtually on Tallent's doorstep. As Alex Worrall explains:

Based on our track record in automotive components we became one of Nissan's first 67 approved suppliers. Soon we were supplying parts to the Sunderland plant and since then we've developed an excellent and cooperative relationship.

Nissan helped us move towards even more efficient systems and introduced us to the benefits of 'partnering'. We've now become part of a highly efficient local network in which virtually all critical inter-company communications – ordering, requisitions, payment – are conducted electronically. We work together with our suppliers to restrict stocks, minimise waste – keep 'work-in-progress' to an absolute minimum. Our stock-turn is now the envy of our industry.

Encouraged by Nissan and Ford, Tallent turned next to the benefits of strategic partnering, an approach which was not new, but which has seen a considerable recent revival of interest, especially in globalising and ever-more-competitive industries such as automotive manufacture (see Figure 7.1).

By 1986–7 Tallent were doing very well. The cash flow problems were well behind them and rapid growth was continuing. Further investments were being made in the latest plant and processes. Bernard Robinson's belief in people and in the advantages of getting people involved, was beginning to show real benefits.

Yet he and his Board still felt they could do *more*. Tallent began to focus more and more on the manufacture of chassis-structural motor components as the restructuring of the automotive industry in Britain, and worldwide, continued.

Tallent's formal partnership approach started quite modestly – and quite close to home. In 1988 they formed a simple strategic *technical partnership* with the DEA Group in Swindon. DEA provided precision testing equipment and Tallent – through their quest for ever-more-efficient operations – had developed a continuous investment programme using the latest test equipment. Initial

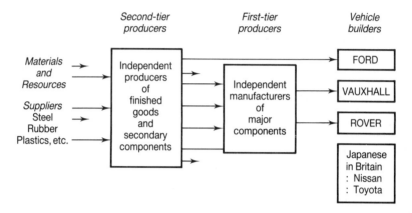

'As both American and Japanese manufacturers target Europe, a recent report says that component manufacturers face a choice between going global or going under', *Distribution*, February 1993.

Figure 7.1 The UK motor industry — the supply chain

arrangements with DEA were for a one-year trial but a permanent and very worthwhile long-term relationship developed, which reflected the value to each company of this alliance.

Tallent's move into strategic 'partnering' on the international stage began in 1989 when, encouraged by Ford's move towards their first truly 'global' motor car (the CDW27, Mondeo) a partnership with A.O. Smith Corporation — a Fortune 500 Company based in Milwaukee, Wisconsin, USA — was announced.

A.O. Smith was formed in 1874 and had grown with the US automotive industry. Today it is North America's leading independent manufacturer of chassis-structural components and automotive suspension modules. A.O. Smith is a Tier I supplier to the big three US car manufacturers — Ford, General Motors and Chrysler — and to leading independent truck manufacturers including Kenworth, Peterbilt, Freightliner and PACCAR. A.O. Smith Automotive Products division's annual sales totalled $528 million in 1992, making them approximately *seven* times the size of Tallent Engineering.

Like Tallent, A.O. Smith's Automotive Products division had been contracted to Ford for the manufacture of major components for the Mondeo. Ford positively supported this alliance because they wanted their 'first-tier' suppliers to *share technology* and to work together with them in areas such as design, research and development. Like many other manufacturers Ford were becoming, increasingly, *assemblers* of motor cars. They would still produce major sub-assemblies such as engines and gearboxes themselves but increasingly they would offer more and more production of other items such as interior components, instrumentation and chassis-structurals to suppliers who were prepared to invest in new plant and equipment, new technologies and processes. Following the Japanese integrated supplier/contractor approach, Ford wanted to encourage their major suppliers to become more involved, more integrated into the entire design and production processes.

On a recent visit to Detroit I spoke to Frank Eischen, Vice President responsible for A.O. Smith Automotive Products' sales to Ford in America. He told me of the progress which has been made:

Our people meet perhaps six–eight times each year, and work together on various projects between meetings. The primary focus is on product design but we also share information on production and processes. Although Tallent are very much smaller than us they are, like us, world-class exponents of robotic arc-welding – we also found that we follow remarkably similar cost-accounting, pricing and people policies. When we agreed this cooperation back in 1989 Tallent's design function was very small – so we provided them with the benefit of our expertise and acquired knowledge. *Our* main benefits come in because the CDW27 was launched in Europe earlier this year but, due to Ford's global scheduling, we don't go into production in the US until early 1994. We're learning with Tallent right now as they move into full-scale 'live' production. Each side stands its own share of costs on this partnership. Our regular meetings are normally two–three day affairs and usually involve our main suppliers – such as the TI group – as well as key Ford personnel. We discuss problems, share successes. It's a very active partnership with specific objectives. We've nothing else at all similar to this partnership with Tallent – it's unique at present. The whole thing seems to work extremely well for everybody.

Tallent's developing relationship with Nissan led increasingly to exchanges of staff and of information, and to closer cooperation in critical aspects such as design and testing. It was through this relationship that Nissan encouraged Tallent to form a *strategic alliance* with the Yorozu Manufacturing Corporation in Japan. Under a 'technology transfer agreement' negotiated in 1990 Nissan agreed to provide assistance to Tallent to help them to develop chassis-structural components for Nissan's new Euro models.

Bernard Robinson told the press at the time:

By combining our own expertise with that of Yorozu, we will be able to offer Nissan unparalleled production capacity. It's a big step forward and our commitment to the venture is underlined by our £18 million investment in new state-of-the-art production equipment over a three-year period. [see Figure 7.2]

And Yorozu's Managing Director, Akihiko Shito said

Tallent has the sort of high-tech culture that makes them ideal partners for a venture of this kind and we are delighted to be working with them.

Robinson is certain that this venture has been beneficial to both parties:

We have an almost constant exchange of technical information. The Japanese rate our welding and paint capabilities very highly and we know there is much we can learn from them in areas such as press-work. We exchange managers and key workers, allowing each to learn from the other at practical grass roots levels. With Yorozu we also jointly develop critical 'benchmarking' initiatives. It is this, and our clear intentions for the future, that have recently earned us our 'world-class' tag.

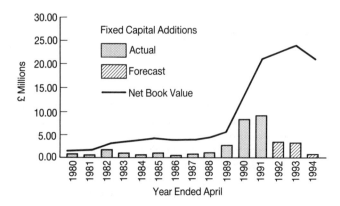

Figure 7.2 Tallent Holdings plc – capital expenditure/net book value

Despite our cultural differences the relationship is excellent and each company is constantly encouraging the other to seek further improvements. We share information and experiences. Nissan also benefits, of course, through ever-increasing improvements in the quality and reliability of products – both in Britain and in Japan.

Recent developments

In 1988 Bernard Robinson received the 'North-East Businessman of The Year' Award. In the following year he received the OBE. He also became Chairman of the Durham Training and Enterprise Board, an organisation set up to encourage better training and improved enterprise in the north-east of England.

In 1989 Robinson, Worrall and Flunder *bought out* Tallent from Colston and the company became largely their own as they embarked on another major phase in their development. Later, continuing success and further rapid growth brought the company to the attention of a number of larger industry players and in 1992 Tallent were taken over by Thyssen Unformtechnik, part of the German steel and industrial conglomerate.

'But, even though we now have new owners nothing's really changed,' concludes Bernard Robinson, now Chief Executive.

We stick to the area of chassis-structurals that we know and we strive continually to do things better. We use our partnerships and alliances to best advantage and we ensure our people receive the best training and we provide the best information to enable them to play their full parts.

Shortly, his company will develop their focus still further by implementing the 'Investors in People' approach in their Aycliffe factories:

To be world-class you have to excel on quality and cost. That means you have to invest heavily in people as well as machines. You have to recruit people as an investment and then manage them. You have to get them used to change, but change for the right, positive, reasons. Not change for the sake of change. The most sophisticated machinery and processes in the world are useless without the right people.

The secrets of success

I have spent quite a lot of time at Tallent recently, talked to management and workers and given a lot of thought to what has been achieved. Delighted that the company I supported all those years ago has done so well, I have looked closely to identify the key reasons for their remarkable and unqualified success. The following are the most important:

- It is difficult to describe Tallent's success without paying tribute to their commitment to the management of *change*. This has been a constant 'success factor' during their 12-year development in the modern automotive components industry.
- Their focus on processes has been a fundamental part of this: the ability to consider the entire production process and how its various sections fit, flow and work together. Tallent's preoccupation with quality and the needs of their customers have also been important here. Flexibility has been important too – the ability to adapt to changing conditions, to overcome obstacles, to adopt and adapt new technologies.
- Leadership has clearly also been a prominent feature. Bernard Robinson's shop-floor background, his willingness to learn – and to listen – and his open, yet positive, management style, all have contributed to Tallent's undeniable success.
- Also teamwork – the dedication displayed by Robinson's small but totally committed management team over the years. And the ability to get the workforce involved, to encourage them, through techniques such as 'cell management', to take ownership of the company's quality philosophies, has been important too.
- When back in 1981 the new strategies were adopted there was little talk of supply chains and the term *business process re-engineering* had not been invented. But the ability of Tallent's management to look at processes, to amend and redesign them, to craft and reshape their work-practices, their 'organisational architecture', has undeniably been a cornerstone of their success (see Figure 7.3).
- Through 12 years of rapid growth it has been Tallent's focus on partnership and cooperation which has helped the Company make some of its biggest strides forward.
- Also, by working closely with the Department of Trade and Industry they were able to source funds to facilitate implementation of new strategies. Then by working ever more closely with major companies like Ford, Rover and Nissan, by integrating the benefits of EDI alongside JIT, by cooperating closely with

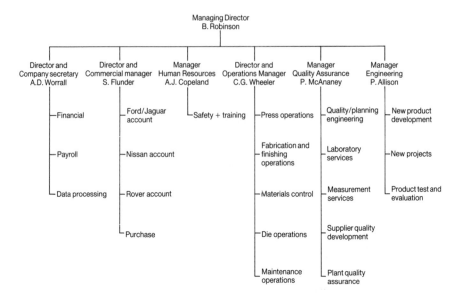

Figure 7.3 Tallent Holdings plc – capital expenditure/net book value

suppliers and by developing positive international alliances with the likes of A.O. Smith and Yoruzo, Tallent have displayed an aptitude for *cooperation* which has helped them develop into a truly world-class manufacturing company.

'Only through increasing cooperation and continuing investment in technology and in people could this have been achieved,' Bernard Robinson told me recently. I asked him if he had developed any 'golden rules' during this remarkably successful 12-year period. 'Adopt a clear and simple strategy and never, ever give up,' he said. 'Get the workforce working with you and never stop looking for better ways of doing things. Its the only way to stay ahead.'

He explained to me what he describe as his 'three Ss':

Standardisation – a set of clearly defined standards and objectives which everyone understands; *Specification* – clear, concise technical quality descriptors which reinforce the standards set; and *Simplification* – make everything as down-to-earth and understandable as you possibly can.

Tallent's achievements in the last 12 years have been remarkable. Annual growth exceeding *30% compound* is excellent by most people's standards and profits have improved at an even more impressive rate (see Figure 7.4). But, even using high-tech equipment and the most modern of production processes, the Company have also provided over *500 new jobs* in an area of traditionally high unemployment (see Figure 7.5). For me, Tallent's is one of all-too-few long-term successes in British manufacturing. I salute them.

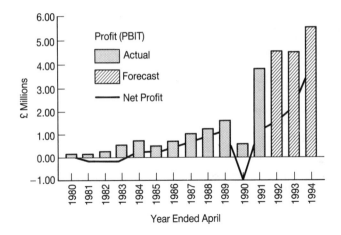

Figure 7.4 Tallent Holdings plc – trading performance

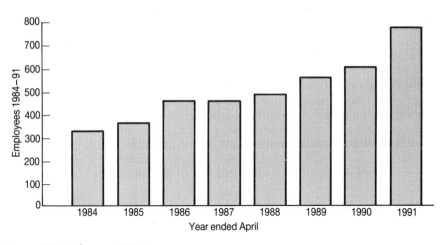

Figure 7.5 Employees, 1984–91

Note

1. Five times in every hour an operator would take a component from the machine and check it for alignment. The results of these checks were recorded over a period of time and if it was found that the machine was straying beyond limits, it would be re-calibrated and the reasons for it straying beyond limits investigated and rectified. If the machine remained in true, then in theory no unacceptable parts would be produced – output would remain of constant quality, thereby avoiding the need for quality inspectors.

8 Competing on service delivery through business process re-engineering

Patrick Moylan

'The most important marketer in our company is the man or woman on the loading dock who decides not to drop the damned box into the back of the truck.'
Executive of a high-tech company, quoted by Thomas J. Peters and Nancy K. Austin, *A Passion for Excellence*, Random House, 1985

Executive summary

This chapter provides a rationale and a systematic approach to improving service delivery of fast-moving consumer goods which are sold through retail outlets.

1. *Why?* Maintaining a competitive edge will require a fundamental appraisal of systems, attitudes and relationships, particularly with regard to supply chain management.
2. *How?* The whole purpose of efficient consumer response is to shorten the supply chain dramatically, making it a system whereby decisions on what to make and deliver are driven by consumer demand.
3. *What?* The approach focuses not on people and productivity, but on improving the process, getting rid of functional specialisation and eliminating delays. The effect is to galvanise business performance.
4. *Who?* A key factor in influencing the behaviour of individuals is the system used to measure and reward performance. This is a critical task for top management.

In the 1990s a new more discerning customer has emerged. During the recession many consumers discovered just how much they could do without. Although purchasing confidence is returning, spending decisions are being carefully considered and lack of availability and poor service will threaten the survival of consumer goods and retail companies.

It was clear in the mid-1980s that Britain was going to have too much retail space relative to demand. After four years of growth, demand faltered in 1987, as people spent less on consumer goods when they needed their money for other things. But all the extra retail space needed stocks to fill it. Did this extra inventory please the consumer? No, they became confused with declining service, interminable mark-downs and promotions, and a diet of bland product.

Despite the worst ravages of the recession being over, these problems remain and are compounded by the entry of new aggressive competitors like Toys R Us, Ikea, Aldi and soon some powerful low-cost discounters like CostCo.

What should companies do in the next five or ten years to face up to the challenges posed by a more demanding consumer and stronger competitors? The issues are as follows:

Quality   Quality is not synonymous with a high price. From a technical point of view it is about consistently meeting the specification, whether the specification is for a high-priced product or a low-priced product. From the consumer's point of view it is about a perception of a product as 'good' quality. In the case of Marks & Spencer, Britain's best-known retailer, quality is an integral part of the offering. Other retailers are reconising this.

Service   This can sometimes be a meaningless concept. As Mike Hammer, an American consultant drily observed, 'I don't care that the driver is smiling if the taxi is broken down.' Undoubtedly the most important facet of service is availability of product and for this retailers depend to a great extent on the effectiveness of their suppliers. A study carried out by Kurt Salmon Associates (KSA) in the textiles and clothing supply chain clearly showed that *improved service is consistently cited by retailers as the most important demand they would make on their suppliers in the 1990s*. Figure 8.1 shows that not only is it important but it is increasing in importance.

Price   The price to the consumer is dependent firstly on the cost price to the retailer. Price has been and will continue to be important. Retail buyers will continue to seek low cost sources for the product, often outside Britain and

*Clothing, footware, home textiles

Figure 8.1 European retailers'* perceived importance of suppliers' success factors

the Continent. The low prices they pay are used to mitigate the effects of poor buying decisions. At top management level there is increasing recognition that long-term interests would be better served by re-defining the role and pattern of purchasing because this search for the lowest cost does not always produce the best overall result for the consumer or the retailer.

The other aspect of price is to do with the efficiency of the retailer. Most retailers believe that low cost retail formats present an increasing challenge, especially American formats. Their success has been based upon a close look at all activities and the elimination of those that do not add value. According to Keith Ackroyd, Managing Director of Boots, in reviewing the next five years, *'A key factor will be the increasing use of management information to control costs and make assets sweat.'*

Uniqueness   Merchandise that is different, ideally unique, can provide a real competitive advantage to a retailer. It can be obtained in two ways. First, by having a franchise or a relationship with the consumer that cannot be replicated easily by competitors. Examples include the Body Shop which, although imitated, is rarely surpassed, Levis whose brand loyalty is stronger now than ever, and Burberrys whose 'house brand' raincoat is recognised worldwide as distinctive.

The other way of having differentiated merchandise is by being quick. A trend is spotted, and the product is developed and delivered quicker than competitors' products. Eventually the competition may obtain a supply but the cream of the market has been taken. When a retailer develops a reputation for innovation and fast reaction, their shops become a first port of call for consumers.

Product innovation is about new and different merchandise being made available quickly and time is of the essence. *Shortening cycle times is one of the most important changes in current management thinking.*

The Shop Floor   Service as described by choice and availability is important but there is another vital aspect – the interface between the staff and the customers. This alas has deteriorated. Technologies like bar code scanning and central ordering may have saved time but they have reduced further the essential contact required on the shop floor. Branch managers and their staff also feel alienated from the centre. They feel under-informed and powerless.

So there are a handful of issues that ought to concern management. Maintaining competitive edge will require a fundamental appraisal of systems, attitudes and relationships particularly with regard to the supply chain.

The opportunity for suppliers and retailers of consumer goods that know how to source globally, create equity with their customers, merchandise stores to meet local needs, distribute efficiently and be cost efficient has never been greater.

The supply chain

The purpose of the supply chain is straightforward enough. It is to satisfy consumer demand. The process however is not so straightforward. In theory demand should pull products from the supply chain and products should flow to meet that demand. In practice it is problematical. Demand fluctuates because of seasonality, changing fashions, competitor activity, weather, and so on. Goods move down the chain slowly and in batches. Imagine a situation where a retailer finds that a particular item is selling well but there is insufficient stock in the business to support the sales potential. Can they order more? Should they order more? In many cases the possibility of resupply does not exist because the lead time is longer than the selling cycle. Even when the lead time permits a reorder there is a possibility that when the quantities are received demand may be falling again.

The result will be a cancelled or amended order, or an excess of retailers' stock and price mark-downs to shift slow-moving merchandise. The effects of this are felt throughout the supply chain between retailers, wholesalers, factories and material suppliers. And this is just one example. Because of delays and discontinuity in supply and demand there is surplus inventory at different stages of the supply process, loss of business at the retail end through non-availability, and invariably mark-down loss and profit loss on residual stock. Whatever way you look at it performance is poorer and loss of profits is higher than it ought to be.

Quick Response

An awareness of the extent of these profit leakages was the springboard for Quick Response which, along with allied practices like Just In Time (JIT), Time-based Strategies and Speed Sourcing, has become the touchstone for advanced consumer goods management thinking. It started in the USA where import penetration in textiles and clothing had brought industry leaders together who formed the Crafted with Pride in America Council. Among its activities to promote domestic products to the consumer was an advertising campaign which has significantly raised the consumer awareness of home-produced products.

The Council also committed part of its budget to research into the supply chain. A study by Kurt Salmon Associates in 1986 revealed that although individual parts of the supply system were efficient, the overall efficiency of the system was very low. In seeking to minimise costs independently of each other the fibre, textile, apparel and retail industries were inadvertently pursuing practices that added significant costs to the overall supply chain. The magnitude of the improvement opportunity surprised everyone, and one key finding in particular caught everyone's attention – the length of the supply chain and the impact this had on the efficiency of the system.

The supply chain from raw material to consumer purchase was 66 weeks. During 80% of this time, the product was either in warehouses (fibre, textile, retail) or in transit. In fact time, during which the product was being added to, could be measured in /urs. Clearly something was wrong. Further research confirmed this. The long supply chain was expensive to finance – all that inventory sitting adding cost but not value. Major losses were incurred as either too much or too little product was produced and distributed based on inaccurate forecasts of future demand.

The consumer market, especially in seasonal and fashion goods, is not conducive to exact science. Even so we make things difficult for ourselves. Traditional time-hallowed methods are still commonplace with individuals being captives of the twice-yearly discrete seasonal planning mentality dealing with lead times of up to, and often more than, a year. This approach is totally inappropriate to today's market and requires retail buyers and merchandisers to be geniuses, trying to predict a year in advance, what styling, colour and accessories will appeal to consumers.

The pity is that with many consumer goods supply chains this is the way the system is designed to work, and participants work extremely hard at making it work the way it has been designed. The logistical system is thus complex and institutionalised – and ineffective. Just how ineffective was demonstrated by two studies into apparel and home textile markets, one in the US, the other in the UK. *The overall loss to the system was estimated to be 20% of overall sales. Overall profitability was about one third of what it could be.* This should help answer the question 'Why Quick Response?'

Efficient consumer response

The whole purpose of Quick Response is to shorten the supply pipeline dramatically and to transform it into a 'pull' system whereby decisions on what to make, supply and deliver are driven by consumer demand. It is consumers that will drive this new vision of a supply chain. Efficient Consumer Response will become the guiding management principle for consumer goods in the 1990s.

The last five years have seen more activity in trying to change and improve the responsiveness of suppliers and retailers to consumer demand than had happened since the 1940s. Experience has been gained, some routes to success have been forged, blind alleys are now known. A mid-term report on progress suggests that there are five major constitutents to making real progress. They are the following:

1. Partnership.
2. Short cycles.
3. Information Technology.
4. Re-engineering processes.
5. New ways of measuring performance.

Partnerships

One of the chief obstacles to truly efficient consumer response is the idea that a company's enemies are its suppliers and its trade customers. How else could one explain the adversarial relationship that exists between companies up and down the supply chain? It is a two-way war with none of the partners being entirely innocent. One example is the battles between retailers and their landlords. Focusing on the length and terms of leases, it sets institutions who want continuing growth on their investments against retailers who must respond to shorter-term change in consumer demand and the cost implications. Retailers would like their landlords to be more flexible and take some of the risk of volume going up and down. This is happening to some extent with turnover-based rents.

Flexibility is also key in relationships between retailers and third party distribution companies. The image of the distributors has become tarnished in the eyes of retailers in the past few years. Peter Walter, Comet's Distribution Director, said, 'Contractors will try to lock you in, so every time you try to change the operation, you will have to pay. Retailers need to get as much flexibility as possible into the operation.'

But attitudes are changing. Real progress is now being made between retailers and their merchandise suppliers. The really interesting by-product of closer partnerships to meet the future demands of the consumer is that they favour British-based suppliers. Alan Smith, Managing Director of B & Q, has stated that in the long term the company would probably move towards British manufacturers. He said, 'Customers want to buy British goods and from our company's point of view there are shorter lead times from British suppliers, which could lead to a greater net margin.'

Perhaps the best-known example of supply partnership is that between Marks & Spencer and its suppliers. Clinton Silver, the Deputy Chairman, stated that the company's close supplier relationships which included information sharing and frequent face-to-face meetings, have helped it to sell products at full price in recessionary times. The bulk of suppliers are based in Britain, which means a short supply chain. He described M & S as a 'manufacturer without factories' and its suppliers as 'retailers without shops'.

Sharing of information is crucial, but until comparatively recently there has not been that much information to share. Even retailers like M & S did not have timely or accurate information about demand, rate of sale and stockholdings at the levels that it really matters – by store, by stock-keeping unit (SKU). The revolution in information technology, particularly in point-of-sale data capture (POS) has brought dramatic improvement. Data captured by retailers is invaluable. It should become the common currency of a logical, responsive and rapid information pipeline. When suppliers are allowed effective access to what is selling and what is not, they can schedule their production accordingly. Lee Jeans, part of the vast VF Corporation, place their Market Response Systems (MRS) at the heart of their consumer-driven philosophy.

In the USA this sharing of information has extended to some suppliers actually taking responsibility for ordering and maintaining stock levels – and guaranteeing to deliver demanding returns on space occupied by their product and inventory invested. And why not? because at the end of the day it is as much in the interests of the suppliers as the retailers that the ultimate consumer gets what they want. Procter & Gamble supply Wal-Mart and own the product until it is actually sold to the consumer. Stock control is thus the responsibility of Procter & Gamble.

Among British retailers like BhS and the hitherto opportunistic Burton Group, there is a real and growing awareness of the need to view suppliers as a corporate asset. The idea is to identify 'key' suppliers were mutual prosperity can be achieved by managing the business practices of both parties to provide maximum value to the ultimate consumer. Management of the supply chain means more than anything else planning to manage the risk inherent in consumer goods, especially fashion-influenced products. Characteristics of this approach are long-term planning to make sure that capacity is available when needed but that the capacity is taken up as late as possible when as many clues as possible, ideally through knowing actual demand, are available. Decisions are made as late as possible, but at planned points. Problems are communicated quickly, confidence is built up and a long-term relationship is developed.

Short cycle times

One of the main objectives of managed relationships with key suppliers is to develop and exploit short cycle times. Time is crucial. By making changes in the way of developing products, in ordering them, in processing them, in delivering them and in exchanging information, it is possible to cut cycle times to a fraction of their current duration.

One example was provided by Mike Hammer, in a presentation to the National Retail Federation conference in New York in January 1993. It concerned the IBM Credit Corporation that provides credit to people wanting to buy IBM equipment. The process involved four functions: credit checking, calculating interest rates, terms and conditions and issuance. The cycle time was six days. Not surprisingly the salesmen in the field were unhappy about this and were always on the phone enquiring about the status of the deal. The current system could not provide accurate status so management successfully installed a control desk function which was able to report progress on each deal.

Unfortunately, but perhaps not unexpectedly, the cycle time lengthened – to ten days and the field representatives became even more frustrated. The prospect of the customer changing their mind, or going elsewhere, increased. There were a series of other improvements to try to remedy the situation. Most notable was a motivation scheme based on measured standards. Within a few weeks almost everyone achieved 100% compliance with the standards but the overall cycle time went up to 12 days! The operation was efficient but not effective in terms of customer service.

According to Hammer, two people had an idea. They took a deal and literally walked it through the current process. At each stage they waited while the relevant transaction was completed and found at the end that the actual work consumed no more than 90 minutes. What was happening for the rest of the 11 days, 6-and-a-half hours? Nothing – the deal was waiting in the queues between the four functions.

An important point emerges here concerning our definitions of efficiency. Suppose by some magical means it were possible to double the efficiency of the people working on this operation. What would that do to the cycle time? Would it halve to six days? Of course not. It would reduce the work content from 90 minutes to 45 minutes but this would have an inconsequential effect on the cycle time.

The issue at stake here is not the people or their productivity. It is the process; and by re-engineering the whole process the cycle time was eventually reduced. How was this done? By getting rid of the functional specialisation approach and training individuals who could deal with *all* aspects of the transaction. By eliminating the queues and delays the cycle time was reduced to one day. The effect on the business was galvanising with the volume of business transacted increasing fiftyfold. This is the power of reduced cycle times.

In consumer goods markets reduction in cycle times of this order are achieved. The Limited, a large American apparel retailer have reduced the time from production inception, through ordering to receipt in stores from nine months from Far East suppliers to an average of just one month.

Information Technology

If we examine the information systems in place in retailing, we will find the following:

- EPOS capturing product level sales data.
- A large central processor which holds copious data.
- Purchasing systems to bring goods into the business.
- Stock management systems.

These systems were originally defined in terms of their operational capability, and they do the operational job well. However, going forward, a retailer's focus must be on Efficient Consumer Response and these existing investments in systems need to be viewed as an infrastructure upon which new consumer-focused applications will be developed.

Allied Maples, a British furniture retailer, views technology as a strategic resource. It fundamentally affects the way the company is managed and is improving their ability to deliver a quality service to their customers, in partnership with their suppliers. According to Managing Director, Graham Winter, 'the focus must be on using technology to add value by reducing the time it takes to respond effectively to changing market needs, improving the quality of products and services and limiting the administrative burden of the business'.

EPOS hardware, by definition, is at the point of sale. It is the key point at which the business comes into contact with its customer and represents an opportunity to capture information about the customer and their buying habits. Liberty, the London-based retail group, is totally committed. Tony Salem, their Managing Director, says, 'our branch operations have EPOS terminals relaying product information to the centre and providing merchandise data. This enables us to ensure that the best mix of product is distributed to the branches.'

A further development from EPOS are loyalty schemes. Customers are provided with cards which when scanned enable selected customers to obtain discounts not available to other customers. The benefit to the retailer is to be able to track consumer purchases against socio-economic and demographic profiles and build up valuable insights into consumer purchase patterns. BhS has such a scheme, 'Choice Card' which has greatly helped their marketing department and generated significantly increased sales volume.

The future may see some interesting partnerships between non-competing retailers who are targeting the same customers exchanging information collected through loyalty schemes.

Technology will also allow retailers to improve their sourcing arrangements and rationalise their traditional ordering and distribution processes. Time-scales from sales transaction through supplier reorder to replenished stock on the sales floor is being cut from months to days; from days to hours. The use of electronic links to suppliers will become commonplace. Sears in the UK is a case in point. It has installed EDI (Electronic Data Interchange) services which allow computer-to-computer transfer of orders, invoices and sales and stock reporting with its suppliers throughout the world. Sears' Chief Executive, Liam Strong, says,

Correct partnership and sharing of information provide tangible benefits for both parties with increased sales, a decrease in total stock, higher product availability and reduced mark-downs. With our Quick Response initiative we can sell more by stocking less. It is essential to buy what we sell, not just sell what we buy.

One of the greatest challenges faced by organisations with gigabytes of sales data is to turn this data into information which can support the Buying and Merchandise functions. Retailers, particularly those with strong seasonal patterns: clothing, sports/leisure, toys, luggage, gifts, are investing much thought and effort into producing merchandise plans which will more accurately reflect what their customers are going to want to buy, and which will ensure that the best use is made of available retail floor space. These planning systems will become the focal point for planning the business, driving merchandising activity and the allocation of space from a single, common plan.

The use of product level sales data will also be used to help forecasting. In-season statistical re-forecasting will become better developed, driven by the need to use actual selling patterns to modify purchasing commitments and distribution decisions. These replenishment systems will become more sophisticated akin to the 'intelligent' system used by foreign exchange dealers to take trading decisions automatically. The timescales demanded and the volumes of data involved mean that human intervention, apart from exceptional situations, is not practical.

Re-engineering processes

It should be stressed that it is not systems but people that will deliver Efficient Consumer Response. Systems enable us to achieve improvement but no piece of hardware or software has ever delivered any benefit on its own.

The essential focus for the future in providing Efficient Consumer Response will be on people and radical changes in the working lives of most individuals. The banner under which these changes will take place is Business Process Re-engineering (BPR). BPR challenges the very foundations upon which traditional business operates.

Industrial and commercial processes are based on two principles. The first is the principle of task specialisation. The basic idea is that if a process like making a shirt, or building a house, or fulfilling an order is broken down into a lot of individual tasks, those tasks can be made simple. People can be trained to work fast at simple tasks and high productivity, especially with long production runs, is obtained. Secondly, large task specialisation units need levels of supervision and management and support from specialists, like personnel, purchasing, stock control, quality inspectors.

This is the process and organisation that served the needs of a post-war society; labour efficiency, economies of scale and layers of management to control the process. It does not meet the needs of the 1990s' consumer goods market. As we saw with the IBM example earlier, it is slow, rigid and stifles flexibility and innovation. It is also expensive because organisation structures based on it have a tendency to develop high costs in non-value-adding activity and overhead.

In clothing manufacturing in Britain there has been a rapid take-up of new processes. The assembly line system based on task specialisation operated by garment manufacturers is no longer inappropriate to the needs of a market which is increasingly looking for faster response. Because the components spend so much time waiting for the next operation it takes several weeks for a garment to be produced. Retailers require garments to be made available much more quickly, especially for lines which are known to be in demand and where supply can be tailored to known appeal.

The solution is team working or modular manufacturing. At its best it involves little, if any, buffer between operations. Normally a team of perhaps five to eight multi-skilled members will make an entire garment. The garment goes through the whole process in a matter of hours, much quicker than the traditional assembly line. Apart from great advantage in making the job more interesting, reducing strain (particularly repetitive strain injury – RSI), reducing absenteeism and labour turnover and improved quality, the principal outcome from the point of view of the customer is that the right goods are available when they are in demand. For retailers sales improve, with minimal stocks and reduced costs.

In retailing there is a radical business change going on. Over the years a plethora of specialist functions developed; corporate planners, marketing departments, advertising, promotions, buyers, selectors, merchandisers, managers, allocators, distributors, planners, visual display specialists. Progressive retailers are now looking at their core business processes and seeing them as essentially consisting of two elements: creating demand through marketing and merchandising and satisfying demand through sourcing, logistics and operations. We are seeing, therefore, simpler structures based on small cross-functional teams, based around products and customers, and energised to achieve new benchmarks of performance.

One of the ironies of technology and centralised systems is that it can reduce the role of the people at the store-end, the people in the front line. A one-way communication system from the centre to the local store overlooks the unique insights that only the people in the store can provide. For example, a store manager will know about local developments such as new job creation in a town, or knowledge about growing or disappearing competition, that no central planning and replenishment system based on numbers can possibly deal with. Yet with the trend towards centralisation the people at the store can become detached, unempowered and demotivated.

The challenge, which successful retailers are facing up to, is to allow an effective association between those at the centre with a wide market perspective and those at the store with a local viewpoint. Testament to this is given by Jim Maxmin, Chief Executive of Laura Ashley who maintained that the reason why his company survived the turbulence that it went through in the late 1980s was because of the commitment and loyalty to the product shown by people in the store and to the loyal Laura Ashley customer.

Measurement of success

We have talked about partnerships, shortening cycle times, information technology and redefining business processes but there is still the question of what constitutes success. No factor is more important in influencing the behaviour of individuals and organisations than the system used to measure, and reward, performance. One of the most important tasks for top management is to ensure that there is a very close correspondence between the objectives of the business and the measurement and accountability for their achievement. To employ a time-honoured phrase, 'What gets measured, gets done.'

Any organisation that attempts to re-engineer its processes and change them to provide better response to its customers' needs without changing its measurement and reward systems will fail to achieve its objectives. There will probably be an initial burst of enthusiasm but this will wane as people realise that performance is still being evaluated on the old measurements.

Traditional measurement systems are allied with the profit maximisation model which is the foundation of the functional management structure. This assumes that if top management organises resources to maximise sales, minimise material costs and minimise operating costs, then the organisation's profit goals will be achieved. The validity of this assumption is now questionable as the following examples show:

Physical distribution has been viewed primarily as a cost centre with the objective to reduce the cost per unit or cost as a percentage of sales. This is how management's performance has traditionally been measured. Yet the needs of the market may be for more frequent, smaller drop deliveries. Whilst this may add cost to the distribution function, the overall benefit to the business in terms of sales increases or inventory reduction may be much greater.

A Retail Buyer's objective is to maximise gross margin, which is why they put great emphasis on the cost prices they pay. They compare suppliers on this basis, ignoring other factors. For example, buyers are encouraged through price incentives to purchase products in pack sizes that lead to higher stock levels than sales justify. But whilst the measurement system easily recognises the cost advantage of the purchasing decision, the overall cost implications of excessive stock levels are obscured.

Many of the changes required in an Efficient Consumer Response mode of working involve trade-offs which may increase costs in one department to achieve more than offsetting savings or increased revenue across the whole organisation. In order to evaluate these trade-offs, it is essential to have in place appropriate measures of performance and service levels; measures which are congruent with Efficient Consumer Response. These need to be non-financial and financial, but not just the financial measures that support a functionally based organisation.

Financial measurement

Traditional measurements required for financial reporting have severe limitations when it comes to managing Efficient Consumer Response. For example, a meaningful comparison between the merits of different suppliers ought to take account of the true costs of dealing with a supplier, including inventory-carrying costs and the cost of shelf space occupied. Similarly, to find out the true profitability of a product, it is helpful to have Direct Product Costing (DPC) which seeks to allocate on a rational basis all of the direct and indirect costs associated with marketing and retailing a product.

A variation of this is Activity-Based Costing (ABC). This is based on the premise that costs are related to activities rather than products. This requires that all activities, and the costs associated with them, are determined. These costs can then be assigned to whatever is being measured: an organisational unit, a supplier, a product line; on the basis of how much of the activity it consumes.

Non-financial measurements

These important measures are directly associated with an organisation's implementation of Efficient Consumer Response.

Service levels   Systems that measure the availability of product to customers.
Customer satisfaction   Regular, structured reviews of customers' perceptions of quality, delivery, product appeal.
Cycle times   Cycle times and the individual steps within them can be determined for most business processes. These can be measured against goals for cycle time reduction.
Fulfilment   This is a measure of the output from a process relative to its input. An example is the actual quantity delivered relative to a detailed order.
Forecast accuracy   Measuring how close forecasting techniques came to accurately predicting actual demand.

Conclusion

Efficient Consumer Response is a strategy for the future. The last few years have shown that complacency in the face of a changing consumer, and innovative, aggressive competition, are fatal. Efficient Consumer Response is a strategy for companies to strip time and cost from the supply chain to achieve a responsive, demand-driven system in which companies can work together as business allies, sharing information.

Efficient Consumer Response necessitates changes in business processes, in corporate culture, in organisation structures, in relationships with customers and suppliers, and in measurement and reward systems. The most important requirement is to break down the functional boundaries that exist, both inside companies and between companies. Only top management has the authority and power to make these changes and to move the organisation towards a different way of doing business.

III   Developing a continuous improvement culture

9 Establishing a high-performance work culture – merging British and Japanese approaches

Gerald D. Radford

'They recruit their managers from the factory floor; we get ours out of law schools.'
John Gibbons, Chairman, Congressional Office of Technology Assessment, on Japanese success in world trade, *NY Times*, 28 July 1985

Executive summary

Sumitomo Rubber Industries took over the Dunlop tyre operation in 1985, at a time when the business was in decline and the workforce was demoralised. The changes which followed were dramatic.

The new management team began a programme of continuous improvement, where employee commitment and involvement were the priority. But it was not simply a matter of selecting a new workforce imbued with 'Japanese work ethics'. This approach was based on investing in the existing workforce and encouraging teamworking.

In time, a structured Total Quality programme was introduced, making sure that some early, if modest, successes were achieved, and using *kaizen* groups for problem solving and continual improvement assessment. Over a two-year period waste was reduced by over 70% at the same time as raising quality standards. Each worker is now responsible for assuring the quality of the products in process. Continuous learning is encouraged through a wide range of company training courses and by supporting participation in external courses leading to a qualification.

Among workers at the plant there is now no distinction between Japanese and British methods. They are logical concepts which make good sense.

As every good gardener knows, successful cultivation requires careful preparation of the soil before planting begins, yet this basic principle is frequently overlooked by managers in their anxious pursuit of an instant 'quick-fix' technique, preferably validated in the Far East.

In the 1970s and early 1980s quality circles, which were thought to be the secret of Japanese industrial success, were eagerly adopted in Britain without in most cases producing significant benefits. The reason was that results-orientated managers were trying to impose on their bemused and often unwilling workforces an activity which should be voluntary and participative. Quality circles are merely the blossoming of a cultural change with much deeper roots. Tinkering superficially with systems and structures serves little purpose unless the fundamental values, beliefs and attitudes of the company are receptive to the changes.

The take-over of Dunlop

This was the problem faced by SP Tyres UK Limited when it commenced operations in 1985. It was the largest Japanese employer in the UK at that time, with almost 3,000 employees, and it was unique because it did not enjoy a greenfield site which it could model to its own requirements. In taking over the Dunlop tyre operations Sumitomo Rubber Industries inherited an ageing and loss-making manufacturing business with a demoralised workforce and nine unions. The one advantage it possessed was that the take-over itself created an expectation and an acceptance of change.

Performance improvement was not therefore a matter of simply selecting a new workforce imbued with the so-called 'Japanese work ethic', nor of investing heavily in new technology and equipment, however necessary that might be. Investment in human resources was, and has remained, the most important priority, the first of the '4Ms' to which our Japanese colleagues sometimes refer – *men, materials, methods and machines*. The focus was not on compliance with any superimposed management formula but rather on seeking commitment and a shared sense of purpose. This can only be cultivated by a long and continuous process of transforming ingrained attitudes and beliefs, starting at senior management level.

The old style of management was largely hierarchical and autocratic. Contact between senior management and the shop-floor was limited and the main channel of communication was through union representatives. The declining state of the business meant that they usually heard bad news about cutbacks and redundancies, indeed, what other reason was there to talk to them?

Open communication

Our new approach was to give employees directly as much information as possible, both good and bad, in the belief that the more they understood the needs and problems of the company, the better they could contribute to its progress. Union representatives were included in this process but they were no longer the mouthpiece of management nor the sole source of information. *The directors led the effort to improve communication* through regular formal briefing sessions and informal contact ('walking the job') at all levels. The emphasis was on listening as well as informing. Suggestions were strongly encouraged and remunerated, so that everyone would think constructively about their job and the company could tap the collective wisdom and experience of all employees. This did not happen overnight, and one of the keys to maintaining interest is to respond rapidly to each suggestion, whether it is significant or not. This is not always easy.

People from different functions were brought together, often for the first time in years, to share in discussion groups and training. A particular effort was made to bring the salesforce and its customers into contact with employees in the production and technical areas so that there could be a greater understanding of mutual needs and everyone could feel part of the customer chain. The extension of the customer concept to mean the next stage in the process made each job less remote and more personalised. At the beginning of each day shop-floor workers and managers met in small departmental groups to review current problems and priorities, and openness in recognising deficiencies or mistakes was encouraged by focusing on the solution without unnecessary recrimination. It is impossible to resolve problems which are regularly ignored or covered up.

Teamwork

Teamwork was essential and managers had to lead by example, becoming 'player-managers' instead of just giving directions from the sidelines. This was only possible if psychological barriers such as status were removed, hence the adoption of common canteens, car parks and workwear, and a progressive move towards the harmonisation of terms and conditions for all employees. Our surviving eight unions now participate in joint working parties and negotiations. Management had to restore its credibility by practising what it preached and through consistency and transparency gradually creating a climate of trust. Managers had to share their knowledge with their subordinates and seek their opinions and participation. It was no longer just a matter of telling people what to do. Not surprisingly *it was middle management who felt most threatened by this change*, which eroded their hierarchical authority and obliged them to adjust to their new roles.

Taking care of the employees

The general welfare of the employees, the so-called 'human resource', has to be cared for even more than the other assets of the business. The removal of the threat of redundancy and the creation of job security, with the expectation of a brighter future where we could all prosper together, led to greater flexibility and a more relaxed acceptance of change. The satisfaction of career and pay aspirations is dependent on our joint success and consequently there is a common interest in strengthening the company so that everyone can share the benefits. Tangible meaning was given to this philosophy at an early stage by the introduction of a *profit-sharing scheme for all employees*. This has already paid out handsomely and is tax free under existing government legislation.

Employee welfare also includes the working environment, which has a strong effect on both motivation and productivity. Our approach to housekeeping is based on the '4Ss' (*Seiri, Seiton, Seiso, Seiketsu*) which signify *sorting, orderliness, cleaning and cleanliness*. A major effort was required initially to clean up and repaint work areas, including plant and machinery, and to provide satisfactory rest and changing facilities. A location was chosen for every item and the factory floor was marked out accordingly. As this was done each employee became responsible for keeping his or her own area clean and tidy, particularly in the factory. Attention to housekeeping provides a more attractive environment in which to work and, since every item is in good order and in its assigned place, efficiency automatically increases and there is less risk of error. The possibility of accidents is also reduced, supporting our strong campaign to promote health and safety, which appears high on every review agenda. It is significant that the areas with the best accident record are often also those with the most consistent quality achievement, which suggests a close link between safety and quality discipline.

Total Quality

The focus of SP Tyres from the very start was on customer satisfaction, but it was only after three years that we made any formal move to adopt Total Quality (TQ). We were simply not ready for it earlier. *Total Quality cannot be introduced successfully unless the corporate environment is receptive to it and even then it requires long and determined management commitment.* The principles and merits of TQ have been amply documented, and were well suited to our changing culture. External help is usually needed to introduce the concept and create the structure necessary to carry it forward but TQ cannot be delegated, it must be led by the directors and senior management. We appointed our own Quality Improvement Executive to help us promote and guide this development but line management must take full ownership of TQ, it is not some 'bolt-on' technique and must become a way of life for everyone.

It takes years for this culture to grow and flourish and it can be assisted by the nomination of a number of 'champions' or coordinators who are available to assist their colleagues with guidance, training or simply encouragement. We initiated a programme of TQ training for all employees, which included planning, effective communication, SPC (statistical process control) and problem-solving techniques. This last item is particularly significant in order to encourage employees to collect and analyse data carefully without jumping to conclusions or working merely on hunches.

Our structured approach to problem solving is close to Deming's formula, and is based on EPDCA – *evaluate, plan, do, check, amend*. The basic techniques involved in evaluation range from brainstorming to Pareto analysis, cause-and-effect diagrams ('fishbone analysis') and the six-word table (what, where, when, why, how, who?). We have not so far attempted to move beyond this into more esoteric areas such as lateral thinking.

Rather than Cost of Quality we refer more positively to *Potential Profit from Quality Improvement* (PPQI) but we resisted the temptation to develop new and sophisticated financial reporting systems or targets. Participation in the TQ process is more important than target setting and excessive bureaucracy could destroy motivation. It is essential to get away from the strictly results-orientated approach of traditional management although theory must be accompanied by practice. Everyone is happy to talk about quality and few will deny its importance but employees must experience it in action as soon as possible after being trained in the concepts. Nothing motivates them as much as *early and tangible success*, however modest.

The key was to encourage our employees to take ownership of the problems and this was achieved through the formation of small problem-solving groups (*kaizen* groups). The significant thing about *kaizen* is that it involves frequent small incremental improvements without disrupting the process or putting quality at risk through radical innovation. After initially being management-led, this activity is now self-generating. Individuals identify problems in their own area, select their team, which is usually multi-skilled, and they set their own improvement targets, which are not necessarily expressed in financial terms. The only control is the formalisation of the process. Using a standard format the problem and the team are identified, and meeting action points and progress are recorded. Success depends not on the amount of financial saving but on the number of problems solved which little by little add up to a significant improvement in efficiency and profitability.

The effect of this activity on performance and on employee motivation has been amazing, and has gradually snowballed across the whole company (see Figure 9.1). In one product area alone, over a two-year period the cumulative effect of *kaizen* activity *reduced waste by over 70%* whilst at the same time quality standards were being raised. As *kaizen* groups multiply throughout the Company team spirit and motivation are strengthened and ideas for further improvement bubble up in increasing numbers, affecting all areas of the business. No financial reward is given for *kaizen* activity as it would be contrary to the spirit of participation. *Kaizen* is considered to be an integral part of the job. The main satisfaction for the individual is the sense of involvement and empowerment. Ample and frequent recognition is given to the teams by directors and senior managers. An annual *Kaizen* Day is held to permit teams representing a cross-section of all departments to make a formal presentation of their achievements to the Board and senior management. There are no winners – 'we are all winners' is our slogan – but each participant receives a small commemorative gift.

Continuous improvement

Kaizen, or small step improvement, is fully integrated with the company philosophy of continuous improvement in everything, which we inherited from

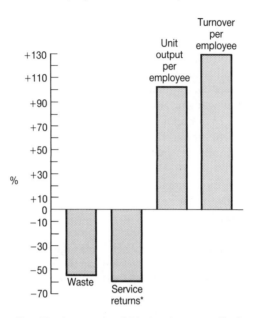

Note *'Service returns' are finished products returned by the customer.

Figure 9.1 SP Tyres UK Limited – performance improvement 1984–92

our Japanese colleagues. Every piece of plant or equipment, however new, can be improved and each time a quality or productivity target is consistently met the goalposts are moved, creating a continuous challenge for further improvement. A similar attitude is taken to costs and efficiency. The results and achievements of sister companies are regularly communicated to the workforce and stimulate a healthy rivalry to do even better. Frequent exchange visits, based on the principle of 'seeing is believing', reinforce this motivation.

Involving suppliers

Quality, especially in production, has a profound significance for profit and productivity. The reduction of waste and rework automatically cuts direct costs and increases output but the full benefits can be realised only on a 'right first time' basis. Quality must be built in during the process rather than defects being inspected and taken out at the end. This principle commences with external suppliers, since defective or incorrect raw materials and components compromise the whole production process.

The selection and quality auditing of external suppliers are the first link in the chain of quality and productivity. Our stated aim is to establish a long-term relationship with suppliers 'based on full and open communication and on the closest possible cooperation so that we may progress together in a mutually successful partnership based on continuous quality improvement'. A full quality audit programme is followed for all major suppliers but, as the relationship develops and trust grows, *quality control responsibility is left increasingly with the supplier on a self-certification basis.*

The responsible worker

In our own factories each worker has full responsibility for assuring the quality of the product in process and for passing on only products of specified quality to the next stage or 'customer'. Defects create a rapidly escalating cost as they move through the production and supply chain. The 'right first time' approach assures quality in the finished product at the lowest cost and supports the aim of zero defects. There is no 'in process' inspection, only a final quality check.

The operator is assisted in a number of ways. The discipline of preventive maintenance, conducted according to a fixed programme, ensures that all plant and machinery is kept in prime condition to forestall any problems and the operator has personal responsibility for the care of his machine, minimising time lost on breakdowns and ensuring a smooth workflow. Each employee, especially on the shop-floor, must have pride of ownership of his equipment and his work.

The *kanban* approach

Although there has been no company-wide adoption of Just in Time, the *kanban* technique is applied in many areas of the factory. Through the use of simple indicators on a signboard, 'coin' systems or even the space allocated to a given component, *kanban* eliminates paper bureaucracy and gives each worker an immediate visual check on when his 'customer' requires further material, and how much, to keep the process flowing. In this way goods are pulled through the production chain as required without the unnecessary accumulation of semi-processed material at each stage. The reduction of in-process stocks frees more space, cuts capital employed and supports quality by ensuring the continual use of fresh materials and components at each stage. This is particularly significant in an industry where semi-processed materials are subject to ageing.

Plant layout is carefully studied to facilitate the movement of materials and semi-finished products and to ensure correct handling in the interests of quality assurance and optimum utilisation of labour. Whenever possible *poke yoke* (failsafe) systems are applied supported by the use of CIM (Computer Integrated Manufacturing) which, for example, automatically adjusts the process if variations are detected and gives rapid feedback to the operator.

The implementation of systems such as SPC (Statistical Process Control) and 'lot control' further assist operators in monitoring the quality of their process work, permitting them to correct machine calibration before problems arise, and to quickly trace and isolate any potential causes of defective production. Each operation is standardised, on the basis of the best and most efficient method, since any deviation must put quality or productivity at risk. A process designed for quality is one which will optimise productivity and contribute to the motivation of the workforce. Variability in the product is usually caused by the process and not by the worker.

This principle is equally applicable in non-production areas. By improving invoicing procedures the sales office increases customer satisfaction whilst improving cash flow and productivity. Likewise, as a result of *kaizen* activity, our salaries and wages department modified its systems and dramatically reduced the number of queries, with benefits all round. The fundamental requirement is that employees everywhere should be motivated to seek continuous improvement and trained in problem-solving techniques. The status quo, or repetition of past achievements, is not enough in today's rapidly changing world, challenging targets must be set to extend the ability of all employees even beyond what they believe is possible. This helps them to savour the fulfilment of their development potential, as well as producing outstanding results.

Continuous learning

Continuous learning plays an important role in employee development. Once more, attitude and motivation are crucial because effective learning begins with the individual's own desire to increase his or her knowledge and skills. If this is lacking no amount of training will achieve the desired objective. Much learning can take place in the employee's own time, and the company supports this by sponsoring participation in external courses leading to an approved qualification. Internal computerised self-tuition and a well-stocked business library are also available. It is always an encouraging experience each year to present so many awards to employees who have achieved a professional qualification and to discover how many of them are keen to continue the learning process.

A wide range of Company training courses is programmed each year covering subjects as diverse as multi-skilling, TQ, FMEA and leadership development. The modest size of our training budget belies the amount of training undertaken for the simple reason that much of it is organised in-house, where the main cost (not attributed) is the time of those involved. Most companies have an enormous wealth of untapped knowledge and experience, as well as a surprising number of potential trainers, once they have been given the help and the opportunity to discover their talent. The trainers sometimes learn as much as the trainees from this experience! An additional benefit is that the training programme provides a further excellent opportunity to bring together employees from different levels and backgrounds within the company.

It will be apparent from what has already been said that we firmly believe managers must have a genuine interest in the welfare of their employees if they wish to achieve results. Reference has been made to many aspects, ranging from open communication, mutual respect and training, to a favourable working environment and performance recognition. Managers must both lead and support their subordinates, encouraging their initiative and responsiveness in searching constantly to improve the process. Managers should also take pride in the growth and success of their subordinates without yielding to the temptation to retain capable employees when opportunities for career development occur in other areas of the business. Regular job rotation, especially for younger employees, broadens their understanding of the business and develops new talents, whilst reducing the risk of over-specialisation. As people move round the company, functional barriers begin to disappear and instead of being a confederation of little fiefdoms, each with its own parochial priorities, a more united team with shared objectives begins to take shape.

Investment for quality and productivity

Although human resources are by far the most important element of the 4Ms to which I referred earlier, capital investment does none the less play its part (m = machines) and in this respect we have benefited from both the strength and nature of our parent company, Sumitomo Rubber Industries. Our plant and equipment were in a poor state when we took over, but it would have been impractical from a financial or operational point of view to correct that in a short time span. Consequently, a long-term investment plan was drawn up for the modernisation of our production facilities and is annually updated. Characteristically, our long-term plan has not been affected by fluctuations in the economy nor in the market-place, it is not subject to the exigencies of short-term profit. This consistency and stability, supported by generous financial assistance during the start-up period, have permitted us to focus with confidence on the goal of long-term growth and performance improvement. Our capital investment has been totally orientated towards quality and productivity rather than increased capacity, though capacity has indeed grown as an inevitable consequence of our progress in efficiency. We followed a logical pattern of upstream investment first, to upgrade primary processing capability and achieve consistently good component quality. Without this, product quality is impossible, and automation is unthinkable. The same principle applies as with computers, garbage in equals garbage out and massive investment is not the answer to problems of quality, nor productivity. To quote Taiichi Ohno of Toyota, 'Use your head, not your money.' Moreover, it is essential to ensure that, when new equipment has been installed, projected quality and output targets are met, before further investment takes place.

British and Japanese styles

Some of the differences in our operation between the Japanese and the traditional British style of management will be immediately apparent but after nine years of working together there has been such an effective merging of British and Japanese approaches that we are no longer conscious of the distinction. In the early days our emphasis on improved communication, housekeeping and teamworking was inherited from our SRI colleagues, but such sensible and logical concepts were not difficult to adopt. The Japanese frequently coin expressions to identify and promote their fundamental ideas – the 4M and the 4S have already been mentioned, whilst 2G (*genchi gembutsu*) neatly expresses the meticulous approach to investigating the facts on the spot, including the 'benchmarking' of good and bad features, in order to resolve problems and to satisfy the customer's requirements promptly. These are all very effective management tools. TQ, however, was a purely local initiative, growing out of the changed environment of the company and leading naturally into the *kaizen* activity. Our experience confirms that managers worldwide have much to learn from each other, and that cultural differences are not an obstacle to the adoption of 'best practice'. Visitors to our plants will not hear any company song echoing through the site, nor are they likely to meet any Japanese personnel, though we do have one or two SRI colleagues assisting us in specific technical and production areas. What the visitor *will* find is a motivated and responsible workforce keen to do better. We have already come a long way since 1985, but we are conscious of how much more still remains to be done. We approach this task with confidence because we have learned that the potential for further improvement is infinite.

10 Increasing profit and market share through total quality management

Graham Pearson

'It is an immutable law in business that words are words, explanations are explanations, promises are promises – but only performance is reality.'
Harold S. Geneen, former Chairman, International Telephone and Telegraph

Executive summary

When Rank Xerox discovered that its Japanese competitors could sell equivalent products for less than Xerox could manufacture them, and still achieve 100% profit margin, the management realised that radical change was needed if the company was to survive.

Graham Pearson describes how Rank Xerox moved from crisis through quality to achieve excellence, the management revolution that this involved, the impact of quality on human resources, how 'closed-loop customer satisfaction' works, the impact of process management and how to use self-assessment as a means of continuous improvement.

This chapter is based upon the experience of implementing Quality Programmes with Rank Xerox (UK) Ltd. These experiences are not necessarily applicable to all other companies, and there is no intention that any of the following information should be used in a prescriptive manner, rather that an understanding of what has worked and also what has failed in Rank Xerox may stop other companies from embarking on the wrong route to Quality.

To many organisations, Quality is something to be managed, another programme that the organisation is following, and which can be controlled in the same way as, for example, a marketing programme or a manufacturing programme. Indeed, this was the approach initially taken by the Xerox Corporation and by Rank Xerox, in its European operation, but we soon realised that this would not allow us to achieve our goals. We had to make Quality a fundamental cornerstone of the business, built into the culture and style, an automatic part of everyone's job, and over time we realised that there is a very simple explanation of TQM that encapsulates our approach: TQM means Total Quality *of* Management.

This may seem a rather pedantic and semantic point but we have found that it is actually very important. When Quality was managed in the same way as other programmes, it was regarded by many of the organisation's employees as a temporary phenomenon, the latest fad, the 'flavour of the month'. When we started to address the quality of our management, it was seen by the employees as a much more serious and fundamental approach to the business, and one which would have widespread impact on the whole company.

The history

Rank Xerox adopted Quality for a very simple reason: *survival*. The company was built around a new technology (Xerography uses an electrostatic process which enables office workers to make copies of documents on plain paper without the use of fluids, special papers or heat treatment) that had itself revolutionised the office, and which had succeeded beyond the wildest dreams of our staff (the initial marketing estimates were that 274 machines would saturate the UK market-place!). We were in a monopolistic situation with a product range that was extremely successful, and so we became very complacent about ourselves, our business, and, above all, our customers. Whatever we produced we could sell. Efficiency was not a top priority, and if we had a problem we could use our huge cash-flows to find a solution. There were no fears for the future because there were no competitors visible on the horizon.

Then the patents ran out

Competition moved in in force and our market share slumped. Our profits started halving year-on-year, and we were rapidly going out of business, but the complacency in management continued. The assumption was made that the Japanese were dumping in Europe and the USA in an attempt to gain market share, so the response was to try to increase shipments and wait until our competitors pulled out.

Our Chief Executive, David Kearns, was not so sure, so he visited Japan to look at our competitors more closely. What he found shattered our illusions. We had nine times as many suppliers, ten times the assembly line reject rates, double the product-to-market time, double the indirect/direct cost ratio of our competitors, but the crucial fact was very simple: *our competitors could sell equivalent products at a 100% profit margin yet at a price that was LESS than our manufacturing cost!* Our strategy of riding out the storm was doomed to failure.

However, this led to an interesting observation. When this information was relayed to our senior managers, there was disbelief. The belief that the Japanese were dumping was so strong that it was not until a number of senior managers visited Japan and saw for themselves that the truth was accepted in the company. Ever since then we have tried to involve our people in all our fact-finding and analysis, and this policy of employee involvement has paid tremendous dividends to us over the years.

Leadership through Quality

In 1980 the first of a number of Quality programmes was launched, but these had limited success. We adopted some basic tools such as the Quality Improvement Process and the Problem Solving Process, and developed others such as the Benchmarking Process. By 1983 these tools had been consolidated into a single portfolio, and a worldwide programme called 'Leadership Through Quality' was launched. To ensure that everyone used these new tools and procedures, we launched a worldwide training programme to train all our 125,000 employees, and this training programme alone cost somewhere between $150 million and $250 million.

The results of all of this work were soon visible in our manufacturing plants and in the quality of our products, and the table in Figure 10.1 shows the impact of our drive to improve Quality. But in the Sales and Marketing parts of the company, very little changed. People were trained, but having been trained they did not use the new tools and techniques and continued to work as they always had. In retrospect, we did have a number of key benefits; we had introduced a common language (of Quality) worldwide which means that we can take any group of

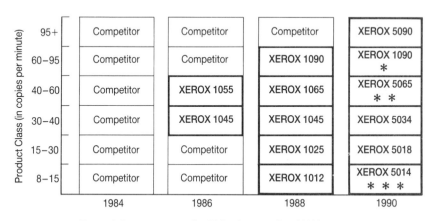

* Buyers Lab–most outstanding high volume copier of 1990
* * Buyers Lab–Copier of the year
* * * Buyers Lab–most outstanding very low volume copier of the year

Figure 10.1 The results: Xerox products ranked 'best in class'

- Rank Xerox is a Quality company.
- Quality is the basic business principle for Rank Xerox.
- Quality means providing our external and internal customers with innovative products and services that fully satisfy their requirements.
- Quality improvement is the job of every Rank Xerox employee.

Figure 10.2 1983 Rank Xerox quality policy

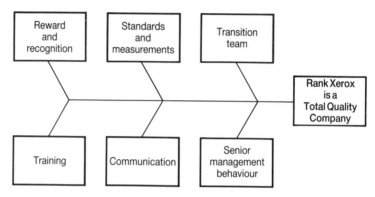

Figure 10.3 The impact of human resources

employees from any grade, any function, any unit, any country, and they know how to work together; we had introduced a number of key policies such as the Quality Policy (shown in Figure 10.2); and we had introduced the concept of a shared mission and goals.

As it became apparent that we were not gaining the expected benefits of this investment in Quality, we had two basic options open to us. We could have abandoned the programme, as many companies appear to be doing today, or we could analyse the root causes behind the lack of success. We chose the latter route, and the result was the Ishikawa diagram shown in Figure 10.3.

Our Chief Executive refers to this model as the revolution slide, because a very similar parallel can be drawn with a revolution. What makes a successful revolution? First, there is a change in government behaviour, with quite possibly a change in the members of the government. Secondly, the revolutionaries take over the radio and television stations, together with the newspapers, and saturate the airwaves with details of the new culture and standards of behaviour. Thirdly, they take over the schools, colleges and universities, so that the courses are geared to the requirements of the new state, and all 'new' citizens are trained in the new cultural ideals. Then new standards of behaviour are introduced, using communications and education to provide the reinforcement. Adherents of these new standards are put in key positions (maybe in the new government), and those who object are removed from positions of power, and possibly imprisoned or deported.

Finally, there is some form of interim government to help the transition to the new culture.

The transition to a total quality company has many parallels with this scenario, and it highlights the reasons why 'Leadership Through Quality' did not give us the expected benefits. We had provided training in Quality but nothing else had changed; we still had the old management style, the old ways of working, the rest our training still emphasised the old approach, and the old success factors were the ones being rewarded. The revolution had not taken place.

The new revolution

Using the analysis shown in the Ishikawa diagram in Figure 10.3, we decided to relaunch the revolution, realising that this time we had to address all the issues simultaneously. But there was also a need to define the end-point vision so that the revolution could achieve a positive goal rather than simply destroy the old culture.

We had already defined our Mission Statement (see Figure 10.4) in such a way that it showed what we were attempting to achieve and how we hoped to do it, but this needed to be developed further to allow people to focus on the specific needs of the company. We had to define some corporate goals and priorities, and these have been refined and reordered since their initial launch. At the start of 1993 they are (in priority sequence):

1. Customer satisfaction.
2. Employee motivation and satisfaction.
3. Market share.
4. Return on assets.

This sequence does not imply that return on assets is not important, rather, we believe that if we address the other three goals first, then we are well on the way to achieving our return on assets targets.

Provide Xerox shareholders with a total return on their investment that is competitive with the returns provided by other leading information industry corporations:
- *By meeting customer requirements* in targeted markets to improve the performance of their document-based business and management processes with competitively advantaged document management products, systems and services.
- *Through the efficient work of skilled employees* who have been attracted, motivated and empowered by Quality Organisational and Managerial Practices.

Figure 10.4 Corporate mission

1. Visibly demonstrates support and promotion of leadership through Quality.
2. Personally uses problem solving, the Quality improvement process, benchmarking, and cost of Quality in key business areas.
3. Uses customer satisfaction as a key measure in all business decisions and assures that unit activities improve customer satisfaction.
4. Encourages and uses feedback from peers, superiors, and customers to modify personal style and behaviour.
5. Establishes expectations and communicates progress for the Quality Plan, its implementation and measurement, and the inspection process. Meets the goals set.
6. Hires and promotes people who actively practise Leadership Through Quality. Counsels and instructs those who are deficient towards the role model standard necessary for promotion.
7. Recognises and rewards individuals and teams using Leadership Through Quality to achieve improved business results.
8. Through regular inspections, identifies weaknesses and provides coaching and guidance to improve use of the quality process.

Figure 10.5 Standards for a role model manager

Having company goals is fine but unless all employees know what they are and, more importantly, what their individual role is in achieving them, then not much will happen. They must be communicated and then used, and we have a process called Policy Deployment which cascades the goals, the shorter-term objectives, the measurements and the targets. This process will be covered in more detail later.

We had already launched various standards of behaviours such as the Quality Policy, but these were reinforced with other standards such as a set defining a Role Model Manager (see Figure 10.5). As can be seen, these standards are simple and clear yet very specific in their definitions of required behaviours. But simply having standards is not enough – they must be used and respected, so the appraisal process was changed to ensure that all managers are formally checked and appraised every year against the standards. A range of ratings was introduced, so the individual can be rated as role model, competent, or needs improvement, and to give this process some teeth, the role model rating became a requirement for promotion, initially for the top 200 managers in the Corporation but then it was extended to include all managers.

We also introduced a process for *upwards appraisal*, the Management Practices Survey, where every manager's 'direct reports' complete an anonymous survey on their manager's style and behaviour. The results are collated by the Human Resources department or a member of the Quality Group, compared with the manager's self-assessment against the same questions, and feedback is provided highlighting major variances across the group or between the group assessment and the manager's self-appraisal. Then a half-day feedback session is facilitated between the manager and the group to explore the variances and to generate an action plan to remedy them. Many managers found this a stressful experience, but it is a good way to highlight and resolve issues in management behaviour.

Our whole training strategy had to be re-evaluated. Every course was checked and upgraded to reinforce the new cultural issues. The induction course for all new employees was rewritten so that all new staff are immersed in the Quality culture from their first day in the company. All staff and management development courses were rewritten so that each course is built round the requirements defined by the Quality culture and to remove all references to the previous culture. Quality modules were then built in to all sales courses, all administration courses and all service engineering courses, so that there is a consistent message given to all employees regardless of their function or grade.

It was also apparent that we had to relaunch specific training in the use of the Quality Toolkit, and this was done through Quality Application Workshops (QAWs). This training was implemented as a cascade starting with our Board, and involved a menu of 16 modules, each module addressing a specific Quality tool. The Family Group Manager is interviewed prior to the workshop to determine which six of the modules are most appropriate to his or her group and to identify a project or issue on which the group is currently working. This then becomes the case study round which the workshop will revolve. The workshop takes three days. Then the attendees repeat the exercise with their own Family Groups. The manager is an essential part of the cascade process and his or her involvement in the training of the Family Group has two real benefits; it retrains the manager in the tools and their usage, and it emphasises to the group that the manager is involved and committed to the use of Quality in their everyday work.

Eighteen months after the launch of this first cascade we launched a new cascade of QAW2, a follow-on workshop that uses the same principles as QAW but with extra modules available, and soon QAW3 will follow. Thus there are many cascades of courses running simultaneously at different levels of the organisation, all reinforcing the message of the new culture and its implications.

The emphasis on training has provided a good communication medium for the company but we do not believe that this is sufficient. We have an in-house magazine which reinforces the Quality message, with articles on Quality and Quality projects and also highlights success stories where people have gained benefits for the company and themselves by using Quality. We have regular 'communication meetings' at management level, by function or by group to let all employees know what has happened, the current status of projects and the business, and the latest plans for further developments. 'Slice meetings', where managers meet groups of employees from across the company, allow managers to communicate their messages but also allow them to receive immediate feedback from all levels of the company. Communication must be a two-way process.

Policy deployment

The most important communication process that we use is Policy Deployment. The company's mission and goals are irrelevant unless they are used within the organisation, and policy deployment is the vehicle used to develop and deploy them.

Every year the planning process is used to evaluate the current state of the economy, the market, the business, etc., to develop the business plan for the coming year, and this business plan is built round the four common goals of the company. We have a series of objectives and targets for customer satisfaction, and similar sets for employee satisfaction, market share, and return on assets.

We then carry out a situation diagnosis which compares our current state and achievements with the objectives defined in the business plan. An analysis of the gaps leads to the development of a series of programmes that must be implemented so that the gaps can be closed and the objectives reached. These programmes are known as 'The Vital Few', and we ensure that there are no more than five such programmes for each company goal. Each Vital Few programme is sponsored (or championed) by a Board member. The specific objectives and measures of progress are determined, and then targets for those measures are set. So, we have a clear definition of what must be done, how we will measure our progress, and how we will evaluate our success.

These definitions are then passed to each of the Functional Directors within the company so that support plans can be put in place. Each function takes each of the Vital Few programmes, together with the supporting information, and states what specific functional work will take place to achieve the objectives of the programme. Each support plan must define the function-specific objectives of the programme, the individual within the function who 'owns' the programme, the specific measures to be used, and the targets for success. These support plans are then given to the 'Champion' who checks for gaps, i.e. that the sum of all the support plans will achieve the desired state for the Company, and overlaps, i.e. that there will not be duplication of effort across the functions.

On agreement of the support plans each function can then develop its Roles, Responsibilities and Objectives document (its RRO – a typical layout can be seen in Figure 10.6). This document defines what the function intends to do in the coming year for each of the company goals, to support the Vital Few programmes and to complete the 'business as usual' activities. Again the measures and the targets are specified. This document is then be used as a personal statement of RRO by the Director concerned.

This document is then issued to the first line managers within the function, who, in negotiation with each other and with the Director, agree their own personal roles and responsibilities. The negotiation ensures that there are no gaps or overlaps, and that the sum of the first line managers' responsibilities will achieve the responsibilities of the whole function. Individual targets are negotiated within the overall framework so that the individual manager agrees with his or her objectives, measures and targets. This document is then issued to the manager's 'direct reports' and a similar process is followed to ensure that they all have personal RROs, and then the cascade continues through the organisation. In the

| MISSION STATEMENT: | XXXXXXXXXXXXXXXXXXXXXXXXXXXXXXXXXXXXXXXXXXX |
| | XXXXXXXXXXXXXXXXXXXXXXXXXXXXXXXXXXXXXXXXXXX |

1993 Goals	1993 Objectives	1993 Measurements
CUSTOMER SATISFACTION • _____		%
EMPLOYEE SATISFACTION • _____		%
MARKET SHARE • _____		%
RETURN ON ASSETS • _____		%

Figure 10.6 Functional mission and goals

UK with approximately 4,500 employees the whole cascade from the Director downwards can be completed in six weeks.

At the end of this process, every employee has a personalised, negotiated and agreed RRO which details exactly what is expected of that individual in the coming year. Every activity is described under one of the four common goals so there is a direct link between the work being done and the Company's objectives. All the employees therefore know the company goals and can relate their individual work to the goals. If an employee is asked to do work which cannot be linked to one of the goals then an immediate challenge can be made, questioning the value of the work.

Policy Deployment is the primary means of ensuring that the basic values of the company are understood by all the employees, that they know and understand the common goals, and can relate their personal work to those goals. The output from Policy Deployment, the personal RRO, also becomes one of the key documents used in the annual appraisal process, when the performance against the agreed objectives can be measured and assessed. The appraisal then produces a formal development action plan – an agreement between the individual and the manager which identifies specific training and other learning experiences necessary for the development of the individual (a minimum of 40 hours formal training per year is mandatory for all employees).

Management process

In order to assess progress against the company's goals, some sort of management process is necessary. Over time many formal and informal processes had been

Historical trend versus plan	Current month & YTD deviation from plan
Root cause analysis	Recommendation & action

Figure 10.7 Quadrant charts

developed, but we realised that we had no logic to these processes, and that they were not very efficient at using the time of our managers. Too much time at too many of our meetings was spent discussing the validity of data, and not enough time was spent in decision-making. We therefore had to redesign our management process. We also realised that the forums and their frequencies have a large influence on the behaviour of the people involved, and that the specific data used and the decisions that result shape their thoughts. Since the Ishikawa analysis had shown that we needed to change the behaviour of our managers, a redesigned management process seemed to be an appropriate mechanism to help implement this change.

First, we looked at the ways in which information was presented, and we developed a standard layout which is now used at all our management meetings. We call it the quadrant chart (see Figure 10.7), and it is a simple yet effective way of showing performance. The top left quadrant displays performance over the past months together with the targets for that period and the targets for the months ahead. The top right quadrant then analyses deviations from those targets looking at the current month and year-to-date, and splits the data in the most appropriate way (for instance, by sales region or by product group, etc.). The bottom right quadrant then shows the causes for those deviations, both better and worse than the plan, and the final quadrant shows the actions that are recommended to address those deviations. We have found that this layout is very useful as the results of actions can then be tracked in the performance quadrant in subsequent months.

To determine which meetings were really needed we went back to our common goals, and the requirements became obvious. We now have a monthly meeting that looks specifically at customer satisfaction and employee satisfaction, our top two priorities. A second meeting looks at market share. A third looks at the financial performance, concentrating on our return on assets. These meetings run at regional and national level, with the national meeting being a 'roll-up' of the information used locally. To explain this more fully, let us look at the business goals review, the meeting that examines customer and employee satisfaction.

Every month we receive information from our customers from customer satisfaction surveys. This data is delivered straight into the local offices, so that trends and performance can be analysed by the people dealing directly with those customers. Quadrant charts are used to display the results. These quadrants can then be accumulated to obtain a regional view and accumulated again to obtain the national view. This upwards accumulation ensures that the root causes are identified within the Company. So the executive board members can simply approve the actions that have already been agreed. Thus the time spent in the management process meetings has been dramatically reduced, and the right decisions can be made at the right place in the organisation.

Customer focus

Over time we realised that we needed to focus on the customer to develop our business. At the time of our crisis the customer had been almost incidental, but by 1987 customer satisfaction had been elevated to be the top priority for the company, the position it still holds today. We then implemented a 'closed loop customer satisfaction process' to ensure that we really understood what our customers were telling us, and then to make sure that they knew and understood our response. This process is shown in Figure 10.8.

Market research information coupled with the responses from our customer surveys is analysed using the basic Quality tools. Corrective actions can then be taken to address specific issues, and these actions are monitored to ensure success. Feedback is then provided to the customer. Other issues, for instance, the customers' requirements for new products and new features, can be fed back into product development, or in the case of market changes, may result in organisational changes. The feedback loops are provided to ensure that we really address the issues and that we inform customers and the distribution channel of these changes.

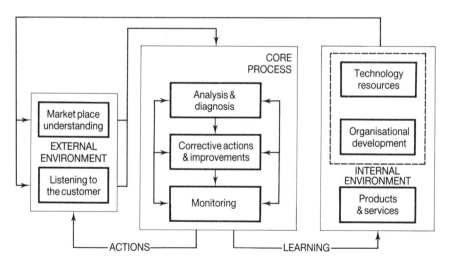

Figure 10.8 Closed loop customer satisfaction

Performance-related pay

The 'revolution analysis' had shown us that our recognition and reward systems were designed to support the old management style, so these also had to be changed. The first change was to widen the use of performance-related pay, and this has now been extended to cover all our employees. All employees receive a bonus dependent on our performance against our customer satisfaction targets, with performance being taken directly from the monthly customer satisfaction surveys. This bonus starts at 3% of salary and is paid quarterly. As we move into the management grades the bonus is raised to 10% and is based on both customer satisfaction and financial performance. At senior management grades the bonus increases to 15%. The same basic measures are used for our Directors but the bonus is raised to 30% and now the bonus includes an element based on employee satisfaction.

We expect people to achieve their targets, so for all management grades and Directors there is a 'buy-in' aspect to the bonus. We use benchmarking against other companies' salary levels to determine the total planned earnings level for each job, but this assumes that all the targets are achieved; so the guaranteed pay is the total planned earnings less the bonus. If the manager exceeds the targets then his or her earnings will exceed the benchmark levels, but if the targets are not reached then his or her earnings will be below the benchmark.

We have also emphasised the requirement that all managers should recognise good performance. Recognition can range from the simple and immediate 'thank you' to the more formal recognition at one of the management or communication meetings. Usually this will be reinforced with a tangible reward, a certificate, a plaque, a cheque, or, for outstanding performance, a more valuable reward such as a skiing holiday. The application of Quality tools and excellent work are prerequisites for these formal recognition awards.

Process management

As mentioned in the Quality Policy (Figure 10.2), we expect all employees to be involved in improving their work processes. We classify these 'basic tools' under the heading 'business as usual', but there are two other approaches that we have developed. The first is Simplification where we look for major improvements to be made to cross-functional processes, and the second is Re-engineering, a fundamental 'vision-led' approach to key processes. We expect (and receive) improvements of 10–20% in efficiency from the 'business as usual' approach, but simplification is providing 100% improvements and re-engineering 1000% improvements. A description of these three methodologies is shown in Figure 10.9.

Many of the techniques used here are similar if not identical to those which were used in O&M or Work Study back in the 1960s, although they are now used in slightly different ways. But there is one crucial difference. In the 1960s we used

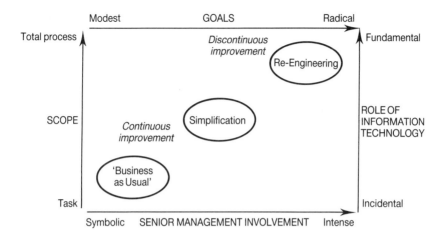

Figure 10.9 Process management

specialist groups to do the work and then we tried to impose the results on the workforce, usually in a confrontation. Now we use the people who are involved in the process in their normal work, to do the analysis and to make the recommendations. We have found that this approach of employee involvement increases employee satisfaction. It also increases the acceptability of the results and recommendations to the other people involved in the process, and because of the detailed knowledge of the people who make the analysis, the results have been of a high standard.

As we became more involved in this work, it became apparent that the crucial processes which deliver value to the customer operate across the internal functional boundaries. We are organised by function, and the functional groups are responsible for their parts of the process, but there is nobody who 'owns' the total process. As functions improved the process, we were obtaining some benefits but not at the levels we needed. Functional specialisation was letting us down. The delays in the processes were at the cross-overs between functions. Function A would work very well (apparently) but somehow failed to deliver the information necessary for Function B to work correctly. The remedy was to introduce the concept of process owners at Board level, so that a Director is responsible for the process regardless of the functions that are involved in doing the work. We anticipate that this approach will develop to the stage where we no longer have functional Directors but instead the whole Company will be organised on a process basis.

Much of the development work has now been done, and a 'map' of all the key processes and their interactions has been developed. Process owners at different levels have been assigned, and the move towards full process management is under way.

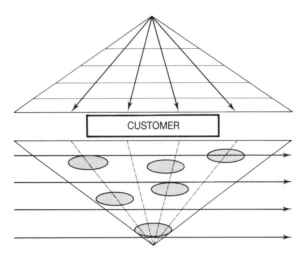

Figure 10.10 Organisation development

Organisation development

It was also necessary to look at the organisational structure from a different viewpoint. The classical company structure is the pyramid, a hierarchy that defines status, pay levels and power, etc., and which has some important benefits to the company. However, it is interesting to place the customer in this structure, and the normal position is right at the bottom (see Figure 10.10). This leads to frustration as the front line staff, the salesforce and the service engineers, are rarely allowed to satisfy the customer's requirements.

We are trying to invert the pyramid to the 'ice-cream cone' of management, where the customer is at the top. Then the most important employees in the organisation are the front line staff, and the role of the managers changes from directing and controlling into coaching, counselling and facilitating. The managers remove the barriers which are stopping the front line staff from satisfying their customers. This change in management role can only be achieved by detailed training for both managers and staff. The management practices survey discussed earlier is a powerful tool to use as the pyramid inversion takes place.

This approach also encourages the introduction of *self-managed work groups*, groups of staff who share a set of tasks and goals and who are allowed to allocate work among themselves. To do this effectively they must be given the authority to make a number of key decisions without recourse to senior management – the *empowerments* that allow them to work to the best effect. We have defined a number of empowerments that the groups will ultimately need, but these are being introduced on a phased basis. Each group on its formation is given specific training

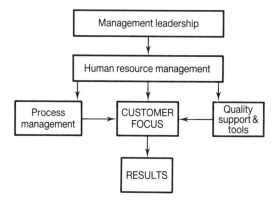

Figure 10.11 Business excellence

to enable it to start work, and it is given a basic set of empowerments. As the group develops and demonstrates its ability to handle this authority, it can ask for further empowerments, thus steadily increasing the scope of its decision-making and enlarging its range.

Self-managed work groups can also be used at other levels in the organisation. At the geographic region level, there is a senior sales manager, a senior service engineering manager and a senior administration manager, each responsible for the functional activities in the region. They have now become a *partnership*, sharing common goals and targets, and also sharing in a common benefits approach. Each partner is paid on the overall performance of the whole region, with the measures including customer satisfaction, employee satisfaction, sales performance, service performance and administration performance. This ensures that all three partners concentrate on the total business in their region and not just on their functional performance. A number of empowerments have been delegated to them from the Board, so that in effect they are running their own local business.

It is important to remember that empowerment is delegation in action, but it must not be an abdication of responsibility. Put simply, it is trying to ensure that the right decision is taken at the right place at the right time.

Business excellence

Quality is only a means to an end, and should not be the end itself. We believe that we must strive for excellence, and so have developed a model of the company, our business excellence model (see Figure 10.11). It is used to prioritise work and it covers most of the topics already discussed. The customer is at the centre of the model. Human resources focus on the customer and are directed by management leadership. The focus is driven by process management, and the processes are improved by Quality support and Quality tools. Business priorities and results then 'fall out' at the bottom of the model.

It is interesting to compare this model with the classical Western approach, where, if the financial results are not adequate for the shareholder, companies immediately start cutting costs. This usually means cutting human resources, which leads to less focus on the customer. This leads to a drop in business results, the classical downwards spiral. In our model, if the financial results are not what are needed then 'Root Cause Analysis' is used to determine what are the failures in the customer focus. If the customer focus is correct then root cause analysis is applied to process management, or to human resource management, etc., working back through the model. Therefore the corrective actions taken are those that address the heart of the problem and do not simplistically remove costs.

This model then becomes the centre of our self-assessment process. Each of the six elements of the model is divided into its major components (human resources would be split into recruitment, education and development, compensation, benefits, etc.), and for each of these elements a desired state is defined. If we achieved the desired state this would make us the 'benchmark organisation' in that particular area. Every year we complete an assessment of our position on a scale to achieve the benchmark, using a combination of results (hard measures that must show trends towards the goals), processes (and there must be a provable link between the processes and the results) and pervasiveness (are all the necessary people involved?). Finally, year-on-year improvements must be demonstrated. Examiners are then brought in to check that the self-assessment is accurate and to provide consistency of assessment across the company.

Since all the results are published internally, this process has proved very effective at sharing best practices. An entity with a low rating in one area can immediately see which entities have high ratings, and can then investigate and learn. This approach has reduced the amount of time spent in resolving problems that have already been solved elsewhere.

Finally, the results from this exercise are used as the primary input for the planning process that was discussed earlier. The business excellence ratings immediately indicate the strengths and weaknesses in the entity and provide strong indications for the formation of the Vital Few programmes.

The lessons learned from this exercise proved to be invaluable when we applied for the European Quality Award in 1992. We were used to assessment and examination. We already had most of the data required for the application and in the required form, and we had the communication processes in place to ensure that all employees knew their personal role in the examination. The application for the award was still a useful exercise to complete, though it was a great relief to us when the announcement was made that Rank Xerox Ltd was the first winner of the European Quality Award.

Results

Has all this emphasis on Quality actually paid any dividends? On a worldwide basis customer satisfaction has steadily increased, and customer loyalty has increased by over 40 percentage points. Employee satisfaction has steadily increased. We have regained much of the market share which we had lost to the Japanese, and we have steadily improved our return on assets.

Within the UK, the number of potential buyers for our core business products has dropped by approximately 25% each year for the last three years, yet we have shown a steady increase in market share, in revenues and in profits. We attribute this to Total Quality.

Lessons learned

The key lesson that we have learned is that the system-wide approach is absolutely essential. The adoption of Total Quality requires a revolution and must encompass all areas of the organisation. The second lesson is that the top management of the organisation must always 'walk the talk', i.e. must always act as role models to reinforce the Quality message. Finally, you must have patience, and approach the revolution with a good sense of humour – you will need it.

Recommended reading

William C. Byham, *Zapp! The Lightning of Empowerment*, Century Business, 1988.
Robert C. Camp, *Benchmarking*, Quality Press, 1989.
Colin Coulson-Thomas, *Transforming the Company*, Kogan Page, 1992.
Gary Jacobson and John Hillkirk, *Xerox: The American Samurai*, Macmillan, 1986.
David Kearns and David Nadler, *Prophets in the Dark*, Harper Business, 1992.
David Oates, *Leadership: The art of delegation*, Century Business, 1993.
Rachel Ross and Robin Schneider, *From Equality to Diversity*, Pitman, 1992.

11 Strengthening customer relationships and building customer service in a major bank

Kevin J. Bourke

'Coffee stains on the flip-down trays mean [to the passengers] that we do our engine maintenance wrong.'
Donald C. Burr, Chairman, People Express Airlines Inc., quoted by Thomas J. Peters and Nancy K. Austin, *A Passion for Excellence*, Random House, 1985

Executive summary

Faced with rigid traditions of conformity, hierarchical management and entrenched, rule-driven employee attitudes, how does an old established company, such as a bank, go about changing its corporate culture to become customer-centred and entrepreneurial?

Kevin Bourke shows how the AIB Group managed this process by involving middle management in developing the new core values, investing in professionalism and prompting market-orientated thinking, supported by a new corporate identity and an unusually open advertising campaign describing the changes (and bravely asking for feedback!). Internal and external resources were combined to translate the AIB mission statement into a reality.

Retail banks provide a fascinating example of culture change. This is not just because of the large staff numbers involved, but because the scale of change needed is enormous. The lesson could be 'if banks can change successfully, then any organisation can'. *AIB in Ireland is an example of a retail bank that has tackled the need for culture change head-on.*

A strongly entrenched tradition

Why is change such a challenge for banks? The fundamental reason lies in our long tradition – surely unique in what is now called the service sector – of being focused *away* from their customers. Many banks have histories stretching back over several centuries, and the retail banks of today inherit a culture that springs directly from their role as a clearing bank in an era before modern communications existed.

If nineteenth-century manufacturing was overwhelmingly production-orientated, nineteenth-century clearing banks were similarly fixated on their own production process – making the money-transmission system (the 'clearing') work consistently throughout their far-flung network of branches. Many bank offices were in distant locations, with little day-to-day contact with their head offices. The culture was therefore driven by the need to perform in a standardised and predictable way within a nationwide system of clearing payments.

Conformity became a traditional core value of banks. Going with this was a rigid, top–down management style – with a carefully defined pecking order from top to bottom.

Activity within the typical bank was *rule-driven*, with considerable emphasis on traditional methods. Individual initiative was actively frowned on, and promotion up the ladder was related to an individual's years of service rather than his or her performance.

The closed nature of the culture was reinforced by the practice of recruiting only at school-leaver level and promoting from within. This approach had the effect of cutting the organisation off from the different perspectives of specialists trained to different norms and in different cultures.

Banks with this tradition were anything but customer-centred. The notion of actively competing for the customer's business was rather alien to the clearing banks. Until recently, banks were somewhere the customer came to get a set menu of services, rather than organisations vying for the customer's attention and custom.

Time for change

It is a testament to the rigidity of strongly based cultures that this clearing-bank tradition imbued the ethos of retail banks until the present generation. In AIB's case, a formal process to change our culture radically did not begin until 1984, and even today many banks have not yet grasped the nettle.

This is not to say that over the years banks had not changed. They had indeed. The point is that their underlying culture had remained intact, a culture that had developed in conditions that now no longer applied.

In our own case, wide-ranging change had been on AIB's agenda since the merger in the late 1960s that had brought together under its umbrella three of Ireland's leading banks. The merged bank grew quickly, expanding into new territories (mainly the UK and the USA) and into new activities (such as merchant banking).

By the mid-1980s the need had become obvious for a cultural change that would match the new kind of organisation AIB was rapidly becoming. *Essentially, the need was to supplant the rigid conformity of our inward-looking clearing-bank culture with one that was entrepreneurial and customer-focused.*

The foundations for change

Three elements provided a platform to base the change programme on which: a new structure for the organisation, a formal statement of our mission, and a specific approach to fulfilling the mission.

In line with its focus on what we did rather than on the market-place we served, AIB's old organisation was functional in its thrust. At the operating level, there were separate divisions for domestic banking, international banking, merchant banking and industrial banking. Within these divisions lurked sub-cultures that were quite different from each other. There was little interplay between them.

In a two-stage restructuring that lasted from 1986 to 1989, we developed a new structure that grouped together those activities that naturally went together *from the customer's perspective* – even though this meant mixing together in one division a variety of different cultures and practices. The final organisation resulted in four operating divisions that were clearly market-based – three of them (Ireland, Britain and USA) geographical, the fourth (capital markets) organisation-wide in scope.

The second pillar of our foundation for change was a mission statement that would provide an agenda for the newly structured organisation. The different parts of the old organisation had been driven either by the outmoded clearing-bank tradition or by the sub-cultures of specialised subsidiaries like merchant banking and industrial leasing. Now, with the desire to focus on the market-place and to take a unified approach to customer needs, a new vision became an imperative for us.

In its most recent version, the AIB Group Mission statement is:

Value and Service are at the heart of our business. We aim to provide real value to every one of our customers, and to deliver the highest standard of service in Banking and Financial Services.

This clearly reflected our new desire to put the market-place first. But in isolation, it ran the danger of all such statements – of being merely aspirational. After all, any bank could choose to say these things. How could we be sure that we delivered them, and were seen to be different as a result?

Hence the need for the third pillar in the foundation – a specific approach that would use our new organisational structure to realise the vision implicit in the mission statement. This approach emerged as we considered the crucial issue: how was AIB to differentiate itself in the market-place? The mission statement gave the first part of the answer: it reflected our conviction that the way to be different was by providing what the customer would recognise as superior value and service.

But how to do this? On the value front, we could not hope to achieve a sustainable competitive advantage through pricing. Neither could we do it through innovation alone, vital though an innovative approach would certainly be. The reality of the world we operated in was that in the future we would provide services that were broadly similar to those that others provided, at prices that would not be too different.

Competitive advantage, we realised, must come from *how* those services were provided. Superior service was the key. In that we saw not only our potential for future growth, but also our potential for future profitability – because, we reckoned, customers would be prepared to pay a premium for what they perceived as superior service.

From this, it was only a short step to realising that AIB's people were central to achieving the market-place differentiation that we sought. Superior service in our business would inevitably mean relating to the *individual* needs of customers. This called for flexibility and innovation in delivering services, at the point where those services were actually experienced by the customer. Our market-driven approach could only be led from the top; to be effective, it had to be followed through by everyone in the organisation.

The third pillar of our foundation was, therefore, our decision to *differentiate through people*. Adopting this third pillar was perhaps the most far-reaching decision in the change programme – because along with it went the realisation that the change needed was deep and fundamental. To achieve this differentiation through people, we had no option but to bring about a radical change in the values and practices of the entire organisation. In short, we had to change the culture itself. Cosmetic change would not deliver what we needed.

By the same token, we admitted that change such as this would only be achieved over the longer term of perhaps ten years. Consequently, we had to recognise that the time frame for the initial phase would be at least five years, and even then that much would remain to be done after that.

Becoming 'marketing professionals'

The task was to transform an organisation of people who considered themselves as 'bankers' into people who also considered themselves as 'marketing professionals'. We needed to change the way people think about the job of banking and then how they do the job. In effect, we were facing the difficult situation that AIB people 'didn't know they didn't know'. Once they 'knew they didn't know', we would be well on our way.

However, what was at issue was not simply sending people on marketing courses. What was needed was to develop within AIB a marketing *ethos* that would drive every action that we took, collectively and individually. We asked ourselves: in what ways must AIB change, so that it can focus on achieving the goal of any market-centred approach: creating valuable customer relationships? The answer to this had no fewer than the following six interlocking elements:

1. First of all, we told ourselves, we need the right *marketing strategies*.
2. But these cannot be dreamed up out of the blue: fundamental to them is *marketing information systems* to provide us continually with detailed and sophisticated information about our markets and our customers.
3. In formulating and communicating those strategies, we also need effective *marketing leadership*. Management at all levels need to be strongly involved – communicating a market-related message, displaying commitment to marketing professionalism and taking the necessary actions. (In particular, we have found it is vital to involve middle management – which, in banking terms, is usually the branch manager.)
4. *Marketing professionalism* is the most important core skill that needs to be added to the competencies of people throughout the organisation. This involves not just an understanding of general marketing principles, but also the ability to apply them imaginatively in the specific situation that we face in AIB. Professionalism in this sense is quite separate from banking professionalism, which up to then had been the main requirement.
5. In parallel with this skilling of people, the jobs themselves need to be restructured so that they are orientated towards the customer. (It became obvious early on that *job roles and structures* that are not orientated towards the customer tend to stifle any initiatives that arise from training and development programmes. Both jobs and people need to face in the same direction.)
6. With all the emphasis on people, it is also vital to build the change programme on a clear recognition that marketing professionalism in the future will depend critically on *market-orientated technology*. The task facing us includes the reshaping of delivery systems – extending automated services, redesigning the physical layout of bank branches, forms and procedures – all with the ultimate aim of tailoring what we do to the needs of our various customer groups.

Strategies, information systems, leadership, professionalism, job roles and structure, technology – this was a complex recipe, and deliberately so. For part of our analysis was an acceptance of the fact that there was no single solution to our need for cultural change – instead, our way forward had to be through making a complicated set of interlocking factors work together. Cultural change is not just a matter of turning one's back on the quick fix; equally, it involves *rejecting the single fix*.

The complexity of the change recipe was one reason why we decided to package the programme and even 'brand' it internally. We called it *The Marketing Action Programme* (MAP), and gave it its own logo and design style. This was not communications gimmickry, but an essential part of ensuring that over a long period the multiplicity of initiatives that formed part of our change programme would be seen as parts of a whole – a whole that was heading in a specific direction.

Branding the change programme was also a response to what was a critical initial need – creating a high level of awareness throughout AIB of the need for change and of the direction in which we had to go. Creating this awareness called for an unprecedented level of *communication* throughout AIB. At the time we started the programme, we employed 9,500 people in 500 locations in eight countries. This included no less than 1,200 managers.

In early 1987 we held a series of mass meetings of managers at AIB headquarters in Dublin. To reach staff throughout the group, we used a combination of media: videos, print material and face-to-face briefings delivered to staff by their own managers.

These were some of the milestones of the initial change programme.

Developing core management values and practices

We set out to discover, through *internal research*, the core management values that would be appropriate to the new, market-focused AIB. Then having established what those values were, we identified the management practices that would support the values. And finally, we put in place whatever training and development that was necessary to put those practices into action, day-to-day.

This process was carried out by AIB's middle management in a programme directed specifically at them, and which lasted two years. These people we recognised as pivotal to the entire change process: if they didn't change themselves and become the driving force of change, then what happened above or below them would have no lasting effect.

The four core values we identified as necessary for the new AIB were as follows:

- Concern for the individual.
- Taking personal responsibility.
- Developing open communication.
- Commitment to goals and standards.

Again, like mission statements such principles risk remaining mere aspirations unless there is a clear follow-up. This was provided first of all by 34 management practices we identified as necessary to support the core values. The 34 practices fall under the following six headings:

1. Demonstrating commitment and purpose.
2. Allocating and developing responsibility.
3. Developing customer awareness.
4. Managing and rewarding performance.
5. Managing the work atmosphere.
6. Managing and developing the team.

Each manager attended a week-long seminar specifically to develop his understanding of these practices, and to receive feedback on the extent to which he did or did not use them already. This feedback was provided by means of a questionnaire which each manager was invited to distribute to his own staff (nearly all of them did).

We discovered through this process that while managers were all the time *saying* to their staff that the customer was king, the staff themselves did not consider that the manager's *actions* fully supported the statement!

Drawing on the creativity of staff

A problem in any change programme is creating involvement down through the various levels of the organisation. Since the first tasks are inevitably strategic and planning ones, the appropriate place to begin is at the top. Then, the crucial task of enrolling and involving middle management will take a further considerable period of time. In all this, staff at the operational level may begin to wonder what is happening to the change programme. Indeed, cynicism may set in as time passes and they see no change at the level of their own jobs.

AIB's change programme did not escape any of these problems, but a major counter-balancing element in it was an initiative called *Superthought*. This was a staff ideas project that was carefully integrated into the overall change programme: it was intended as a practical demonstration that management did genuinely want to hear ideas from staff, would implement them whenever practicable, and would reward them appropriately.

The very existence of the initiative was in itself a demonstration that AIB had changed. Such an approach would have been unthinkable in the old 'clearing bank' culture. Superthought became for the staff a practical expression that the winds were changing.

The project differed from the usual run of suggestion schemes in that it involved team rather than individual activity. It was conceived and delivered on a massive scale: 98% of the staff and management were involved over a three-month period, during which the entire focus of the organisation seemed to be on the scheme!

No fewer than *1,200 ideas* were selected for implementation, and their authors rewarded. They spanned three areas: customer service improvements, income enhancements and cost savings. In terms of eliciting worthwhile business ideas, the scheme was successful and cost-effective. However, it was even more valuable in developing understanding of the market-led approach and enthusiasm for it, and also in demonstrating the sincerity of management's commitment to a new way of doing business and of running the organisation.

Bringing the public in on the act

A temptation that AIB resisted was to present its planned change to the public as a promise, rather than as an accomplished fact. In other words, what needed to be resisted was the premature publicising of the change programme outside the organisation. The reason for this initial reticence was twofold: internal and external.

Internally, early publicising of the change programme outside AIB would have undermined the sincerity and the long-term thrust of the initiative. Viewing the publicity from within, staff might well have been tempted to see the programme as nothing more than cosmetic – for external consumption only, while the underlying reality remained unchanged.

Externally, to rely on promises rather than performance would be to invite customer cynicism. Since in the long run the aim was to convince customers that AIB's offering was genuinely superior, it was vital not to make claims that could be seen merely as the usual external posturing without a solid foundation in the reality that was perceived and experienced by the customer.

For these reasons, it was decided very deliberately to lead the change programme from within. Two publicity initiatives were, however, undertaken during the first phase of the programme. Both had the same objective: to signal that AIB was changing, in a way that was relevant to the customer.

The first initiative was a *corporate television advertising campaign*. This campaign was remarkable not just in that it avoided any attempt to promote directly AIB services. Much more unusually, it frankly admitted the need for change in AIB. It said in effect: 'To serve you best, we need to change. We see that, and we're working on it.' In addition, though the campaign itself was allegorical in approach and featured an emerging butterfly as its central image, there was no doubt about the positioning of AIB as an organisation of *people*, rather than as an impersonal monolith.

The advertising programme had two further elements. A corporate message in print media explained the commitment to change, and our understanding of the need. We also took the adventurous step (with some trepidation) of asking the public through press advertisements for their ideas on the kind of change and innovation they would like to see in AIB.

The openness and indeed humility of this approach achieved a high awareness for the basic message that AIB was changing. This was then built on with *a new corporate identity* which was launched in 1990 with a threefold purpose: to symbolise the change taking place; to be a mark of differentiation in the market-place; and to be a flag for the future.

The specific imagery of the identity was intended to reflect the new kind of organisation that AIB was becoming, but from the customer's perspective its launch had perhaps the more immediate effect of underlining the fact that change was in train.

In both these external publicity initiatives, however, we were careful to avoid over-promising. We saw communications of this kind as providing the background for change, and reflecting the reality of change, rather than constituting the change itself.

The never-ending task: connecting change to the market-place

In a way, the initiatives sketched out above are the preliminary and more easily documented precursors to the real task of change, which is the *living* of the new culture in the day-to-day business of the organisation.

From the beginning, we were clear about two things. First, that the groundwork for change had to be laid carefully and correctly – and that this was something that could not be hurried. Secondly, that change would never become a complete reality until everyone in the organisation and everything the organisation did reflected the new culture.

So the focus of later phases of a change programme such as ours is on connecting the new philosophy with the realities of the market-place. In an organisation like ours, this can happen only at the level of the individual business unit. If a marketing culture is not centred at the point where the company interfaces with its customer, it is a contradiction in terms.

After the initial phase, which in AIB extended over a period of about five years, the centre of gravity shifted downwards in the organisation. Within the broad framework of the original grand strategy, each division and each business unit has to do its own searching for a way to make the new culture a reality in its operation. As it does so, responsibility for change is pushed further and further down the line. The ultimate point of arrival is when everyone is engaged. But to say that is to mislead, because in a sense this is a road with no ending.

Change is never over

In AIB, we started from an awareness that effecting change is a long-term process. From this we have evolved to a conviction that the process of change is in fact a permanent one. To say that is not to argue that change should be embraced as an end in itself, but to accept the reality that over the course of a long-term change programme the outside environment will also change – and in doing so demand further change on the part of the organisation itself.

This is certainly true of AIB. The competitive world in which we find ourselves now, nearly a decade after the need for cultural change was first recognised, is a very different one to the world that sparked off the process. Competitive forces have become fiercer than many might have forecast; the pace of technology development and of deregulation within our business has accelerated; uncertainties in the world economy, paralleled by massive geo-political changes, have dramatically changed the background against which banks operate.

But these changes have not led to any need for AIB to change its course. Nothing that has happened in the past decade has suggested that the basic strategy was wrong. Instead, what we see is a continuing need to accelerate the process, and to deepen the commitment to a market focus.

A vision for the future

Just now we are communicating to our people the output of an extensive review of AIB's direction for the rest of the decade. This aims to consolidate the progress made under the Marketing Action Programme by setting out *a vision of the organisation in the year 2000* and the values that will characterise its operations together with a clear view as to how stakeholders' interests can be balanced.

This vision is intended to be action-guiding, and therefore moves quite quickly from generalities to specifics. On market positioning, for instance, the overall aim is to be recognised as Ireland's leading bank, with significant operations in the USA and the UK. At divisional level, this is then expressed in more concrete terms as follows:

- In Ireland, to be Ireland's No 1 bank in all AIB's chosen markets – distinguished by superior service value, operating effectiveness and profitability, high credit standards and the professionalism and involvement of our people.
- In the USA, to maintain (through our wholly owned subsidiary, the First Maryland Bancorp) a strong competitive presence in the greater Maryland market-place, generating a growing stream of quality earnings.
- In the UK, to be a focused retail and commercial bank, developing in and from the natural markets serviced by our branches and committed to professional credit management, operating efficiency and quality customer service.
- In capital markets, to be a market leader in Ireland and have a reputation for excellence in our international markets – distinguished by a superior ability to create value for customers.

In relation to balancing the interests of AIB's following four sets of stakeholders, the vision is equally specific:

- *Customers*   To consistently score No 1 in our chosen market segments, on a basis measured by market research, in perceived service value.
- *Shareholders*   To achieve consistently a return on equity superior to all other publicly quoted Irish and UK clearing banks; to provide the basis for long-term capital growth by growing dividends consistently above the rate of Irish inflation (together with appropriate dividend cover); and to widen significantly the shareholding base outside Ireland.
- *Staff*   To foster a spirit of unity and professionalism among all staff, provide fair and equitable treatment with the objective of maintaining optimum levels of employment, address the challenges of change in a balanced way and manage the consequences of change to ensure a balance between the needs of individuals and those of the organisation.
- *Community*   To be a company admired for its values, standards and the contribution it makes to the economic and social development of the communities we serve.

Success?

AIB's change story is not finished. But an essential part of the continuing process is to assess progress so far. Has AIB succeeded in changing its culture?

There are several ways of looking for an answer. Far from the worst of them is to assess the way the organisation looks and feels at an intuitive level to those who work inside it. By that yardstick, AIB has indeed changed radically. The stakes in an operation like this are too high, however, to rely on intuition alone. From time to time AIB commissions formal *attitude research among its staff*. This is carried out by an outside organisation, and the results – good or bad – are communicated back to the staff.

The results of such probes in AIB have been twofold: on the one hand, they have confirmed that the organisation has indeed moved far and fast; on the other, they highlight (sometimes very painfully) the distance that still remains to be travelled. Perhaps not surprisingly, the outstanding difficulties are those of communication: the central problem remains that of involving everyone in the change process, and of translating aspirations into specific changes on the ground.

Then there is *the market-place test* – the yardstick of the bottom line. In AIB's case, a powerful catalyst for the change process has been that the overall strategy has been clearly seen to pay off in terms of growth and profitability.

In the past decade, AIB moved decisively from being No 2 on the Irish banking scene to one in which it is now the undisputed leader. It has also made the difficult transition from a national bank to one with a strong international presence. Cyclical hiccups apart, the bank has continued to grow, to expand its market share, to increase its net worth and its return to shareholders – and to do this during one of the most difficult periods for banks in this century.

None of this would have been possible without a decisive rejection of the outmoded 'clearing bank' culture which had long outlived its usefulness.

12 Building a creative culture for a growing organisation

Henry Curteis

'Innovation is the specific instrument of entrepreneurship . . . the act that endows resources with a new capacity to create wealth.'
Peter F. Drucker, *Innovation and Entrepreneurship*, Harper & Row, 1985

Executive summary

This chapter is written from experience by an owner/manager who has built a medium-size high-growth business from scratch.

Henry Curteis describes his philosophy for developing a business which combines individualism with creative teamwork and control. He points out some key pitfalls in the development of a company culture and describes the role of intuition in the growth of a business. Finally, he explains the need for a common purpose to achieve growth and suggests a way to achieve it.

Curteis Chains has recently been identified by 3i as belonging to the 'Superleague' group of companies, i.e. privately held, profitable medium-size companies achieving a turnover growth of at least 25% per annum over a two-year period.

In 1975 I dropped out of my Law Degree course at Oxford and started working as a sales agent in the jewellery industry. The message thrust at me from all sides was that there would be no future without a degree. But by the third year my interest in Law had waned, and the idea of launching into the outside world unencumbered by an excess of traditional learning, had acquired an almost romantic appeal. Like many others among the Oxford spires I dreamed. Unusually I dreamed of a business empire. This, I estimated, would take about three years to complete, before returning to a life of leisure. This was all the funnier because I had no idea in which area of business this empire was to be! I met an old lady in an antique shop who told me that she knew two people who had gone into jewellery recently, and both seemed to be doing well. So, in the absence of anything else, I bought an ageing Sunbeam Rapier, made some contacts at a jewellery trade fair at Earls Court, and proudly set off to call on jewellers, sample bag in hand. Fortunately I had no idea what I had let myself in for!

Any business which grows from scratch to a medium-sized organisation makes an interesting story. But the focus of this chapter is not to pick out critical moments from the story of Curteis Chains. I want to look at the development of our organisation and see what lessons can be learned, or what ideas have sprung from witnessing and experiencing the progress of the last 18 years.

Everyone knows of growing and creative organisations that inspire admiration, and of others where growth has stagnated. The latter seem slow to take decisions, and they no longer focus on customers' needs, although at one time, they must have been creative and responsive. If from our experience I can point out pitfalls and suggest how to avoid them, this chapter will serve its purpose. But first of all, how does the creative business process begin?

Curteis Chains Ltd

Curteis Chains Ltd which makes chains for jewellery began trading in 1977, the year of the Queen's Silver Jubilee in which millions of commemorative pendants were sold. This market enabled the business to make good initial progress. The market for jewellery then collapsed in 1980 with the rocketing of precious metal prices at the onset of the Afghanistan War. At that point there were 31 UK jewellery chain manufacturers. Today there are 6, and some of those face an uncertain future.

During the 1980s Curteis Chains established a market supplying jewellery chains to independent retailers – the only manufacturer to do so until recently. The problems of jewellery multiples which caused some competitors severe difficulties when large orders were cancelled were only felt marginally, as the multiples only represented 20% of turnover.

Within the sector which is predominantly supplied from overseas, Curteis Chains Ltd has a 3% market share. Throughout the recession the company has continued to grow by launching new product ranges, entering export markets and increasing penetration of the UK market. A new factory has been built. Much equipment has been purchased at bankruptcy sales both in the UK and in the USA, where a similar shake-out has taken place. While new production and administrative processes are being developed, the company culture and values have been defined to maintain a common purpose, tight control and a high rate of innovation. The company is now poised to increase its market share and to achieve continuing growth in the years ahead.

Entrepreneurship

At the start of this chapter, I left you with a vision of a young salesman walking optimistically down a high street with a bag of samples looking for customers. The task was not easy, particularly for someone with no experience. But before long, his list of customers grew and the vital first few steps had been taken. However, within two months the project folded, the victim of lack of experience and cash flow problems. Although a brave start had been made, the young man's youthful dreams were now starkly confronted with reality. He soon learned that no one can build a business from nothing without *a strong sense of purpose.*

An aspiring entrepreneur must forego current consumption, dedicate all his or her energies to the enterprise, and put most other aspects of life into second place. The commitment to succeed has to be total. Some venture-founding companies which invest in business start-ups prefer to select entrepreneurs who are single or divorced for this reason. Most organisations begin with an entrepreneurial phase as did Curteis Chains, and as this is the start of the growing and creative process it is worth looking at how this sense of purpose comes into being.

It is curious how someone can chance on an opportunity and within a short space of time make it the focus of their life. The process is not unlike that of falling in love! It is certainly far from rational. What starts as a mild flirtation and a detached assessment of possibilities escalates through stages to total commitment. As each challenge is met and overcome, there is the thrill of survival, and commitment grows. The greater the difficulties, the more the satisfaction and the stronger the commitment. To me this process defines *entrepreneurship* and is how most business organisations are created.

But what is the source of a person's commitment? In my opinion it has to be their *inner values.* The idea of an early return to a life of leisure was not enough to inspire the required level of determination in the example of the young salesman. There has to be courage to fight on and not to be defeated, but also the positive view that the results of building an enterprise are of such value that the effort and sacrifice needed are justified. Value in this sense can hardly be money. The things that we really care about are above financial consideration. Qualities such as courage will not be turned on by money alone, or the dream of an easier life, but the feeling that this challenge is the thing to make life worth living – that will drive a business start-up.

If you were to enquire of the average person in Britain what drives the creation of business, they would probably reply that it is desire for status or power. The fact is that creativity and entrepreneurship are rarely driven by a desire for power over other people. It is usually the reverse – a search for independence, and freedom from control by others. It is about achieving *fulfilment* through your own resources. It is something between you and yourself. Your courage is your own. The disappointments are your own, and the satisfaction is your own.

However effective and supportive your team becomes, there will always be periods in the development of a business when an entrepreneur has to face life alone. At these critical times he or she will be thrown back on their inner personal values. Growth requires commitment, and that will only come if the end result is valued. One of the main reasons that businesses cease to grow is that the owners no longer see any value in it. If there is a sum of money or a standard of living aspired to, once that is achieved, growth will tend to stop. If, on the other hand, personal fulfilment is the aim, the process of growth and creativity will continue. The path to growth, however, is innovation.

Intuitive innovation

An organisation that wishes to grow has to compete. This requires not just a single advantage over competitors, which would be identified and imitated, but layers of advantage in all areas of an organisation's activities. An environment conducive to *continual innovation* is essential – one where change becomes the normal course of events. Some ideas on what makes a suitable cultural environment for continual innovation are discussed in more detail later. The first step is to look at the process of innovation itself.

Many studies have been made of the process of innovation, from which three distinct phases have been identified: *initiation of ideas, evaluation* and *implementation*. An individual initiates or proposes an idea. The idea is evaluated, usually in a financial sense, and if it is seen to meet the strategic aims of the organisation, it is implemented. An open and free environment is thought to be best for the initiation of ideas. Evaluation is usually seen as a detailed and analytical process while implementation is considered to require tight controls and structures.

A good example of innovation of this kind from our experience is when a consultant suggested that we ought to consider a change of premises. We had been thinking of extending, but when we sat down and thought about it, the option of moving to purpose-built premises was far superior. Different methods of financing were discussed, and the decision was taken to appoint a 'design and build' company. The implementation of the plan required tight controls to ensure that we came in on budget. Although on this occasion we innovated in a structured way as recommended in the textbooks, I can only say that most of the time this is not how we have experienced innovation.

When innovative ideas are put forward on a subject familiar to the members of a team well known to each other, the process seems to be different. A person who has a wealth of experience in a business or working environment and who has a deep interest in one or more aspects, seems able to access innovative solutions through intuition. Most people have intuition at some time. Perhaps ideas have occurred to you, while in the bath, or in the first few moments of wakefulness in the morning. As if from nowhere an idea arrives in your mind, accompanied by the certainty that it is right, often with a feeling of satisfaction or excitement. It is as if your subconscious mind has been on a thorough search through your past experience and accumulated knowledge, and has come up with an idea. The subconscious then evaluates it before reporting back to the conscious mind, which receives it at a moment of relaxation. Individuals who have learned to have confidence in their intuition are usually happy to project their idea without any further detailed evaluation, as did Archimedes with his bathtime scientific breakthrough. By all accounts he spent no time evaluating. As his intuition gave him his idea, it also told him it was right beyond a shadow of doubt. All he did was project his idea outwards to the world with a flourish!

The intuitive process begins with a sensing of opportunity or a potential problem. This can be a definite or even a vague feeling. This sensing then gives rise to a scanning and focusing sequence in the conscious mind, which appears to set up a parallel process in the subconscious mind. The mind quickly scans around the area in question, related areas or unrelated areas, wherever it senses possible gain, as it looks for a pattern. Every so often the mind will focus in more depth in case it is onto a potential winner. The process can result in a breakthrough quickly in the conscious mind, but if the problem has not yielded a solution, the conscious mind will, of necessity, move on to something else. Not so the subconscious mind. If it senses that there are important issues involved. It carries on working on the problem and eventually reports back when it has found an answer.

The quality of intuitive thought has evidenced itself over and over again in my experience – also in the experience of others at Curteis Chains and elsewhere. I have heard bankers say that if their initial reaction to a lending proposal is negative, they have learned from experience to follow their instincts. Some minds are intuitive about business. Some about engineering. Others about people. The subconscious mind can also issue strong warnings when it feels that your conscious decisions are on the wrong track. When, for example, a situation is not working and you are putting in enormous effort to make it work, it is often the intuitive process which convinces you to change your approach.

One concrete example of intuitive innovation came hard on the heels of the decision to proceed with the new building. The decision to build 20,000 sq. ft of usable space had been taken, and the planning officer was arriving the next day to inspect the site, but we were not happy with the suggested designs for the roof. In the morning I woke up picturing the college buildings at Oxford, and in a flash I realised that the quadrangular approach would solve the problem, and that is the shape of the building I am now sitting in as I write this chapter.

To summarise, intuitive innovation starts by sensing a need. This prompts scanning and focusing. If a result is quickly achieved, there is no further conscious search. If the need is still not satisfied, the scanning and focusing process carries on subconsciously leading to a report back to the conscious mind when it is at rest, if an answer is found. The answer provided is usually accompanied by certainty that it is right, and a feeling of excitement – or sometimes sadness if the answer implies that tough action must be taken. Experience confirms the excellence of intuitive thought, and the process of subsequent evaluation is usually finding out why the idea is good, not whether it is good. The last stage of intuitive innovation is not really implementation. I have called it projection.

In a closely working team, an intuitive person will become recognised as such, and the other members of the team will usually be happy to rely on the ideas deriving from his or her thinking and will quickly assimilate them into the progress of the organisation. The dangers of such an open approach to implementation are, in my experience, far outweighed by speed and effectiveness. If the controls of the organisation are pushed to their limits, it is essential to re-establish structure and direction. With a closely working team this does not present a problem. There is far more danger in damaging the innovative process by excessive control than the other way round. Where the team does not possess sufficient experience of a subject, there is a need to observe caution. In this case a structured approach to innovation would achieve better results.

There is clearly a need for a high degree of trust between the members of a team for intuitive innovation to be given space to work and this makes it vulnerable to change in the social environment. It is crucial that people in the organisation wish to and can work closely. Because of this an organisation that is growing and undergoing continual change needs to develop a strong culture. The answer we have found is the 'Virtuous circle of growth'.

The Virtuous circle of growth

A company culture has two roles. The first is to produce a statement of the purpose of an organisation. This should not merely be a rational assessment of the nature of your industry and how you fit into it, but it should also define the philosophy that drives the activity. It should not just say what you do, but also why you do it. The second objective is to protect and control the organisation. As the role of hierarchy is reduced and working teams are 'empowered', culture becomes an important means of control. Clear knowledge of why you are doing something also informs you of how it is to be done.

As Curteis Chains changed from a one-man-band to team management, it was clear that the values that had driven the growth of the business to that point needed redefinition. We began by discussing the value of our organisation – to the owners, the management team, the staff, the local community and the other stakeholders. It seemed to us that the main value was the contentment which our growth was bringing to the lives of many people.

Then we looked at our teams, which we have always regarded as the building blocks of the organisation. What were their ideals? It was then that we realised that the best team-working individuals were the more content, and the less good at team-working the naturally more jealous. This prompted the idea of a circular model to define our culture, based on contentment as the ideal (see Figure 12.1).

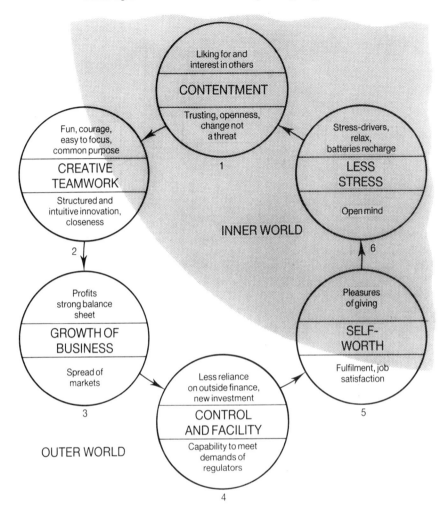

Figure 12.1 The 'Virtuous circle of growth'
(Source: Henry Curteis, 1992)

The model reads from one circle to the next anticlockwise, starting at Contentment. The shaded area represents the Inner World – the world inside a person. The rest is the Outer or Visible World. It explains the relationship between the individual and the team and describes how creative and focused teamwork can reward the individual with a feeling of self-worth and a reduced stress level, bringing a feeling of contentment. The circle also implies that these are not just benefits, but are also necessary *inputs* to creative teamwork.

The Contentment Circle states that our ideal team member is basically content with their life. They do not carry a chip on their shoulder or have excessive interest

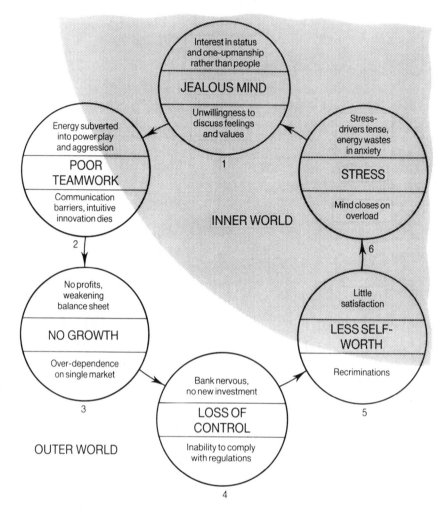

Figure 12.2 The 'Vicious circle of decline'
(Source: Henry Curteis, 1992)

in status. They tend to like and be interested in other people. They are able to trust and willing to be open about their feelings and values, and find the prospect of change interesting rather than threatening.

The Creative Teamwork Circle describes the coming together of the team. Ideally this should be fun. The team should be easy to focus, and show courage when required to tackle a tricky problem. There should be the ability to take part in a structured approach to decision-taking, coupled with an understanding of the value of intuitive thought. It is at this critical point that the Jealous Mind is so destructive (see Figure 12.2). As an entrepreneur has purpose, so *common* purpose is necessary for a team to be creative.

The Growth of Business Circle is not part of the personal or Inner World but the Outer or Visible World. It looks at the need for growth to be balanced. In our philosophy there are three ingredients to financial strength. First, a good Profit and Loss account – preferably featuring the former! Secondly, a strong balance sheet. And, thirdly, a wide spread of markets. If you are overly dependent on one market or especially one customer, how can you confidently project forwards? Similarly, high profits do not bring control without a strengthening balance sheet. Balanced growth enables the organisation to achieve increased *Control and improved Facilities*. There could be new building, better equipment or more stocks. Increased control means less reliance on banks or outside finance, and the ability to comply with demands of regulatory authorities. Control also comes from being able to project the company forwards with confidence. As the direction previously taken by the company is confirmed by financial success, this becomes easier.

As the increase in Control and Facility is achieved, the individual team member should experience an increase in confidence, a feeling of satisfaction and fulfilment. Psychologists talk of *Self-Worth* – the next circle. How does a person see him or herself? As a loser or a winner? A growing business has more winners. The greatest pleasure in life is giving and winners have more to give.

The *Less Stress Circle* – stress can be a good thing, but in business there is a tendency for stress to increase to unacceptable levels. In our model, stress should be controlled to its efficient level, which produces enjoyable work and yet allows the batteries to recharge when a person is at rest. If you feel you are winning, you tend to suffer less stress. You recover and your imagination expands. The end result is an increase in contentment for the individual, which enables them to grow and contribute more to the team next time round.

The Vicious circle of decline

The 'Vicious circle of decline' goes round in less fortunate style than the 'Virtuous circle of growth'. A person who is resentful, has a chip on their shoulder and a jealous mind will tend to see change as threatening. Such people are often unwilling to discuss their feelings or values, and are not generally interested in or fond of others. They generally perform better in a hierarchical working environment, where interest in status or one-upmanship can be more easily accommodated. They are the natural office politicians but in a creative team they are out of place. Communication barriers go up and intuitive innovation dies as energy is subverted into powerplay or aggression. This produces *poor teamwork*. The common purpose is not achievable.

The *No Growth Circle* is produced as the level of creativity is low. Perhaps the Sales Manager is forced into accepting orders at low prices to keep the factory working. Profits are hard to come by. There are no funds available to acquire assets and to develop the business.

The *Loss of Control Circle* describes the bank looking nervously at the increasing overdraft, while the Fire Officer threatens to prohibit the use of your building which he had given a clean bill of health to at the planning stage! Control is slipping away.

It is worth pointing out that many businesses are deterred from growing by the arrogance and hostility of regulatory authorities. The laws themselves are confusing and they can be enforced aggressively. There are now nine government agencies with powers to close businesses.

The Less Self-Worth Circle shows that lack of visible success makes people feel that they are losing. Recriminations are voiced as satisfaction becomes a rare commodity. In the *Stress Circle* stress levels rise and it is hard to relax. Energy is wasted, and the mind closes up on overload. The circle is complete.

The 'Virtuous circle of growth' and its opposite the 'Vicious circle of decline' have proved useful in explaining our culture and the value of Growth to the company, the team and the individual. They define the requirements for team composition, particularly emphasising the need to avoid the Jealous Mind of the circle of decline. If there are difficulties the models provide a basis for discussion or training, and generally they have given a process to maintain momentum.

Developing a common purpose

In our view it is important to look at your business not just in financial terms. To generate growth it is also necessary to develop a broader view of the value of your business. Some may feel that the approach taken by the Virtuous circle of growth is not compatible with the aims of their organisation. Many boards would define their key purpose as achieving a sustainable increase in their share price, and paying increasing dividends to their shareholders. In the era when business interests were threatened by political change this approach made a lot of sense, but I would like to challenge the effectiveness of a purely financial approach to produce growth in today's more competitive business environments.

History shows that people are more motivated to build by creed than by greed, and a problem with a purely financial approach is that in emotional terms the main reference point is greed. This can hardly be motivating to people working in an organisation. As described earlier, qualities such as courage are not easily motivated by money.

Another problem with a monetary approach is that the Directors of an organisation have started to define the value of their organisation in terms of profits and share value. This could deprive the organisation of the opportunity to define and adopt a value such as Growth which could give a *common purpose* to the workforce and the other stakeholders. By focusing primarily on the financial interests of shareholders, Directors are inviting the workforce to see themselves as of secondary importance.

There is a tendency in the human mind to see what it wants to see. A company is a complex and changing organism which is hard for the mind to visualise, and this apparent lack of definition makes it easy for perceptions to be coloured. Directors and shareholders hoping for a financial return from an organisation, a seemingly harmless enough aspiration, will tend to see the relationships of others to the organisation in financial terms. If they perceived an organisation as a group of teams working together, rather than a network of competing financial relationships, the need for a common purpose would become more obvious. Many large organisations declare a wish to become more entrepreneurial, and if they are to do so they need to adopt values which give the same sense of purpose to everyone in the organisation.

In our philosophy there is no need for a conflict between the needs of the individual and the aims of an organisation that is required to grow. The Virtuous circle of growth looks in detail at the perspective of an individual team member working in an organisation and links their needs with the requirements of the organisation. Job satisfaction, less stress and contentment are recognised as intrinsic benefits of work, but they are also recognised as crucial inputs to teamwork and business success. Growth is therefore perceived to be in everyone's interests and is the unifying ideal. A change from a monetary to a growth philosophy such as this could permit many organisations to find more cohesion and grow faster.

The role of intuitive thought in business should be recognised. Many managers in industry have to disguise decisions based on 'gut feeling' to look like the results of analysis and detailed work, because the quality of intuitive thought is not appreciated. The current fashion for empowerment and delayering will address some of the problem, but unless this is coupled with a broader understanding of how people innovate, much intended good will be lost.

It seems to take about two years for a person to absorb enough information about their task to be able to start working intuitively. Businesses that move their staff around frequently will be losing effectiveness unnecessarily. Also the Employment laws which are based on a two-year shaking down period do not allow long enough for people to show their potential.

Today, with rising levels of unemployment there is more appreciation of what businessmen do for society, but the process of changing perception has further to go. As church and community play a lesser role, and family life becomes less stable, people need to find new sources of purpose and contentment in their lives. If business organisations can let go of the old perceptions and find ways to adapt themselves to meet these aspirations, there is a great opportunity.

13 Total innovation management: turning ideas into action[1]

Mark Brown

'Corporate risk takers are very much like entrepreneurs. They take personal risks to make new ideas happen.'
Gifford Pinchot III, management consultant, *Intrapreneuring*, Harper & Row, 1985

'Today we make 50% of our current turnover with products which did not exist 5 years ago. Thus if we are not creative in time, we cannot employ 50% of our workforce within 5 years. This is the continuous burden of innovation for our company.'
Dr. Kaske, Siemens, August 1990

Executive summary

Total Innovation Management aims at the successful achievement of 'customer obsession', releasing people's energy and motivation, involving and applying their creativity, and empowering them within a broad framework of objectives and policies.

It goes beyond new product development by encouraging everyone to do things better and differently in developing products, processes and procedures that will delight customers and increase profits and performance.

The chapter explores proven and practical ways to stimulate creativity and innovation. It shows how to tap people's ideas and translate them into profitable action whilst simultaneously running a highly efficient organisation.

Innovation matters. Directors know this. The question is how to engineer your organisation for the appropriate levels of innovation. This chapter explores this question of how to promote innovation in your organisation.

The Total Innovation Management approach rests on the successful understanding and implementation of the following four principles which help to ensure the success of all collective enterprises, public and private:

1. *The focus – other people's worlds* Ask what it is that your current and potential customers want. Don't assume anything. Don't assume that you know what they want. Ask them. Try concepts, products and services out for size. Become

obsessed with 'quick and dirty testing'. Achieve a Copernican revolution and put your customers at the centre of your organisation. Rotate everyone around your customers. Study, involve and compulsively listen to them. Try to provide what they want in the way they want it.

2. *The energy – meaning* Try to give people meaning in their work and they will become passionate and committed. Try to match people's jobs to their interests and energy. There is little you can do externally to 'motivate' people. People are motivated from inside. Humans are 'ert' – not inert. The problem is that what 'erts' them is often not what we ask them to do in their jobs. Align their work to their 'ert' and they become unstoppable. As Mark Twain said – 'make your vocation your vacation'. People with passion can provide excellent quality and they will automatically care for their customers. You never had to send Picasso on a quality seminar.

3. *The intelligence – ideas* Establish a framework for turning ideas into action. Tap every individual's creativity and intelligence. Involve everyone in the search for doing things better and differently in pursuit of delighting customers. Ensure a constant flow of ideas into action to improve and revolutionise products, services, systems and procedures – with customers at the centre of your universe.

4. *The action – situational empowerment* Establish freedom within a framework. People want to have control over their lives. They like varying degrees of self-determination. Empower everyone within a framework. Empowerment without control creates chaos and anarchy. Empowerment within a framework creates synergy and a coherent organisational output.

Turning ideas into action

Open an umbrella. Call that umbrella 'innovation', not elitist 'new product development' but *Total Innovation*. Total Innovation can be defined as 'putting ideas into action for increased profitability and performance'. Total Innovation therefore can apply equally to a product, a process or a procedure.

What therefore fits under the heading of this 'Total Innovation' umbrella? – TQM, Continuous Improvement, Customer Care, Cost Management and other such quality-type initiatives. These are all focused attempts at 'Total Innovation'.

Some of these initiatives, especially those that focus on quality and continuous improvement, may have their own built-in 'glass ceiling'. Terms like 'continuous improvement' suggest the principle of 'doing things better' – that is, evolutionary changes – and may exclude much needed revolutionary changes – that is, 'doing things differently'.[2]

The focus for various initiatives (some might say fads) will continue to change. However, the underlying need for tapping the intelligence of people throughout the organisation, and empowering them to translate that intelligence into action, will not change.

So how do you achieve 'Total Innovation'?

The process

Here is a simple and practical way of thinking about generating ideas and putting them into action. Think of four simple stages: Goals, Ideas, Selection/Control and Action.

Minds begin to tick once they are presented with a problem goal or an opportunity goal. Many individuals, unfortunately, only begin to think once they are presented with a problem — cloudy, overcast 'grey' day. Less often people try and seek out an opportunity — 'white' thinking — like white light which is always present yet difficult to see.

Once a goal is suggested, you start to generate ideas, coded 'blue' for 'blue sky thinking'. You then start to select among the various ideas. 'Red' thinking captures this selection/stop phase — red traffic lights — time to stop, think through the implications, check your ideas against various decision criteria. Lastly, minds and bodies act on those ideas — go — 'green'.

So you have a *goal* — which can be 'white' or 'grey', 'blue' ideas, 'red' selection/control and 'green' — action.

The individual

Individuals may show some preference for different parts of the Ideas Into Action process. For example, an individual may be more drawn to the 'blue'/ideas phase, or the 'red'/selection or the 'green'/action phase of thinking.

A strong, divergent 'blue' thinker may see the more applied 'red' convergent thinker as a barrier. Vice versa, the 'red' thinker may see the 'blue' as unrealistic and 'pie in the sky'. 'Blues' and 'reds' in their turn may see 'greens' as impulsive and headstrong. 'Greens' may feel that 'blues' and 'reds' waste interminable time in purgatorial meetings.

Once you begin to reflect on the question of which is the most important colour, you realise that they are all equally important. It is only together that these colours create the process for turning ideas into action. Together they can create 'Total Innovation'.

The team

Many teams fail to differentiate between information sharing meetings, on the one hand, and creative problem solving meetings on the other. In creative meetings, the teams can work more effectively by consciously distinguishing between and moving through the 'blue', 'red' and 'green' phases.

The organisation

The full process is: GISA: Goals, Ideas, Selection/Control, Action. But many organisations are stronger in one stage than in others. Let us consider some different organisational profiles:

ISA – 'all dressed up with nowhere to go'.

Here you have an organisation without vision, or at least with no vision that is capable of being simply and effectively communicated.

GIA – 'every idea is foolhardily actioned'.

This is a more dynamic profile perhaps, as there is a vision, and ideas – and all these ideas are translated straight into action. This profile may suggest a younger organisation, perhaps an entrepreneurial start-up. This type of profile may remind you of Apple Computer in its youth. John Sculley appears to have provided a 'red' counterbalance – and perhaps offended some of the 'original ideas' people.

GIS – 'the whole is less than some of the parts' – this is a disempowered organisation which cannot take action.

This profile is present in many large organisations. Though there are many talented individuals, the output from the organisation is disappointing. When you probe beneath the skin of such an organisation you usually find that managers feel they are powerless to change things.

The terms 'empowerment' and 'disempowerment' are so much 'in vogue' that they suggest yet another fad. But the ideas have a noble pedigree. 'Locus of Control' is a term used by psychologists to describe the extent to which people feel they have control over events in their lives. For example, someone who has an 'external locus of control' will probably believe that such external forces as luck, fate, chance control their lives. They use expressions like 'It is not what you know, it is who you know'; 'Getting on is a question of being in the right place at the right time'. Believing that the 'Gods' control their lives, they remain passive and sure enough 'luck, chance and fate' do control their lives. This is a self-fulfilling prophecy.

In the corporate version of an 'external locus of control', individuals say that although they may have many good ideas they feel incapable of translating them into action because of 'the company', 'the system', 'the boss', 'marketing', 'finance', etc. In such a powerless environment, individuals point an accusing 'rigid digit' at other departments, functions or simply at the 'organisation'.

A good indication of how disempowered people feel is the way in which they describe their organisation. They describe it as though there is some monolith that actually exists. Clearly an organisation is no more than a legal figment. All that actually exists is a number of people and perhaps some technology. Sadly, the hierarchy and the culture of many organisations leave people feeling that the problem with getting 'Ideas Into Action' is 'they, them, the organisation'.

The fascinating question is: How can you change the culture so that every time an individual points that accusatorial rigid digit away from themselves they are spontaneously reminded that there are always three fingers pointing back at them and asking: What can *you* do to make things happen?

GSA – no ideas

This is the most common profile we find in organisations. The very spark that originally gave birth to the organisation has faded. Although the organisation has a clear vision, excellent control and a high action orientation, the culture does not stimulate or reward creativity and innovation.

Imagine a new, naive, manager attending his or her first management meeting in such a 'red' culture. They may fail to realise that the organisation reinforces the safer act of 'red' critical thinking. The 'blue' individual may hold forth with some new ideas only to find that the culture is a master of 'idea assassination'. Different organisations have their own polite or impolite ways of 'yes ... butting' ideas.

What will such a new 'blue' thinker do following such an onslaught of 'red' critical thinking? Their choices – turn 'red', leave the organisation, or move sideways into Human Resources!

Company cases

So how do you organise to put ideas into action? It may be useful to describe some real company cases – successes and failures (see Figure 13.1).

Creative problem solving teams – without any top–down blessing

We have had painful experiences in several organisations by encouraging individuals and teams to act in more creative and empowered ways. In these companies, as there was no top–down blessing for such an activity, we ultimately

> *Thomson Holidays* – 'Leading Edge Teams'. Teams were encouraged to focus on PISCES, <u>P</u>rofit, <u>I</u>mage, <u>S</u>ervice, <u>C</u>are, <u>E</u>xcellence, <u>S</u>avings. Every team to focus on any opportunity or problem that was within its zone of control that helped it achieve any part of PISCES.
> *Apple Europe* – 'Communication Teams' – 'In-country' teams. The focus was to improve European corporate communications.
> *Owners Abroad* – 'Winning Teams'. The second largest UK tour operator wished to involve everyone in thinking through and achieving their vision and newly established corporate values.
> *Manweb plc* – 'Ideas Into Action Teams'. A successful UK electricity utility wanting to involve people in thinking through and achieving 'extraordinary customer service'.

Figure 13.1 Ideas into action programmes

came to see such interventions as 'counter cultural' and largely unhelpful, both to the individuals involved (except perhaps personally) and to the organisations.

Generating ideas

A large leisure company invited us to help them do a 'blue' trawl. The aim was to stimulate a wealth of business-focused ideas around customer care and service. We ran a range of structured creativity sessions, some helped by a new piece of creativity software entitled 'Brian' that we had developed.

Several months passed before the complaint came back that although there was now a flood of ideas inside the organisation, managers were literally drowning in the sheer volume of them. We generated too many ideas and we had also failed to find sponsors, champions and homes for them. This is a problem inherent in many suggestion schemes.

Think-tanks

A board may request the formation of think-tank or 'NPD' teams. In such cases the goal to be tackled is fairly clearly defined by the board or top team and then passed to the 'blue/red' team which has been appropriately skilled in a range of analytical techniques. The teams themselves may not act but they may make suggestions or recommendations. Think-tanks have been created to find innovative solutions for a wide range of products and services from submarine design/repair through to new kinds of foods.

Blessed blue/red/green teams

Following the criticism by the client that we had flooded their organisation with ideas, the leisure company invited us to create and help them implement a

1. A greater sense of involvement, empowerment and motivation – 'I am the company'.
2. Creation and implementation of new ideas for:
   (a) money saving
   (b) quality improvement
   (c) business process engineering
   (d) continuous improvement
   (e) new products
   (f) 'delighting' customers.

Figure 13.2 Results from ideas into action initiatives

mechanism to put the ideas into action. In their case the mechanism was focused on the quality of customer care and service. We produced the GISA model which has become the basic formula, implanted in other client organisations.

Usually the board or top team decides on the legitimate 'focus'. All natural work teams then generate their own problem and opportunity goals relevant to that focus. The teams can use a range of 'blue' creativity and 'red' *thinking tools*. They then take their ideas through to action. Usually a strong emphasis is put on empowerment. When we first experimented with this approach we had never heard of the word 'empowerment'. Undoubtedly, however, the teams not only became excited about executing ideas, they began clearly to identify much more closely with their own organisation – 'we are the company'.

'Blue, red, green' teams in various organisations have been developed for many different purposes as follows:

- Customer care.
- Improving communications.
- Turning corporate values and vision into a way of life.
- Stimulating quality and ingenuity.
- Salvaging failing quality initiatives.
- New product development.

Some initiatives have been far more successful than others and there are two factors that help to explain those successes. The first of these is 'Situational Empowerment'.

Situational empowerment

The enterprise that does not innovate inevitably ages and declines. And in a period of rapid change such as the present, an entrepreneurial period, the decline will be fast.[3]

Yet:

one of the collateral purposes of an organisation is to be inhospitable to a great and constant flow of ideas and creativity ... The organisation exists to restrict and channel the range of individual actions and behavior into a predictable and knowable routine. Without organisation there would be chaos and decay. Organisation exists in order to create that amount and kind of inflexibility that are necessary to get the most pressingly intended job done efficiently and on time.[4]

One client has a statement of corporate values that include among others the following:

- Get It Right First Time.
- Continuous Improvement.
- Innovation.

Once you reflect on these three values you begin to wonder how they interrelate. Surely 'Get It Right First Time' suggests no errors or mistakes. But can you have continuous improvement and innovation, unless people are allowed to make mistakes? One activity undertaken by this client company is flying thousands of people around the world. When I am being flown into Heathrow I am delighted that the pilot operates by the principle of 'Get It Right First Time' and doesn't try a little 'Continuous Improvement' or 'Innovation', e.g. 'What happens if I land this airbus upside down?'

Clearly we are here discussing the commonly labelled 'tight–loose' properties of any system or organisation. Many clients, having realised that their culture has been historically too tight, too controlling, too 'red', too restraining, then decide that they want to swing 'loose': let's involve and empower the people, encourage initiative, etc. Such organisations often come from a background where the commodity for which they are responsible does need tight control – money, dangerous substances, electricity. Such tight controls, however, have spread to other parts of the organisation where such restrictions are inappropriate. Having encouraged creativity, innovation and empowerment a year or so later, worried by some 'silly mistakes' being made and feeling somewhat 'out of control', the top team/directors decide to reimpose control. This in turn induces scepticism and resentment and worsens the previous levels of disempowerment.

'Tight–loose' was never intended as an 'either/or' concept. It was intended as a 'both' concept – a continuum. Think of the following continua:

1. Total disempowerment/'no go areas'.
2. Mainly disempowered/'yes – then go areas'.
3. Partially empowered/'go then inform areas'.
4. Totally empowered/'go areas'.

Let us label these 1 to 4 (see Figure 13.3). In Box 1 'No go areas' speak for themselves. In the same way that we disempower people from driving on the wrong side of the road, there are certain rules which you must abide by and not violate. If you do violate these – especially if this mistake is repeated – you will be justifiably fired. Box 2 means that you are transgressing some basic principle or

1	2	3	4
NO GO	YES THEN GO	GO KNOW	GO

Figure 13.3 Freedom within a framework

practice and therefore need to obtain clearance before you can proceed. Box 3 decribes the situation where it may be appropriate to let your manager know. Finally, in Box 4 are areas for total empowerment.

If ideas into action teams are going to be successful they need to understand both as teams and as individuals what parts of their jobs fall into these four boxes. They especially need to know for the Ideas Into Action process what they are responsible for, which are the ideas that they can carry through straight into action. Their zone of control must be very clearly established.

This is clearly not to say that you will not have teams that are operating outside those zones of control, as, for example, in the case of business process re-engineering. It is simply that with such teams they will probably be making recommendations rather than acting directly on many of their ideas. Initiatives are much more likely to succeed if creativity and empowerment are clearly established within a framework. Without such a framework you tend to encourage chaos.

Lastly, there is another factor which hugely influences the likely success or failure of various 'ideas into action' initiatives.

Human engineering

The other day, I got into a lift in a client's office. There were several members of staff in the lift with me. There was a large piece of crumpled paper lying on the floor. The lift was otherwise smart, clean and modern. The company had just run an intensive and expensive culture change initiative around quality, customer focus, continuous improvement and empowerment – 'I am the company', 'We take responsibility', etc. None of the employees bothered to pick up the paper.

Experienced human resource and personnel practitioners are not too surprised when a new corporate change initiative fails. They have seen it all before. Initiative after initiative may create a flurry of short-term activity: 'we watch the videos, wear the T-shirts but two years later...'. However, in the light of the strategic importance of many of these change initiatives and the amount of investment made in the process, it should come as a surprise that such initiatives fail – and continue to fail.[5]

Let us explore one brief reason for such failure and see what can be done to overcome it. In many companies senior executives may bemoan the fact that following some grand change initiative (which may make strategic sense) fundamental patterns of behaviour and accompanying attitudes may have changed less than originally intended – maybe not at all. It is clearly a mistake to believe that just because people 'understand' why behaviour should change, that they will change.

Another mistake we may make is to believe that people have not changed because they are not too bright. People are very perceptive. They will tend to do what they see sense in, enjoy doing and are rewarded for. People, in part, do not change because all the old 'reinforcers' that collectively make up the 'implicit rule book' maintain the old patterns of behaviour more successfully than the required new patterns of behaviour. In other words, you may rewrite and communicate the logical needs of the business – but logic does not change people. People are not primarily logical, they are psychological. It is 'psychologic' that changes behaviour – and this requires 'human engineering'.

A simple way to think about human engineering is to imagine a puppet with accompanying strings. If we pull one particular string a limb may move. If we pull another string the head may turn. So it is with 'reinforcers', both positive and negative, in organisations. In order to achieve success with any change initiative we need to identify and understand all the historical 'strings' that motivate people's behaviour. Some of these strings will support the new behaviour, some will be unhelpful and some neutral.

Having understood the present reinforcers – in the light of your desired change initiative – you should strengthen all the existing positive reinforcers, and add new ones, whilst simultaneously cutting and eliminating those reinforcers that are working against the new behaviour. This ideal strategy, in part, explains why it is that those organisations who develop tailor-made change initiatives are more likely to have success than those organisations who simply assume that they can buy 'an off-the-peg change initiative' and expect change to happen. In such cases there is a failure to think through all the reinforcers – and put these in place. There is a failure of the 'human engineering strategy'.

---

1. The Top Team needs to decide on its 'focus for innovation' – products/processes/procedures, etc.
2. The Top Team, and HR/Personnel especially, need to ensure that teams and individuals understand 'Situational Empowerment and Innovation'. People need to understand their 'no-go areas', 'yes – then go', 'go then inform areas' and 'go areas'.
3. The Top Team, having established the 'where to innovate' can now pass this focus on to the next level. They in turn can present the 'where' and the 'how'. Make this a line management and not training initiative – make it credible!
4. Ensure your 'human engineering' is working successfully. Give *soft* reinforcers – 'catching people doing things right' – applauding teams' successes – right through to applauding sensible failures! Also put in the *hard* reinforcers – recognition, rewards and promotion being directly affected by individuals' and teams' achievement in putting 'Ideas Into Action'.

Figure 13.4 A checklist for action

I called the same client whose lift I was in the other day. The switchboard answered fairly quickly. The manner was perhaps a little indifferent. I asked for the person I wanted. An extension rang. 'You've come through to the wrong extension,' a voice barked. He made it sound as though I had deliberately done so. So much for 'We take responsibility'.

Conclusion

The 'Ideas Into Action' approach can work. Decide on the focus. Train teams in the GISA process. Clearly establish freedom, empowerment and creativity within a framework. Rewrite the 'rule book' and put in the appropriate reinforcers (see Figure 13.4 on previous page).

Notes

1. The term Ideas Into Action, and the GISA approach are the copyright of Mark Brown, Innovation Centre Europe Ltd.
2. M.J. Kirton, 'Adaptors and Innovators' in *Innovation: A cross-disciplinary perspective*, J. Gronhaug and G. Kaufmann (eds), Norwegian University Press, 1988.
3. Peter Drucker in *Innovation and Entrepreneurship*, Heinemann, 1985, p. 137.
4. Theodore Levitt in *Harvard Business Review*, 'Creativity is Not Enough', 1963, vol. 41, no. 3, p. 81.
5. The Economist Information Unit, *Making Quality Work: Lessons from Europe's leading companies*, Specialist Report No. P655, 1992.

IV The strategic management of human resources

14 Achieving a dramatic improvement in performance using shareholder value

Brian Pitman

'Chief executives, who themselves own few shares of their companies, have no more feeling for the average stockholder than they do for baboons in Africa.'
T. Boone Pickens, Chairman, Mesa Petroleum Co., *Harvard Business Review*, May/June, 1986

Executive summary

In 1984, Lloyds Bank adopted a strategy which focused on selective market leadership rather than global growth. At the same time, they set themselves the target of doubling the value of the business every few years.

So far, this objective has been achieved. Ten years on, Brian Pitman reflects on the following lessons they have learned:

- Shareholder value as a governing objective demands continuous improvement.
- We can only create value for our shareholders if we create value for our customers.
- Growth for its own sake can produce the biggest loss of all.

What constitutes success?

Every company needs to have a governing objective – a driving force by which it measures its ultimate performance. We have to know what constitutes success for a company before we can measure it. Often, the driving force of the top management team is to be the biggest company in the industry. A bigger size is usually accompanied by a bigger salary, a bigger office and a bigger car. So, size offers a powerful incentive.

There is no denying the fascination of size in banking. For decades the chart bankers first turned to was the one listing size of assets. The top bank was the one with the largest assets and it was not unusual for a bank to go to considerable lengths in order to remain at the top of the list. Yet, to be big is not synonymous with leadership. The largest banks are by no means the most profitable, often because they carry product lines, supply markets or apply technologies where they cannot do a distinct, let alone unique, job. And diminishing returns set in.

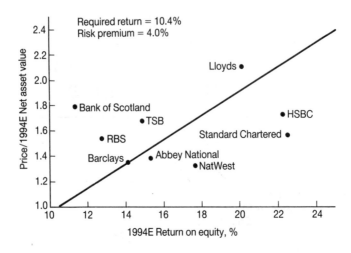

Figure 14.1 UK value map (*Source*: Morgan Stanley Research)

The test of leadership by market share is also deceptive. Examples abound of banks that have the largest market share but are far behind their smaller competitors in profitability. A lower size is often preferable for it makes possible that concentration on specific segments of the market where genuine leadership lies. Attempting to have leadership in everything within the financial services market is a common obstacle to outstanding performance.

These arguments about size and market share are assuming less importance. One of the lessons that bankers have learned is that growth for its own sake can produce the biggest loss of all. Increasingly, the new measure of success is market value and it is resulting in some dramatic shifts in the perception of who is winning. Market value is becoming so important because many observers see the possibility of a wave of bank mergers and acquisitions. Those banks which have strong share prices and high market values will be absorbing the banks which do not. But as many banks are discovering, the task of increasing their market value is much more difficult than the old aim of increasing the size of a bank's assets.

Shareholder value as a governing objective

One of the great advantages of shareholder value as a governing objective is that it demands continous improvement. There is no time when you can sit back and admire your achievements. The measurement is obvious to all, inside and outside the Company. There is no hiding place.

You can set the bar as high as you like. We use the method of asking ourselves how long it will take to double the value of the Company. We set ourselves an objective of doubling its value every few years. It is a demanding target but, so far, we have met it.

Few Chief Executives would deny the value of stretching their organisation by setting the bar higher than people think they can go. If you can generate greater involvement and excitement in the Company, you are halfway there. A big benefit to be derived from seeking to double the value of the Company every few years is that the status quo is never enough. The challenge itself brings forth new ideas and new excitement. In the beginning some may groan and claim that what we are seeking to do is impossible. 'How can we double shareholder value every four years in a mature industry characterised by excess capacity, low growth and irrational competitor behaviour?' Yet, because of the new energy and ideas stimulated by the challenge, the gap between the required and current performance soon gets filled. The sheer magnitude of change required to meet the challenge of the new environment helps to change perceptions, which is a prerequisite of any major change programme.

Lloyds Bank's experience

An investment of £1,000 in Lloyds Bank shares ten years ago, with dividends reinvested, was worth £15,000 at the end of 1992 – a compound growth rate of 31% per annum. Ten years ago, the shares were selling at the equivalent of 66p or 40% of book value: at the end of 1992, the shares were selling at 533p or over 240% of book value. So, we doubled the value of the Company every three years (see Figure 14.2 and Figure 14.3).

This ten-year turn-round involved a number of steps which, taken together, illustrate what can be achieved if the shareholder value concept is fully embraced.

- In 1984, we developed a strategy focused on a vision of selective market leadership rather than global growth.
- We ranked our businesses on the basis of the shareholder value they created. Each activity was viewed either as a creator or destroyer of value. Businesses with permanent negative cashflows became targets for divestment. Altogether, these divestments fetched over £1.2 billion which exceeded the whole of the market value of the company before the process began.
- We faced up to our past mistakes. We made provisions of about £3 billion for problem country debt. This produced accounting losses but no movement in cash. Our share price went up, not down. Research shows that the market reacts

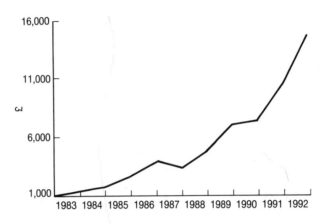

Figure 14.2 Lloyds Bank – total return to shareholders

favourably when companies recognise bad investments, despite the negative short-term earnings impact.

- We entered new businesses. Expansion into life assurance and private banking were examples of higher value strategies which reduced the group's risk profile and increased its cashflow.
- We recognised that in measuring performance cash is king. Earnings per share and other accounting variables should not be used exclusively to assess performance as they ignore the time value of money and they exclude risk. We believe that long-term cashflows are what determine market value.
- Because of greatly improved cashflow, we were able to finance capital expenditure of £2 billion and a dividend increase of 320% over a ten-year period (see Figure 14.4). There has been no call on shareholders since 1976.
- We introduced performance-related remuneration, linking the interests of our people more closely with those of the owners. More than 28,000 employees now own shares in the Company. The senior management have serious money at stake in shareholdings in the Company and/or in share options.

Resistance to change

The adoption of a shareholder value philosophy is a tough discipline. Sceptics argue that the philosophy implies short termism, is just another fad, favours

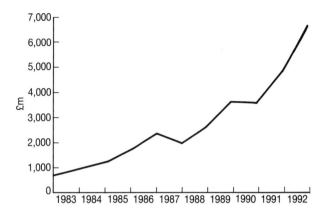

Figure 14.3 Lloyds Bank – market capitalisation

shareholders against other stakeholders and involves too much change ('There will be nothing left if we follow the divestment criteria'). All sorts of arguments are advanced for staying in an activity even though it is a persistent underperformer.

In particular, middle management, recognising the potential implications for poorly performing businesses, may attempt to discredit the process. The barriers to change are most significant when the management's interests and incentives are in conflict with those of the owners. People employed in an underperforming unit find it hard to be realistic about their competitive strengths. Yet, one of the most effective and neglected areas of improved performance is the systematic elimination of all activities which cannot make an important contribution. To attempt the impossible is not good strategy. It is just a waste of resources.

So, the real question for the management of many financial institutions is: 'What collection of divestments, acquisitions and reallocations of capital is necessary to change our return on equity, market value, access to capital and ability to sustain appropriate growth?' These are major risk issues. There are no model answers. Each bank must reach its own decisions.

Misallocation of resources dramatically affects performance. Research shows that it is not uncommon for two-thirds of a bank's value to be generated by less than one-third of its capital. Value is created when the cashflow return exceeds the cost of capital. Performance can be improved either by increasing the return or by reducing the cost of capital. As the perceived risks in the business are reduced, so

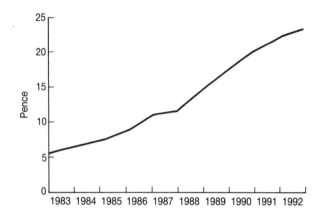

Figure 14.4 Lloyds Bank – growth in dividends per share (gross)

the cost of capital declines. Each business has a different cost of capital. For example, the cost is lower for life assurance business than for the securities business, while lending to top quality companies also attracts a lower cost of capital. On the other hand, smaller companies pose a higher risk, but attract a higher return. So, changing the mix of markets and products can substantially enhance shareholder value.

Shareholder value and customers

Customers are the source of shareholder value. Our aim is to have a leadership position in customer service, costs, asset quality and innovation. So, our strategy starts with our customers. We can only create value for our shareholders if we create value for customers. And customers' needs and expectations are changing rapidly. Today's customers are more selective than ever. They want wider choice. They want better quality. Above all, they want greater value for money.

The constant challenge of any business is to secure and sustain a competitive advantage. Our shareholder value analysis has led us to the conclusion that, in an era of greatly intensified competition, tomorrow's most successful banks will be built on focus not diversity. This requires us to concentrate on the few things that we do very well and then strive to do them better than anybody else.

By concentrating on fewer markets, we can simplify our business and reduce our overheads. Diversity carries with it complexity and complexity creates cost, slippage and delay. Today's world is too competitive for us to handicap our managers with extra costs, extra procedures and slippage in communication and execution. Even more important, today's rate of change is too fast for us to tolerate the delays in decision-making caused by having an excessively complicated mix of businesses.

There is a myth that high quality service means high costs. The evidence is that better relative quality boosts rates of return. Customers are willing to pay more for better quality service. Poor quality service loses those customers that really should be kept. And attracting new customers can be costly.

The following benefits accrue to those financial service companies who offer better quality:

- Stronger customer loyalty.
- More repeat purchases.
- Ability to command higher relative prices without affecting market share.
- Improvement in share of chosen markets.

Market share should not be an object, but a reward: a reward for providing a better service than the competition.

So, customer service is at the heart of shareholder value.

Pay policies to create shareholder value

In most companies it is necessary to revise pay policies to support a focus on creating shareholder value. This is a key element in making the strategy work.

Essentially, our aim is to reinforce the notion that employee interests and shareholder interests are inherently similar. A good way to start is by increasing employee ownership of the Company's shares. We have achieved this mainly through profit sharing schemes, share saving schemes and share option schemes. Over the years, we have substantially increased the proportion of our shares owned by our employees.

Our focus on the creation of economic value requires managers to act like business owners. This has led to a revision of our incentive programme for senior managers. Today, our incentives are tied primarily to their contribution to economic value and they represent a much higher percentage of total remuneration than before.

Creating value by acquisition

Some acquisitions are brilliantly successful in enhancing a company's value, but the odds are against success. About 50% of acquisitions are ultimately divested while fewer than 25% actually create value.

We apply the following criteria:

- Does it in fit with our strategy?
- Does it fit in with our proven skills?
- Is it capable of integration with our existing business?
- Will it enhance customer service?
- Do the acquisition economics stand up to the test?

In our experience most deals are killed by the premium required − 75% of acquisitions simply transfer wealth from the acquiring shareholders to those of the company being acquired.

The use of shareholder value analysis

No planning system guarantees the development of successful strategies. Nor does any technique. The strategy requirements of any business are ruled by the competitive environment and the potential for change in that environment. Only when real competitive advantage exists can real returns accrue.

What shareholder value analysis has given us is a clear discipline. Our goal has been to analyse every strategic decision in terms of its impact on shareholder wealth. We use shareholder value analysis not only to evaluate acquisitions, divestments and capital investment projects, but also in assessing alternative strategies. We know which business units are worth the most to us and how much value each can create. We know which strategies will create the most value in each business unit. We also know that there is always a gap between our current market value and our potential market value. It is not a question of whether there is a gap; the issue is where and how big it is. In sum, we have the tools to manage our company better from a strategic and financial standpoint.

We still have a long way to go, but our aim is to make value creation itself a core competence and a primary source of competitive advantage to Lloyds Bank.

Recommended reading

Publications on shareholder value

E.R. Arzac, 'Do Your Business Units Create Shareholder Value?', *Harvard Business Review*, May–June, 1981.

W.B. Johnson, A. Natarajan and A. Rappaport, 'Shareholder Returns and Corporate Excellence', *Journal of Business Strategy*, Fall, 1985.

Cynthia A. Montgomery and Michael E. Porter, *Creating Shareholder Value: A new mission for Executive compensation plans*, Booz Allen and Hamilton, 1983.

Cynthia A. Montgomery and Michael E. Porter, 'Strategy-Seeking and Securing Competitive Advantage', *Harvard Business Review*, 1991.

Alfred Rappaport, *Creating Shareholder Value: The new standard for business performance*, The Free Press, 1986.

Bernard C. Reimann, *Managing for Value*, The Planning Forum in association with Blackwell, 1989.

Joel M. Stern and Thomas K. Hahn, 'More Value – MVA and EVA measures underscore market perceptions', *The Finance Week 200*, 18–24 March, 1993.

15 Establishing a system of pay for achievement – linking performance and rewards

Chris Gamblin

'I gotta tell ya, with our $2.4 billion in profits last year, they gave me a great big bonus. Really, it's almost obscene.'
Lee Iacocca, Chairman of Chrysler Corporation, addressing market analysts in Detroit, quoted in *Time*, 1 April 1985

Executive summary

In an environment of massive change, linking performance to rewards can help the transition into a period of high achievement. But first the organisation should understand what is involved, how employee needs are changing and how performance-related pay schemes can help management to achieve their objectives.

Chris Gamblin gives practical advice and explains what performance-related pay can do and when to use it, also what it cannot do and how to avoid the pitfalls. He describes Northern Telecom's 'Managing for Achievement' process which is an integral part of the company's corporate vision.

The environment

In talking to managers one thing is clear: there is a shared understanding about winning in today's dynamic business environment. Management is very aware of the challenges that face their organisations and we are all familiar with the much talked about clichés of complexity, ambiguity and unpredictability, but at the practical level how do businesses operate successfully within a global environment which changes so fast it is sometimes breathtaking?

Slowly we see organisations changing to meet this new environment and some of the following features are beginning to emerge in many of our organisations:

- A clear and shared vision.
- An obsession with customers and their needs.
- Relationships shifting from vertical to horizontal and changing from a command structure to networking.
- Distinctions between the managed and the manager diminishing – the empowerment of employees.

- An increasing emphasis on the 'total team'.
- A 'lifelong learning' approach.
- A 'win-win' customer/supplier relationship.
- A 'continuous improvement' environment.
- An open and trust-based system.
- A growth in 'economic participation', employee share ownership and profit sharing.
- Contribution is more important than status.
- Leadership is more important than management.

Many of these indicators are values-based and indicate a growing relevance to individuals of the real motivational issues, and the underdiscussed psychological drivers that make the difference.

The question nevertheless remains: But how do we make the transition? Not through performance-related pay — at least not initially. There are many steps before this.

Strategy not technique

Linking performance to rewards is one technique which an organisation will need to use effectively and carefully in order to *support* the transition. The key to success is not a sophisticated process or a fancy management tool but a clear understanding by the organisation of the following key issues.

1. Do we have a clear understanding of our *customer needs* and the external environment?
2. Do we have a *clear and shared vision* about where we are going and what sort of organisation we want to be?
3. Do we have *a shared and agreed view of our values* in terms of our people, our organisation, our business conduct and our operations?
4. Have we *involved employees* in helping us build these values?
5. Are our *organisation and infrastructure* supportive to these aims?
6. Do we have *measures* to ensure that progress is being made?

Answering these and other questions is an important and essential prerequisite before attempting to link performance to pay.

We must therefore start with the fundamental business issues and set about solving them in different and perhaps informal ways throughout the whole organisation. Experience and success bring about long-lasting change not abstracts, quick fixes or cascades down from the top of the company to the bottom. *Only after substantial success has been achieved should you alter the infrastructure as a means of supporting the behaviour changes which have occurred. Any performance-reward system should therefore come last and not first.*

Another way of explaining this is to try and take a snap shot of the organisation

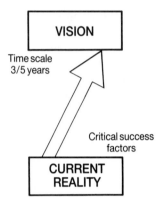

Figure 15.1 The vision and the current reality

five years hence. What is the Board's vision for the company? What will it look like? What will it feel like? Where will it be placed competitively? Imagine that this future situation is *already* a reality and then come back to the 'current reality' and look at the critical issues in between. One of those critical issues could be the realignment of the company's performance and reward structure (see Figure 15.1).

In other words this key move is an important infrastructure change which supports the Company's strategic intent. It is not a fundamental change mechanism in its own right.

Understanding not perception

A further point to consider is: 'Have management a clear understanding of what performance-related pay can and cannot do? At this point there are some important references which should be considered.

Maslow's Hierarchy of Needs and Herzberg's Motivation Theory concepts are both founded on a belief that the real motivators are embedded in the worth of the work itself, and that the movement is towards 'self-actualisation' rather than pay or material rewards. Pay and material rewards can be dissatisfiers if they are perceived as being inadequate, unfair or insufficient for your needs. They are certainly not motivators and if used as such normally only produce very short-term results (see Figures 15.2, 15.3 and 15.4).

The philosophy of Dr W. Edwards Deming is also very significant. At this point I will refer to two documents which may make useful further reading. The first one is a booklet produced by the British Deming Association and entitled *Performance Appraisal and All That*.[1] It discusses the twelfth of Dr Deming's 14 points which can be summarised as follows:

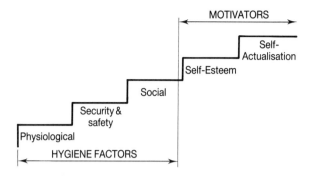

Figure 15.2 Hygiene factors and motivators
(Source: Frederick Herzberg)

PRIMARY CAUSES OF SATISFACTION
- *Achievement*
- *Recognition*
- *Responsibility*
- *Growth and advancement*
- *The work itself*

Figure 15.3 Motivators
(Source: Frederick Herzberg)

PRIMARY CAUSES OF UNHAPPINESS
- *Company Policy and Administration*
- *The Supervisor*
- *Relationships*
- *Working conditions*
- *Salary*
- *Status*
- *Security*

Figure 15.4 Dissatisfaction
(Source: Frederick Herzberg)

- Ranking individuals on the basis of performance is fundamentally unsound.
- Individual and departmental targets and objectives are nearly always destructive of customer-focused teamwork.

- Formal performance appraisal reinforces management's reluctance to regularly coach and develop individuals.
- Reliance on pay as a motivator destroys pride in work and individual creativity.

The Japanese philosophy on rewards and performance is to be found in the papers of Professor Kosaku Yoshida who is a professor at the School of Management, California State University. His subjects include *Sources of Japanese Productivity: Competition and cooperation.*[2]

The Japanese philosophy closely relates to the teachings of Dr W. Edwards Deming but we can learn more about the cultural differences from reading this short paper. It explains why the Japanese find it so easy to follow a philosophy of Continuous Improvement or *kaizen* and why we in the West find it so difficult. In Japan competitiveness within a company is subordinated to cooperativeness and consequently people who are cooperative and get along with others are preferred to aggressive and competitive people. In Japan their only natural resource is people and throughout the centuries and during the education process of their young people all roads lead towards a competition for respect, status, recognition and praise. Even so, the competition for these social values is highly constrained and implicit within a company.

This type of reading is essential to understand *why it is impossible to copy the Japanese and so vitally important to understand them.*

Potential pitfalls

A recent study[3] undertaken by Stephen Bevan and Mark Thompson of the Institute of Manpower Studies, University of Sussex showed the following:

- *Individuals are frequently concerned about the unfairness of the system* and the way money is allocated and, as a result, can be seriously demotivated. Many employees feel performance pay awards are based on patronage rather than on merit, and that quiet diligence is less likely to be rewarded than high visibility.
- *Attitude surveys consistently show that employees are in favour of being paid according to their individual performance* – the problem arises when employers try to make this a central feature of their remuneration policy. Research suggests that the way in which schemes are administered can quite often frustrate these (often over-ambitious) objectives.
- *Performance pay is often part of an appraisal process* and when the two are linked some organisations find the staff development side of the appraisal is often devalued or ignored, with deleterious long-term results.
- *Performance pay is sometimes used by employers to tackle skills shortages and retain specialist staff*, instead of ensuring that base pay remains competitive. This serves to undermine the pay–performance link and discredit it in other employees' eyes. In addition, performance pay often increases the salary bill.

- *Many organisations introduce such schemes without consulting their employees.* This often signals the failure of the scheme from the start as staff feel they have no ownership and therefore are not motivated.
- *Firms tend to keep information secret,* with individuals often overestimating the pay of their peers and underestimating the pay of their superiors.
- *Many companies introduce performance pay too quickly.* Indeed, very few employers get it right first time, with many having to change the scheme several times in the first few years.
- *Defining targets and objectives that can be measured objectively is a recurrent problem* – particularly in service sector companies where output can be less tangible than in manufacturing.
- *Few organisations audit their performance pay schemes* and many have no idea of the impact on employee attitudes and motivation (whereas changing attitudes is apparently the reason most companies introduced performance pay in the first place!).

The message here is that *withdrawing* from a scheme is far more difficult than introducing one.

My point is to help companies to avoid the pitfalls of using performance-related pay as a quick fix solution and secondly, to ensure that management have considered the different philosophies and have the information and education they need to make a decision before introducing new schemes or changing existing ones.

No one has the perfect system but I have had the fortune to work for two leading global companies over the last ten years, Hewlett-Packard and Northern Telecom. Both of these companies have strong values and an obsession with customer satisfaction. It is not surprising, therefore, that their performance management systems are very similar. I will focus on the Northern Telecom process.

The core programme

The Northern Telecom 'Managing for Achievement'[4] process is the core of the Company's belief in the concept of pay for achievement. It is surrounded by other mechanisms which reinforce or add to it. This can be seen by the model in Figure 15.5. I will explain the modules surrounding the core process later in this section.

The company has a very strong corporate vision and a clearly stated set of values. Its vision, known as VISION 2000, is 'to be the world's leading supplier of telecommunications equipment by the year 2000'. The core values supporting this are shown in Figure 15.6.

The MFA process provides a means of translating the vision and the values into work plans, actions and behaviour for the coming year. It also provides the opportunity for employees to initiate and to participate in performance

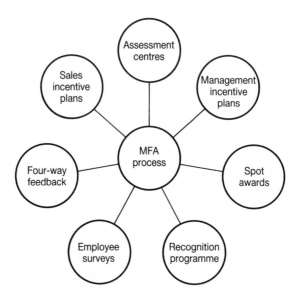

Figure 15.5 Managing for achievement
(Source: Northern Telecom)

Excellence
We have only one standard – excellence

Teamwork
We share one vision/we are one team

Customers
We create superior value for our customers

Commitment
We do what we say we will do

Innovation
We embrace change and reward innovation

People
Our people are our strength

Figure 15.6 The core values

discussions, and for managers to give feedback to employees on their progress, and the achievement of business and personal objectives. Figure 15.7 demonstrates how the vision and values of the company flow down into individual and team objectives.

There are five key components to the process which employees and managers jointly need to work to each year. These components are as follows:

Figure 15.7 From vision to objectives

1. Core Values.
2. Excellence Initiatives.
3. Job Purpose and Key Responsibilities.
4. Objectives.
5. Development Plans.

Let me take each one of these in turn:

1. Core values

These are the values stated earlier in the chapter and at the start of each year managers will discuss with the employees reporting to them the significance and importance of these values as they pertain to their job. Necessary actions and behaviour to support these values can then be built into the current year's planning. The emphasis is very much on behaviour since only through the behaviour of managers can core values be brought to life. It is vital that management behaviour supports and strengthens the Company's core values otherwise the perceived values will not match the stated values and the process becomes incomplete and flawed (see Figure 15.8).

2. Excellence initiatives

The purpose of stating this separately is to emphasise the importance of the principle of continuous improvement at every level of the corporation. Here again, at the beginning of the year managers should discuss with employees ways of building the continuous improvement philosophy into job objectives. Northern Telecom have recently embarked upon a company-wide programme to institute the philosophy of continuous improvement throughout the company on a global basis. Millions of dollars have been invested in skills and philosophy development programmes for all employees. The measurement of progress along this path has therefore become a key issue in the Company's performance management system.

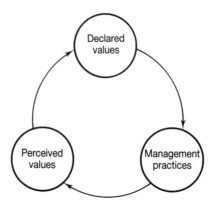

Figure 15.8 Live the values

3. Job purpose and key responsibilities

As with all fast moving industries the importance of flexibility in coping with change is critical and therefore the job purpose and key responsibilities should be reviewed with individuals at least once a year, probably more frequently. This emphasis on flexibility recognises that it is no longer feasible to talk in terms of the traditional job descriptions which are reasonably static but more in terms of job roles where *knowledge and competencies* are the key drivers.

4. Objectives

The specific objectives which are set for the year concentrate on a few key issues which are critical to achieving success. These objectives are split into three categories: operating objectives, people development objectives and strengthening of the business objectives.

Operating Objectives are the tangible, measurable and challenging objectives which connect directly to the implementation of the operating plan, budget and department plans. *People Development Objectives* are those which enhance the capabilities, skills and future contributions of the individuals. *Strengthening of the Business Objectives* relate to those longer-term issues which lead to greater competitiveness and improved operational strength. This could include, for example, continuous improvement programmes, upgrading of systems or equipment and other activities which make the work unit stronger.

5. Development plans

This is a critical part of the process which should blend the employees' interests with the immediate and future needs of the corporation. It relates to the employees' individual needs in terms of strengthening them for their current job or for a future job and ties in very strongly with the company's manpower planning review which identifies critical and key resources.

The annual cycle

The process starts in January/February when the company objectives for the coming year are discussed and formulated into individual objectives and development plans. In February/March these plans are reviewed with peer managers and others who have the opportunity to comment on employee development needs. During the year there is continual and informal feedback on progress against objectives but in addition at least twice a year there is more formal and written feedback. Lastly, in December/January an annual summary is completed for every employee, which is then used as input to compensation, training, staffing and career development. A flow diagram of the process is shown in Figure 15.9.

At year end a formal performance rank for each employee is agreed, based upon

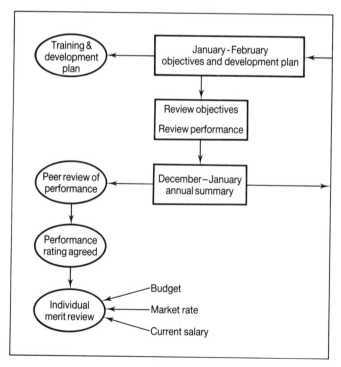

Figure 15.9 The 'Managing For Achievement' cycle

the previous year's performance, against the objectives set at the beginning of the year and of course against the overall backdrop of the Company's value statements. The performance rank is determined by the individual assessment, carried out by the employee's manager/supervisor in conjunction with a comparative assessment to others doing similar work at a similar level. The rankings are as follows; Exceed, Achieved and Needs Improvement.

The majority of the Company's employees would find themselves in the achieved category and approximately 10% in the exceed and 10% in the needs improvement. A small percentage of employees would fall outside these categories either because they were unsatisfactory or they had been in the job too short a time for a ranking to be made. This distribution is used as a *guide* and 'force fitting' is not used as it serves no useful purpose except to produce a statistically perfect distribution curve. It also results in demotivation and is destructive to continuous improvement. Dr W. Edwards Deming refers to this at length.

The key elements of the Performance Management approach can be summarised as follows:

1. The whole process is founded on a *clear purpose and direction*, a very strong set of company values and a vision of where the Company wants to be.
2. The process is *holistic* in its approach and relates not only to compensation but to development, training and the setting of objectives.
3. It is a *joint* process between employee and manager and not a one-sided event.
4. It is a *flexible* process in that it can emphasise or de-emphasise the importance of its constituent parts. For example, it is becoming increasingly important for us to operate as a team and therefore there is a heavy emphasis within the process currently to measure the effectiveness of team work. Continuous improvement is another example.

There are two further important points to make. First, the performance-ranking process must be kept separate from the development planning stage. The development discussion looks forward and is designed to strengthen the employee's contribution by agreeing action plans for further development, training skills programmes, different but lateral experience, secondment, etc.

Secondly, the conversion of the company strategy into individual objectives is a critical part of the process which comes early in the year and must be done carefully to ensure accountability. These objectives can be described by the acronym, SMART:

Specific
Measurable
Agreed
Realistic
Timely

Specific

Do the objectives clearly spell out the result required? Do they differentiate between *activity,* and *end result?* What the person does from what he or she achieves?

Measurable

Does the objective contain measures which allow you and the employee to assess achievement? What are those measures? Quality? Quantity? Resources? Cost?

Agreed

Have you gained the employee's agreement and commitment to the objectives?

Realistic

Is the objective achievable? Are the resources required to achieve it available? Does the objective provide a degree of challenge for the individual?

The degree of challenge needs to be directly related to the time in job. For a person new in the job the challenge would normally be restricted to getting the job done in an acceptable way. People who have been in the job some time and have already reached the acceptable level could be given a much greater degree of challenge and possibly 'stretch' objectives outside of their job and in other areas.

Time-Related

Have time scales been included? When is the output required? What is the deadline? When will the objectives be reviewed?

Designing reward systems

This last but vital part of the performance management link relates to the design of the reward system. Many companies tend to view their compensation and benefits organisations as control mechanisms or the suppliers of competitive data. Compensation and benefits departments can be and should be used creatively as part of the organisation development initiatives which go towards supporting change from the company's 'current reality' towards where it wants to be – the 'vision'. Pay and reward mechanisms should be seen as major change support programmes which clearly link the individual to the goals of the organisation, both in terms of its customer objectives, its values and organisational culture.

If an organisation has decided that it needs to move towards a flat, non-hierarchical structure which requires trust and empowerment then the reward structure needs to reflect this. If your compensation and benefits system still provides for senior management bonuses, hierarchical schemes, top hat pension plans, two-tier restaurant facilities, etc., then clearly your organisation will not move where you want it to move. So the performance mechanism and the reward philosophy should and must be established by a Board-level decision, to support a major change or a stated philosophy and not a reward mechanism run by the Human Resources Department for control and competitive market purposes.

It is also important to understand this not only from the company perspective but also from the employee perspective. Have you tried asking your employees recently: Why they joined your company? Why they remain with your company? What would it take to get them to move? I find that more and more employees of the type we require are individuals with a high self-esteem as well as very marketable skills and a flexible attitude. These people, I would suggest, are looking for some of the following in their new or potential employers:

- Lifelong learning opportunities.
- Self-fulfilment.
- Involvement and teamwork.
- Recognition of performance (not just in pay terms).
- The opportunity to create personal wealth (as opposed to a monthly salary).

Making trade-offs

There are of course many decisions for a company to make in relation to its reward system and there should be different approaches within the Company according to the particular business needs. Within this there will be many trade-offs and a gradual move towards the desired goal, but some of the following decisions will have to be made:

- Company-wide profit sharing or division based?
- Emphasis on individuals or teams?
- Unitary or multiple systems?
- Short-term/long-term or both?

None of these options are mutually exclusive and well-balanced schemes will have elements of each. If the scheme is to support a changed philosophy however it does ultimately have to show a definite bias towards the way in which the Company is going – *supporting strategic intent*.

In summary, your company's ability to be successful and to attract and retain good people will not be solved by any off-the-shelf consultant's package or process but by a careful and considered view of the fundamental issues which will affect your success. We started the chapter by listing them but I will repeat them here. They are as follows:

1. A clear purpose and direction.
2. An understanding of customers and their needs.
3. A clear and agreed vision.
4. A strong set of shared values.
5. Infrastructure change to support and reinforce.
6. Systems and measures to ensure your critical success factors are being achieved.

Support programmes, spot awards and recognition programmes

One of the most important motivators is recognition. Northern Telecom has a sophisticated recognition programme which encompasses the following rewards.

Spot awards

These are awards which can be made, as required, to recognise exceptional accomplishment by any individual or team of employees. The awards will typically take the form of tickets to an event, functions, dinners, small gifts or vouchers. The importance of these awards is that they can be spontaneous, made very quickly after the event and of course publicly.

Awards of merit

These recognise outstanding contributions by individuals or teams. They are made *quarterly* by the local units and normally take the form of a symbolic award.

President's, function heads' awards of excellence!

These are awards which are made *annually* by the Presidents of each business unit.

Chairman's awards of excellence

These again are made *annually* and recognise a high level of excellence by any individual or team. The awards are presented by the Chairman of the Company and will include a symbolic award, a monetary award and the Chairman's Gold Award of Excellence.

Employee surveys

It is important to keep in touch with our 'internal customers', the employees, and surveys are therefore carried out regularly on a local, regional and global basis. As well as asking questions about the organisation and the strategy of the company they also focus on the How Are We Doing? This is one mechanism which can be used to measure the success of an *internal strategy*.

Four-way feedback

Many of the operating units and divisions use a system known as four-way feedback. This takes the form of a questionnaire which is completed by the managers on his/her view of style, communication, leadership, etc. Copies also go to the manager's boss, his or her peers and subordinates. The total response is coordinated and analysed externally and the results fed back to the manager. Any gaps between the manager's own understanding and the understanding of others immediately become apparent and programmes or development are put into place to narrow the gap. This is a useful tool to ensure that the system is open and working.

Skip meetings

These meetings take place regularly and informally where a whole layer or maybe two layers of management are skipped and an informal discussion takes place about the company, the direction in which it is going, the company's processes, etc.

All of these mechanisms ensure that the company is on track and that its programmes are working.

The future

I have mentioned earlier how our organisations are changing shape in order to meet the fast pace of change. I also touched on some of the changing needs of employees, and the companies they are prepared to work for. We need to be alive

Table 15.1 The changing shape of organisations

Characteristic	From	To
Organisation	Hierarchy	Network
Output	Market share	Market creation
Focus	Institution	Individual
Style	Structured	Flexible
Source of strength	Stability	Change
Structure	Self-sufficiency	Interdependences
Culture	Tradition	Generic core
Mission	Goods	Strategic plans
Identify	Direction	Value
Leadership	Dogmatic	Inspirational
Quality	Affordable best	No compromise
Expectations	Security	Personal growth
Status	Title & rank	Making a difference
Resource	Cash	Information
Advantage	Better	Sameness
Meaningful differences	Motivation to complete	To build

Source: Rosabeth Moss Kanter

Table 15.2 The changing shape of reward systems

From	To
Individual reward system	Team reward system
Many job grades	Broad bands
Short-term measures	Medium- & longer-term measures
Numerical results	Continuous improvement & customer feedback
Performance in present job	Competency profiling
A fixed compensation & benefits offering	Cafeteria approach
Pay for status	Pay for knowledge & skills

to market changes, the flexibility of our organisations to meet these changes, the behaviour of the people within the organisation and finally, the infrastructure which includes performance management.

We are moving very fast towards a scenario described effectively by Rosabeth Moss Kanter[5] and shown in Table 15.1.

If this is the shift then we also need to be moving our performance systems in a different direction and developing new systems which more adequately support the type of companies we want to become. The move from one system to another might take years rather than months, but some suggestions are given in Table 15.2.

It is impossible in one chapter to define all the options. All decisions involving performance-related rewards involve short-term trade-offs and a planned and stepped approach towards the goal of creating a high value, flexible company which will not only survive but win.

Notes

1. The British Deming Association, *Performance Appraisal and All That*, BDA, 1991.
2. Kosaku Yoshida, *Sources of Japanese Productivity*, Occasional Paper, California State University School of Management.
3. Steven Bevan and Marc Thompson, *Studies of Performance Pay*, Institute of Manpower Studies, University of Sussex.
4. Northern Telecom, 'Managing for Achievement'.
5. Rosabeth Moss Kanter, *The Change Masters*, George Allen and Unwin, 1984.

Recommended reading

Steven Bevan and Marc Thompson, *Studies of Performance Pay*, Institute of Manpower Studies, University of Sussex.
Dr W. Edwards Deming, *Out of the Crisis*, MIT Press, 1986.
The British Deming Association, *Performance Appraisal and All That!*, BDA, 1991.
Frederick Herzberg, 'One more time. How do you motivate employees?', *Harvard Business Review*, October, 1987.
Rosabeth Moss Kanter, *The Changemasters*, George Allen and Unwin, 1984.

Masaaki Imai, *Kaizen*, Random House, 1986.

Joyce Nilsson Orsini, 'Bonuses: What is the impact?', *National Productivity Review*, Spring, 1987.

Kasako Yoshida, *Sources of Japanese Productivity*, Occasional Paper, California State University, School of Management.

16 Changing the culture of the W.H. Smith Group

Malcolm Field and Kevin Hawkins

'Changing the direction of a large company is like trying to turn an aircraft carrier. It takes a mile before anything happens. And if it was a wrong turn, getting back on course takes even longer.'
Charles Revson, founder of Revlon, *Positioning: The Battle for Your Mind*, with Jack Trout, McGraw-Hill, 1980

Executive summary

In 1991 W.H. Smith launched its vision statement. One of its aims was to develop a new management style. For Field and his team, the challenge was to change the leadership style to embody the strategic direction and core values of the new culture across the Group, while recognising and preserving the organisational personality of individual businesses.

Commitment and communication have been the keynote. WHS found that to achieve successful change, there must be a critical mass of managers who see themselves as potential winners from the process, and who are willing to grasp the opportunities. Senior management's role, working from the centre, is to communicate the core beliefs and values through a variety of means such as booklets, videos, meetings. But crucially, the most powerful communication link takes place between individual members of staff and their superiors, and unless this happens, any attempt at change will founder.

Corporate renewal or transformation is hardly new. Most large companies periodically ask themselves what they are good and not so good at doing, discard unprofitable businesses and move into new markets. Never before, however, have the questions on the corporate agenda been so fundamental or so concerned with the least quantifiable of all management issues – the purpose, culture and structure of the organisation itself. This partly reflects the impact of recession as companies demand more and more from fewer people. But it may also reveal a growing awareness that traditional ways of organising and managing people are not achieving the desired transformation in corporate performance and are not likely to do so.

Frederick Winslow Taylor, pioneer of scientific management, told a group of students at Harvard in 1909: 'Your job is to find out what your boss wants and give it to him exactly as he wants.' Most companies which have been in business for more than 50 years were founded on the principle of unquestioning obedience to orders. The biggest single challenge facing corporate leaders is how to replace this notion with something much more attuned to the task of competing successfully in the markets of the 1990s and beyond. Managing organisational change is essentially a matter of inspiring and leading the process of cultural change. This means that the people who work in British business – from top to bottom – must think and behave differently from what has traditionally been accepted as normal. The companies who will achieve and sustain excellence in their products and services are those which discover how to unlock the commitment, the ideas and the ability to learn of people at all levels of the organisation.

In embarking on this enormous task, it would be very helpful if corporate leaders could turn to a tried, tested and generally recognised theory of managing change. Unfortunately, one does not exist. All we have to guide us are the trials and errors of other organisations, the guidance of consultants and, of course, an intuitive feel for what will or will not work in our own companies. With these resources at its command, the W.H. Smith Group has over the past three years initiated a process of cultural and organisational change which is now beginning to gather pace. Our purpose in this chapter is not to present proudly our experience to date as a case study in 'how to do it'. What we have started is a process which almost certainly does not have a predictable, finite end and whose full effects will only emerge over several years. We can, however, offer a few – hopefully useful – suggestions to other companies who may be thinking about initiating a similar process.

What is 'culture'?

The culture of any organisation is conventionally and somewhat lazily defined as 'the way we do things around here'. But this begs at least two questions. What *determines* the way in which we do things and why do *we* do them differently here from how *they* do them over there?

A culture has two basic components – a set of core beliefs and values, and certain identifiable characteristics of behaviour and style which distinguish one organisation from another. Together they make up the personality of the organisation. Like the human personality, it is likely to have been shaped over time by different experiences – some benign, others less so. Anyone who is responsible for managing people knows how difficult it usually is to get someone to change their behaviour, especially if their ways are 'set'. If this is true at the individual level, it is true many times over in large, complex organisations.

Changing any culture, therefore, requires, first, that we should be very clear about *why* we want to change it. The first question an individual will ask is: Why do you want me to behave differently? Unless he or she understands the reason, the message will produce no result. The same applies to changing the culture of an organisation. Managers and staff must know *why* change is needed, *how* they as individuals must change, and what the *benefits* will be.

The group vision

The purpose of trying to change the culture of any business (or, indeed, non-business) organisation is usually to achieve a big and sustainable improvement in its performance. The accepted wisdom, which the W.H. Smith Group followed, is that the process should begin with a declaration of intent, communicated to both external and internal audiences. The primary audience, of course, is internal. Such declarations – commonly known as 'vision' or 'mission' statements – are designed to give employees a clear sense of direction and simultaneously communicate the essence of the changes which senior management wants to make.

The W.H. Smith Group produced its first vision statement in 1989 as part of its internal strategic planning process. In 1991 it was revised and relaunched both internally and externally as follows:

The Group Vision

- Our goal is to offer a range of products and a quality of service which meet our customers' needs more effectively than any of our competitors.
- We want all who work for the Group to contribute as much as they can to its success. We will develop a climate which emphasises directness, openness to new ideas, personal accountability and the recognition of individual and team achievement.
- By attaining our goal, we will achieve a consistent and competitive growth in profits and earnings for the benefit of our shareholders, our staff and the community.

We claim no originality for the ideas and phraseology of this statement. Several other large companies have had very similar 'visions'. This, however, does not matter as long as the ideas in it are regarded by the individual managers and staff as germane both to their own working lives and to the future of the business. The challenge is to make these ideas come alive – to transplant them into the culture of the organisation so that managers and staff actually change their day-to-day behaviour and thereby change the culture.

The statement quoted above is our vision for the Group. Since then each of the businesses within the Group – W.H. Smith Retail, Our Price Music, Waterstone's, W.H. Smith News, Office Supplies and our businesses in the USA – has produced its own 'mission'statement. Each of these statements reflects the business's own view of what its purpose or role should be and what it aims to achieve.

A critically important message in the Group vision is in the second paragraph, which seeks to describe in the minimum number of words the style in which every business within the Group should be managing itself. When defining our vision, we also developed in parallel a fuller description of the style of leadership which we intend shall be the norm throughout the Group. The principles on which this style is based are as follows:

The Leadership Style

- The people who work for the Group should be proud of it and feel responsible for its success.
- All staff should have an opportunity to contribute, learn and grow, with progress based on merit and performance.
- All staff should be respected, treated fairly, listened to and involved.
- Staff should achieve real satisfaction from their achievements and business friendships and enjoy their place of work.

The word 'empowerment' is a convenient shorthand term for the values embodied in the Group leadership style. Empowerment is defined in the statement as something which 'increases the authority and responsibility of those closest to our products and our customers. By actively pushing responsibility, trust and recognition throughout the organisation, we can release and benefit from the full capabilities of our people.'

Any company which succeeds in genuinely empowering its managers and staff will achieve a huge and largely untapped source of competitive advantage. This is our goal.

The process of cultural change

Declaring this aim is relatively easy – achieving it is, of course, a very different matter. Cultural change is a process, not something which can be delivered overnight like a product. The culture of any organisation is not simply 'the way we do things around here'. Most managers spend over half their time *communicating*, mainly by word of mouth. The only way in which a culture can be changed is by changing the content of the communication between people, especially that which takes place outside formal meetings. In a traditional culture, most of this communication reflects a fundamental lack of trust between people. The underlying assumptions are as follows:

The Traditional Culture

- Someone is 'right' and is going to 'win', and that someone else is 'wrong' and will 'lose'.

- When something goes wrong, someone must be blamed.
- Criticism, especially when voiced by subordinates, is a threat to the status and competence of the person being criticised and must therefore be suppressed or otherwise proved to be 'wrong'.
- Mistakes must be covered up or blamed on someone else.

Every manager is familiar with the patterns of behaviour produced by these beliefs. They constitute the most powerful set of obstacles to change in any organisation.

The style of leadership we have adopted for the Group is based on a fundamentally different set of behavioural norms. The kind of communication we want to encourage is based on the following norms:

The New Cultural Norms

- Openness to ideas, whether critical or otherwise.
- The creation of a 'safe space' in which people at all levels feel confident enough to speak out, knowing that what they say will be respected and taken into account.
- A willingness to accept personal accountability.
- A firm belief that mistakes and problems represent opportunities to learn from experience and find out what is needed to make progress. Empowerment means having the freedom to err as well as to succeed.
- A commitment to the success of others and to the team to which every individual belongs.
- A willingness to trust others.

Cynics may regard all this as starry-eyed idealism. These norms are certainly ideals – how can any organisation progress unless it sets itself ambitious targets? 'Starry-eyed', however, they certainly are not. There is enough published case material on the cultures of global market leaders and other conspicuously successful companies for us to know that many of them have managed to achieve relatively high levels of employee involvement in and commitment to their business.

A recent report (January 1993) by a joint CBI/DTI working party on innovation, for example, describes Best Practice Companies as follows:

Best practice companies demonstrate a clear sense of mission and purpose, with a strategy balanced between the short, medium and long term, thoroughly thought out at board level and communicated throughout the organisation. They have an open, cross-functional and multi-level teamworking approach to projects and problem solving and empower employees at the lowest level. Flatter hierarchies are the norm.

There are, of course, numerous examples of companies which have attempted to secure greater employee involvement by one means or another and have either failed or been very disappointed with the outcome. One reason may be that they have put too much emphasis on a particular technique or fashionable 'action programme' (for example, Total Quality Management, Customer Care initiatives, Team Briefing) which consumes a huge amount of time and effort but produces relatively modest results. Initiatives of this kind are often driven forward by external consultants, with consequently little sense of ownership on the part of management. Scepticism and resistance to the idea of employee involvement are more likely to be found among middle managers, who see themselves as potential losers. This in turn emphasises the importance in any organisation of the values and behaviour of management as the engine of cultural change. *A strategy for managing change* must be devised, owned and driven by the 'home team' and should concentrate on the broad principles of *securing employee commitment* rather than on particular vehicles or techniques of communication.

Cultural change

Changing the culture of a relatively homogeneous organisation may seem difficult enough. There are many companies, however, which – like W.H. Smith – are groups of businesses, each with its own culture.

There are two very different cultural traditions within the W.H. Smith Group. The businesses which form the historical core of the Group – W.H. Smith News and W.H. Smith Retail – were until relatively recently the two halves of a family firm. The prevailing style of management was autocratic, tempered by paternalism. The values of the business were hierarchy, loyalty, security and obedience to orders. During the 1980s, however, the company expanded by acquisition and became a Group. The most important acquisitions on the retailing side were Our Price Music and Waterstone's Booksellers and, on the distribution side, the five businesses which now comprise W.H. Smith Office Supplies (see Figure 16.1). While each of these companies had – and still has – its own unique personality, they all had and retain the following common cultural characteristics which distinguished them from the older core businesses:

- They were all relatively new, having been created over the past 10 to 20 years.
- Their original founders were in most cases still running the business.
- Their predominant style of management was essentially entrepreneurial and informal, with relatively few controls and rules.
- They had strong traditions of local autonomy and responsibility. A store manager in Waterstone's, for example, would have much greater freedom to run his business than his counterpart in W.H. Smith Retail.

These businesses were acquired either to enhance W.H. Smith's already strong positions in certain markets (books, music) or to achieve leadership in new markets (office supplies). The acquisition programme had been completed by the end of 1989. The concurrent development of Group strategy focused on:

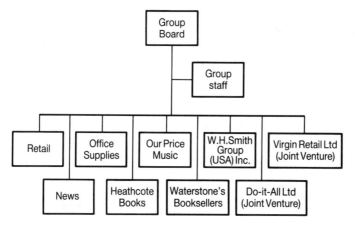

Figure 16.1 The W. H. Smith Group's major businesses

- Achieving the scale economies of market leadership, while preserving the different retail brands in the portfolio.
- Identifying the core skills and competencies of the Group which could be fostered and shared by the businesses.

In short, the strategic thrust of the Group and the need to improve the performance of the newly acquired businesses underlined the importance of achieving some form of cultural synergy. We recognised that W.H. Smith Retail and News could benefit from an infusion of the entrepreneurial flair and devolution of responsibility characteristic of the newer business while the latter, in turn, could benefit from the systems and disciplines of the older businesses.

The development of the Group vision and leadership style embodies the direction and values of the culture we want to see emerge throughout the Group. Within this framework, however, we recognise that each business will continue to preserve and enhance its own brand and organisational personality.

Winning commitment

We recognised at the outset that, in any organisation, there is always likely to be some resistance to change because there are always people who see themselves as potential losers. Resistance can rarely be 'overcome' but it can and must be managed in a way which ensures that the process of change is not blocked. For some managers, particularly those who spent their formative years in the autocratic and paternalistic climate of the older businesses in the Group, the prospect of fundamentally changing their style of management was unattractive. Others, by contrast, welcomed it as a powerful reinforcement of the way in which they were already trying to manage.

Our businesses in the USA have been particularly receptive to the message and process of change. Perhaps American society is naturally more attuned to what ex-President Bush called 'the vision thing'. Certainly, the organisational character-istics of our businesses in the USA have provided fertile ground for the development of 'empowerment'. The Group has two major businesses there – a chain of 350 shops in hotels and airports across the country, and a more compact group of 165 recorded music stores in Pennsylvania and neighbouring states. The latter has grown rapidly from a baseline of 30 stores in 1989 by acquiring four other chains, or parts of chains. Senior management has therefore had a strong incentive to define a vision, a strategy and a set of values as a means of bringing the managers and staff of these recently acquired businesses together. They have produced statements which are consistent with those of the Group but which are written in their own words, with an emphasis which they believe is right for their staff and the environment in which they operate. Having defined their vision and values, they are now seeking to win internal commitment through a series of training courses. Their next step will be to adopt one brand name for the entire chain, based on clear brand values which will closely reflect the core values of the business.

As our American colleagues have clearly demonstrated, *achieving cultural change requires that there should be a critical mass of managers at every level who see themselves as potential 'winners' from the process and are willing to grasp the opportunities*. Bringing this critical mass together requires leadership from the top – not just at Group level but within each business and functional area. It also requires sensitive communica-tion, training and development and, above all, the visible implementation of the desired form of behaviour by all levels of management.

Leadership

The process of change must start at the top. Any organisation which awaits the development of a consensus in favour of change at middle management level will wait for ever. Within the Group, it was a relative handful of people at the top who started the process by changing their own styles and delegating more authority to senior people in the businesses. This happened in response to criticisms from some of the managing directors of the businesses, who felt that the boundary lines between their responsibilities and those of the Group centre were often unclear, resulting in confusion, uncertainty and occasional resentment of what they saw as undue interference.

When drawing up the Group vision and leadership style statements (a process which involved no more than 20 very senior people) we agreed on a formal, written code of behaviour to clarify and regulate the relationship between the centre of the Group and the businesses. The model we adopted, with the assistance of external consultants, was *the centre as coach*. A document was drawn up which clearly defined the role of the centre, spelling out those issues or circumstances where it would act as follows:

The Role of the Centre

- Act as the primary decision-maker.
- Adopt the role of arbitrator between differing opinions on issues which affected more than one business.
- If necessary, vigorously challenge the proposals of a business.
- Comment and offer advice on any aspect of the business.

The agreement of these ground rules, known as 'due process', has provided a framework within which the roles and responsibilities of the Group and its businesses are more clearly understood. Within this framework, each business team is free to manage as it thinks fit.

Communication

Once the businesses themselves had been 'empowered' within the due process rules, it was left to each management team to initiate the same process of change within its own organisation. Given the cultural differences between the businesses and the fact that none of them was starting out from the same baseline, no other approach would have been practicable.

Not surprisingly, the pace of change has varied considerably within each business. One change common to all the businesses, however, has been the flattening out of the management hierarchy. This process has been driven by the need to reduce costs in a difficult trading climate, but the outcome – shorter lines of communication, more delegation of responsibility – is certainly helping to make empowerment a reality.

The Group centre retains the responsibility of continuing to communicate internally the core beliefs and values embodied in the concept of empowerment. This is done partly through booklets, manuals, videos and the internal business planning process and partly by more direct means. There is, for example, a well-established programme of regional meetings throughout the UK in which small groups of middle managers from all the businesses meet the Chairman or Group Chief Executive to voice whatever questions or concerns they may have on any aspect of Group policy. The issue of empowerment regularly arises at these meetings, which gives the Group's top management the opportunity to explain the principles, invite comment and get direct feedback on the progress being made within each business.

The most powerful communication link in any organisation, however, is between the individual member of staff and his or her immediate superior. Everything else must be planned around this link. However much a company spends on the hardware and methodology of communication – videos, newsletters, presentations, briefings, etc. – *the most powerful communicator in any organisation is the day-to-day behaviour of management*. Unless this changes – at the level closest to the customer as well as in the boardroom – the culture will not change.

At some stage, it will be necessary to assess the effectiveness of the internal communication process in terms of how staff perceive the behaviour of management within each business and how far these perceptions accord with the declared Group style of leadership. We will then have a benchmark by which the process of cultural change can be measured.

Training and development

The Group's residential management development centre at Milton Hill, Oxfordshire, has a particularly important role in ensuring that the Group's vision and leadership style are integrated into mainstream development courses. The centre is also concentrating on strengthening the Group's core skills and encouraging the transfer of these skills between businesses. This will help to achieve the cultural synergy which is required to bring the performance of all the Group's businesses to our target levels over the next few years.

Team development is also progressing at senior levels in all the businesses, often with the help of external consultants.

Conclusion

The genesis of cultural change in any organisation is a clear vision of how it should function and what it should achieve. Bringing the vision to reality requires a change in the behaviour – the leadership style – of senior management. Once senior managers are seen to be 'walking the talk', the understanding and commitment of other managers and staff will follow. Many staff are capable of contributing more to the success of the business than traditional management styles have encouraged or enabled them to do. Once this unused potential begins to be unlocked, the culture has changed (see Figure 16.2).

Cultural change is, therefore, a means to an end. We are trying to change the way in which people behave in order to get better results. To argue the case on any other grounds would not normally engage the attention of hard-pressed managers, preoccupied as they are with more mundane matters. We must also recognise, however, that cultural change is a process not a product. Above all, it is a process which is not self-sustaining but needs to be created, pushed forward, measured and, if necessary, re-launched. The more ambitious the goals, the more likely it is that the process will require periodic injections of corporate energy.

The process must be perceived by staff as a genuine attempt to change for the

Figure 16.2 Achieving the vision

better the climate in which they work. Experience elsewhere suggests that while few managers change the way they behave quickly or easily, a process which seems to generate a lot of meetings and memoranda but with no tangible benefits will soon lose credibility in the eyes of staff. If management wishes to persuade staff that their opinions are valued, there must be clear evidence that communication up the line produces results. *Cultural change, therefore, requires not just one champion at the top but many at every level.*

As organisations become flatter and managerial hierarchies are simplified, the lines of communication between staff and top management will grow shorter and clearer. In these circumstances, the quality of leadership will become even more important to the momentum of change and the overall success of the business.

17 Managing strategic and organisational change: the role of the Chief Executive and Board

Charles Allen

'The leader must know that he knows and must be able to make it abundantly clear to those about him that he knows.'
Clarence B. Randall, *Making Good in Management*, McGraw-Hill, 1964

Executive summary

While particular parts of the business may need special attention at certain times, Charles Allen argues that the Chief Executive and the Board must constantly keep the entire picture in view. He describes his approach to his job as Chief Executive and provides the following guidelines:

- Business is a game that you play to win but the Chief Executive must understand the rules.
- The Chief Executive and Board must lead from the front.
- They should create a positive culture – focused on 'how to' rather than 'can't'.
- There must be an ongoing, honest appraisal and commitment to *quality* throughout the company.
- There should be no surprises.
- The Chief Executive and Board need to recognise that they cannot manage all the details themselves. They need to promote responsibility with control for line management.
- Communication is a two-way process. Top management should give quality feedback and recognise and communicate success.
- The journey of change is continuous – there is no final destination. The management of change is *a state of organised, permanent revolution.*

The game

I have always held to the belief that business is a game. This is not flippancy but a truism. Business is a game that you play to win. It has rules, recognition, rewards and failures – even promotion and relegation. In order to win, the participants need flair, stamina, planning, flexibility, skill and the ability to excel at both hard-ball and soft-ball. In an innovative and changing world the major task of the Chief Executive and Board is to create a winning team and to keep it striving to reach the peak of its abilities.

Before we start playing to win we need a game plan. We need *rules, objectives, a plan* and *enthusiasm*. To play the game successfully we need to define the do's and don'ts. We need a clear set of objectives and, as in any game, tenacity and enthusiasm.

The first step in winning is to understand the rules.

The rules

The phrase that underscores every aspect of this chapter is *Keep it simple*. There is no need to cloud one's approach to management with verbose philosophies. You need a clarity of purpose and direction and a simple means of getting the message across. As Chief Executive, I follow these basic guidelines which are my rules of the game.

1. Install only top quality managers.
2. Keep management structures simple.
3. Make quality a real issue – and refuse to accept excuses.
4. Sell our wares aggressively.
5. Seek a full price and prompt payment.
6. Do not waste money.

The decisions that you need to make will grow organically from adherence to these rules.

The player/manager

In putting together a winning team, eventual success depends on the total participation of the Chief Executive and the Board. They fulfil the roles of the Player/Manager, Team Captain and the Coaching Staff.

Their first task is to organise the field of play – the boundaries, touchlines and goals. The second task is to identify talent, pick the team and allocate roles within that team.

To get this team to play to win, you need to be totally committed to training and the creation of a vigorous training programme, one that will broaden vision, deepen understanding, hone skills and build stamina – and one that will also keep enthusiasm bubbling. A skilful mix!

Case study: The Board at Granada

In order to put these points into a proper perspective let us look at a specific company – Granada Television.

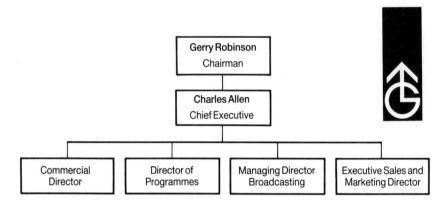

Figure 17.1 The Granada Television organisation

Background/objectives

Granada Group plc had a turnover in 1992–3 of £1.4 billion. The Group Board is structured into four divisions. I am Chief Executive of Granada Television (see Figure 17.1). On joining Granada I defined my objective within the Group as follows:

To achieve a significant improvement in profitability and return on investment and to realise earnings from all businesses through the provision of a high quality service.

It is a statement that follows on from the *keep it simple* rule which brought a proper degree of clarity to many day-to-day decisions.

At Granada we went back to basics to re-examine the structure of the company – a company on the threshold of a highly competitive new broadcasting environment that posed a major threat to a deeply ingrained management culture.

Executive Board and reporting system

An early decision was to create a small executive board of five. With five people there are only ten inter-relationships to manage, with a board of ten there are forty-five such relationships. Tight management information and the ability to make quick decisions must start in the board room. A small executive board operating as a team enhances the forward dynamic necessary for change and helps eliminate the political jockeying that seeks to preserve the status quo and power blocks which are the enemy of change.

To control change the Board needs to have a clear picture of the company's success and failure – of its progress or otherwise. It needs to understand the financial picture and to put this information into a framework that allows analysis and gives the ability to plot the correct course and rectify error. A detailed monthly reporting system was introduced for all managers but starting in the board room.

Planning

However, having decided on the first objective and laid down the rules, the next step was the formation of the plan to achieve that objective. This required a detailed hands-on approach. In short, we needed to change the business attitude of Granada; we needed to run this major organisation as one might run a much smaller business. Stage 1 was to review every aspect of the business: costs, prices, volume, cash and capital expenditure. Stage 2 was forward action.

To summarise, in planning for change you must review each aspect of the business as follows:

Costs	– Overheads
	– Operating costs and cost structures
	– Procurement
Price	– Pricing policy, strategy and tactics
Volume	– Marketing policy, development and tactics
Cash	– Control
Capital expenditure	– Strategic review and control

Implementation

Realising this type of plan requires maturity, professionalism, plain hard work and clear incisive management information in a success-focused culture.

As player/manager the Chief Executive creates a two-to-three year vision, a one-year plan, quarterly sets of objectives and monthly progress reviews. At the end of each quarter, the Chief Executive and Board need to stand back and focus on the achievements and problems and reassess the next quarterly plan.

In my first year at Granada, the quarterly plan broke down in the following way:

1st quarter	– Identify problems
2nd quarter	– Identify the vision and choose the team
3rd quarter	– Implement the plan
4th quarter	– Identify how to move forward

Management style

The new Granada management style is one which promotes a culture of openness and honesty. It is one which reinforces the need for all staff to understand the role that they can play in achieving the company objectives and it is a style that has seen success, not only in profit growth but also in our success in reaching the standards set out in the Business Rules.

However, without enthusiasm, support and understanding, all this could amount to no more than good intentions. In managing change it is important to remember that, seen from above, change is exciting and challenging. Seen from another perspective it may be threatening. You need to take care, therefore, to project your own enthusiasm to your team and to create a positive culture, i.e. to look at 'how to' rather than 'can't'.

It is necessary to ensure that your team understands all the reasons behind the business rules. For example, the professional requirement not to waste money must not deteriorate into penny-pinching, which cuts effectiveness, hits morale and goes against the positive culture. It must go hand-in-hand with a positive approach to management and services.

The Chief Executive and the Board must lead from the front, displaying their own ability to act as a team and demonstrating a passionate commitment to the quality of their product. A devotion to the short-term bottom line at the expense of quality products and services will be to the detriment of the long-term bottom line. There must be an ongoing, honest appraisal of and commitment to quality, throughout the company.

Branding and presenting the plan

A crucial stage is the branding of the plan. To create the ethos that change is exciting and offers opportunity it is necessary that the plan should be easily understood, and that it is divided into digestible chunks with finite targets. It is also necessary that the Chief Executive brands the plan, otherwise during what will be a difficult period for the company in terms of morale, others will do so, and will turn a positive into a negative.

The name given to the Granada plan was *Fit for the Future*. It offered a three-year vision for the company, set targets for change, explained the required company structure and introduced a management training programme which would build the team and introduce management to the rich potential of change, identifying change as an opportunity rather than a threat.

Fit for the Future was written and presented in straightforward language to all the management and staff, by myself as Chief Executive and by the Board. A company in change is about to embark on a difficult and exciting journey but it is important to management and staff – and for maintaining the confidence of shareholders – that it is not a journey into the unknown.

The maxim throughout *Fit for the Future* was, and is, *keep it simple*. Maintaining a clarity of purpose and not overcomplicating the message and the route were imperative. It is also vital that you are – and are seen to be – decisive. The alternative is grey management which will not motivate or inspire change. I believe it is often better to set off full of purpose in the wrong direction which one can adjust from the experience gained, rather than to stagnate because of the fear of change inherent in grey management. It is understood however that if he or she persists in marching in the wrong direction then a Chief Executive will not last very long!

The key factors of the plan are therefore:

1. Keep it simple.
2. Create clear objectives.
3. Communicate the objectives.
4. Create clear management information.
5. Promote responsibility with control.
6. Make training real.
7. Give quality feedback.
8. Recognise (and communicate) success.

Management information and training

The first step in instigating and controlling change and ensuring that the plan stays on course is to create a steady flow of management information. The first tool is a monthly report by all managers to the Board. The Chief Executive and the Board also use this report to measure their own progress.

Monthly reporting ensures that the plan is always kept in focus because it is broken down into manageable chunks of time. In the monthly progress report, the Board must be sure to draw the full facts out of management not just the good news. There should be no surprises. A company management can navigate the most difficult changes provided (a) they are sufficiently determined and (b) they know where they are going and where the bumps are going to come along the way.

It is important to create a hit list of problems to attack and successes to maintain. One way to gain a full picture of progress is to ask management to identify five successes and five failures in their monthly report. I call these monthly 'Highs' and 'Lows'. This will alert the Chief Executive and the Board to problems in achieving the plan but it will also ensure that management is aware of the shortfalls in performance that they need to address and it is an encouragement to avoid that failure in future reports. It is also easier for people to talk about what is not good if they can balance it with what is good.

To evaluate all levels of reports it is necessary to initiate a unified system of measurement. Analysis can then be made on the basis of hard facts such as the volume of production, profitability and product range. It is important that the system of measurement is also introduced in the corporate service areas, e.g. Finance and Personnel. It is also important to ensure that before instigating the reporting system managers will have to identify the measures which will form the yardstick of their success or failure and live by that yardstick.

This naturally leads on to the use of *league tables* to record success in achievement of key objectives measured so that performance can be compared across the company. This is management not only through recognition and reward but also by a powerful motivator – embarrassment.

Management by walking about

The management of change at Granada and elsewhere requires an active management and it is vital in creating the environment for change to remove the mystique from management. You must communicate with one's staff not just by reports and presentations but also by conversation and meetings. In simple terms (that word again) it is *management by walking about*. This involves being seen around the organisation, talking to staff, eating in the canteen, being open to conversation, ideas, worries and ambitions and getting a true picture for oneself of the situation on the ground. Management by walking about is a continuous daily process to get a personal knowledge of the temperature of all sections of the business and to communicate with all sections of the staff. Although not the only way, it is also a direct way of allowing the Chief Executive to recognise and communicate success.

Management by walking about is also a key incentive in ensuring that management informs those under their line command of all aspects of the development plan, and recognises they have a duty as sales representatives both within and outside the organisation.

Training and communication

The key to successful management of change is training. There is no one in the organisation who should be immune to training. The Chief Executive and the Board need to set an example and to stay constantly abreast of developments and outside change. They need to train managers who in turn need to train the rest of the staff.

When making any change, communication and training must be the best. In an industry such as Granada's which employs a large number of people at different locations this is vital. It is imperative that this is always to a national standard and is clearly directed. At Granada Leisure we introduced a Quality Improvement Programme called 'Be the Best'.

Training and staff development at Granada has now become a line management issue – training can be done in situ, where and when it is most needed and is most relevant and it can also be conducted quickly and effectively. *Make training real.*

Training sets the scene and gives staff a route to success. But the Chief Executive needs to ensure that messages are communicated clearly and relentlessly. This gives staff a proper understanding of the required approach and helps them feel good not only about the change but also about the process of the change.

The Chief Executive and Board therefore rely heavily on *internal marketing*. An example is the approach we adopted at Granada Leisure. Having spent a month putting together the restructure plan we devoted a full week to creating a very detailed communication programme which gave everyone a clear part to play in the communication process with very clear messages for all parties who might be affected by the change, e.g. management, staff, unions, suppliers, press and customers.

Training plays an equally important role once the restructure has been completed. Change invariably means some difficult decisions have been made, different roles allocated, a new company culture introduced, jobs reduced, colleagues changed. It is an unsettling and potentially dangerous situation. The Chief Executive and the Board need to recognise these problems of morale and to ensure that management are properly equipped to address the problems and to drive change forward by taking the staff with them.

Training therefore has significance in team building and it is important to take management on structured training and awaydays or longer training courses. The design of these courses is a responsibility of the Chief Executive and the Board. Careful thought must be given to designing programmes that allow management to discover new ways of working together, cooperating to conquer new challenges, to review progress and to identify key challenges for the future. This sort of training is a key stimulus in allowing the Board to recognise individual and team merits and to create the exact combination to achieve their primary objectives.

Individual training is just as important as team building. Managers should be encouraged to analyse their own strengths and weaknesses and to identify training solutions which may, for example, be individual training in man-management; financial analysis or computer literacy.

Conclusion

Our approach throughout the management of change has been to follow the rule *Keep it simple*, to look at the problems facing you and to get right back to basics.
The same simple approach was used as we went on to *create clear objectives*. We need to be very clear with our staff so that they know just where we are going and what their contributions to success can be.

We need to focus very hard on the housekeeping issues, on the need to have the right information to manage the process of change with the introduction of *clear management information*.

The Chief Executive and Board need to recognise that they cannot manage all the details themselves and need to promote responsibility with control for line management. To create these appropriate levels of support for ourselves and for our staff we need to invest time and skill in *making training real*. We need to ensure that support is there for them so that they can identify and achieve objectives.

To ensure that communication is a two-way process we need to *give quality feedback* and *recognise and communicate success*. This can be done through *management by walking about* and also through awards, be it letter or sometimes by a simple telephone call.

Finally, ensure that team building is given early and high priority and continue the process at every stage of the long-term plan. Annual training and conferences can play an important part in this providing they are properly planned.

The journey of change that one has embarked upon is a permanent one – there is no final destination. The moment that the team feels it has reached perfection is the moment that stagnation sets in. The management of change is a state of organised, permanent revolution.

Bibliography

Changing corporate culture

Denis Boyle (ed.), *Strategic Service Management*, Pergamon Press, 1991.

Andrew Campbell, Marion Devine and David Young, *A Sense of Mission*, Hutchinson, 1990.

Andrew Campbell and Kiran Tawadey, *Mission & Business Philosophy: Winning employee commitment*, Heinemann, 1990.

Jan Carlzon, *Moments of Truth*, Ballinger Publishing, 1987.

Charles Hampden-Turner, *Creating Corporate Culture*, Addison-Wesley, 1992.

Masaaki Imai, *Kaizen*, McGraw-Hill, 1986.

Richard Normann, *Service Management: Strategy and leadership in service businesses*, John Wiley & Sons, 1984.

Donald Petersen and John Hillkirk, *Teamwork: New management ideas for the nineties*, Victor Gollancz, 1991.

Peter M. Senge, *The Fifth Discipline*, Doubleday, 1990.

Competitive benchmarking and process re-engineering

Robert Camp, *Benchmarking: The search for industry best practices that lead to superior performance*, ASQC Quality Press, 1989.

Michael Hammer and James Champy, *Reengineering the Corporation*, Nicholas Brealey, 1993.

David T. Kearns and David A. Nadler, *Prophets in the Dark*, Harper Business, 1992.

Preston G. Smith and Donald G. Reinertsen, *Developing Products in Half the Time*, Van Nostrand Reinhold, 1991.

George Stalk Jr. and Thomas M. Hout, *Competing Against Time*, The Free Press, 1990.

Howard Sutton, *Competitive Intelligence*, The Conference Board Europe, 1988.

Gregory H. Watson, *Strategic Benchmarking*, John Wiley & Sons, 1973.

Creating shareholder value

Christopher J. Clarke (ed.), *Shareholder Value: Key to corporate development*, Pergamon Press, 1991.

William H. Davidow and Michael S. Malone, *The Virtual Corporation*, Harper Collins, 1992.

Alfred Rappaport, *Creating Shareholder Value*, The Free Press, 1986.

Bernard C. Reimann, *Managing for Value*, The Planning Forum, 1987.

Peter Thompson, *Sharing the Success*, Collins, 1990.

Customer value and the environment

Andrew Dunham and Barry Marcus with Mark Stevens and Patrick Barwise, *Unique Value: The secret of all great business strategies*, Macmillan, 1993.

John Elkington and Peter Knight with Julia Hailes, *The Green Business Guide*, Victor Gollancz, 1991.

Jacques Horovitz and Michele Jurgens Panak, *Total Customer Satisfaction*, Pitman, 1992.

Directors and boards

Ada Demb and F.-Friedrich Neubauer, *The Corporate Board: Confronting the paradoxes*, Oxford University Press, 1992.

Bernard Taylor (ed.), *Strategic Planning: The Chief Executive and the Board*, Pergamon Press, 1988.

Bernard Taylor and Bob Tricker (eds), *The Director's Manual*, Director Books, 1990–3 (with annual supplements).

R.I. Tricker, *Corporate Governance*, Gower, 1984.

Human resources and organisation structures

Michael Armstrong (ed.), *Strategies for Human Resource Management*, Coopers & Lybrand, 1992.

Colin Coulson-Thomas, *Creating the Global Company*, McGraw-Hill, 1992.

Sheila Rothwell (ed.), *Strategic Planning for Human Resources*, Pergamon Press, 1990.

Philip Sadler, *Designing Organisations*, Mercury, 1991.

J. Rodney Turner, *The Handbook of Project-Based Management*, McGraw-Hill, 1992.

Shoshana Zuboff, *In the Age of the Smart Machine*, Heinemann, 1988.

Innovation and entrepreneurship

Mark Brown, *The Dinosaur Strain*, Element Books, 1988.

Donald K. Clifford Jr. and Richard E. Cavanagh, *The Winning Performance*, Sidgwick & Jackson, 1985.

Richard N. Foster, *Innovation: The attacker's advantage*, Pan Books, 1987.

Bruce Lloyd (ed.), *Entrepreneurship: Creating and managing new ventures*, Pergamon Press, 1989.

Tom Lloyd, *Entrepreneur!*, Bloomsbury, 1992.

P. Ranganath Nayak and John M. Ketteringham, *Breakthroughs!*, Rawson Associates, 1986.

Stuart Slatter, *Gambling on Growth*, John Wiley & Sons, 1992.

Managing change and turnaround situations

James A. Belasco, *Teaching the Elephant to Dance: Empowering change in your organisation*, Century Business, 1990.

Colin Carnall, *Managing Change*, Routledge, 1991.

Pankaj Ghemawat, *Commitment: The dynamic of strategy*, The Free Press, 1991.

Rosabeth Moss Kanter, *When Giants Learn to Dance*, Unwin, 1990.

Richard Pascale, *Managing on the Edge*, Penguin, 1991.

Thomas J. Peters and Robert H. Waterman Jr., *In Search of Excellence*, Harper & Row, 1982.

Stuart Slatter, *Corporate Recovery: Successful turnaround strategies and their implementation*, Penguin, 1984.

Paul J. Strebel, *Breakpoints: How managers exploit radical business change*, Harvard Business School, 1992.
Frederick M. Zimmermann, *The Turnaround Experience*, McGraw-Hill, 1991.

Partnerships and alliances
Jordan D. Lewis, *Partnerships for Profit*, The Free Press, 1990.
Peter Lorange and Johan Roos, *Strategic Alliances: Formation, implementation and evolution*, Basil Blackwell, 1992.

Strategic planning and strategic management
H. Igor Ansoff, *Implanting Strategic Management*, Prentice Hall, 1984.
John M. Bryson, *Strategic Planning for Public and Nonprofit Organisations*, Jossey-Bass, 1988.
Adrian Davies, *Strategic Leadership*, Woodhead-Faulkner, 1991.
James W. Dudley, *Strategies for the Single Market*, Kogan Page, 1989.
Nigel Freedman (ed.), *Strategic Management in Major Multinational Companies*, Pergamon Press, 1991.
Michael Goold and Andrew Campbell, *Strategies and Styles*, Basil Blackwell, 1987.
P.C. Haspeslagh and D.B. Jenison, *Managing Acquisitions: creating value through corporate renewal*, The Free Press, 1991.
John Kay, *Foundations of Corporate Success*, Oxford University Press, 1993.
Toyohiro Kono (ed.), *Strategic Management in Japanese Companies*, Pergamon Press, 1992.
Peter Lorange, *Strategic Planning and Control*, Basil Blackwell, 1993.
Management Analysis Center, edited by Paul J. Stonich, *Implementing Strategy*, Ballinger, 1982.
Michel Robert, *Strategy Pure & Simple*, McGraw-Hill, 1993.
William E. Rothschild, *Risktaker, Caretaker, Surgeon, Undertaker*, John Wiley & Sons, 1993.
Richard W. Sapp and Roger W. Smith, *Strategic Management for Bankers*, Planning Executives Institute, Ohio, 1984.
Peter Schwartz, *The Art of the Long View*, Century Business, 1992.
Bernard Taylor and John Harrison, *The Manager's Casebook of Business Strategy*, Heinemann, 1990.

Vision and leadership
John Argenti, *Your Organization: What is it for?*, McGraw-Hill, 1993.
Warren Bennis, *On Becoming a Leader*, Century Business, 1989.
Stanley M. Davis, *Future Perfect*, Addison-Wesley, 1987.
Max Depree, *Leadership is an Art*, Dell Trade, 1989.
J.K. Friend, J.M. Power and C.J.L. Yewlett, *Public Planning: The inter-corporate dimension*, Tavistock Publications, 1974.
Jeffrey Pfeffer, *Managing with Power*, Harvard Business School Press, 1992.
Benjamin B. Tregoe, John W. Zimmermann, Ronald A. Smith and Peter M. Tobia, *Vision in Action*, Simon & Schuster, 1989.

Index